TYPES OF THE ESSAY

TYPES OF THE ESSAY

SELECTED AND EDITED BY

BENJAMIN A. HEYDRICK, A.M.

HEAD OF ENGLISH DEPARTMENT, HIGH SCHOOL OF COMMERCE
NEW YORK CITY

CHARLES SCRIBNER'S SONS

NEW YORK   CHICAGO   BOSTON

CONTENTS

v

52886

INTRODUCTION

WHAT IS AN ESSAY?

When you write a letter to a friend, you tell him what you and others have been doing, what you have seen, and what you think about various things. People who write books do the same thing on a larger scale. A book that tells what you have done is an autobiography; a book telling what others have done is biography or history, or if it deals with imaginary people, it is fiction. A book telling what you have seen is travel, and a book telling what you think on various topics is a book of essays. Yet not all books giving people's thoughts are essays. If a man writes a book on religion or philosophy, for example, a book made up of various chapters, arrranged in such order as to form a systematic and complete treatment of the subject, that book would not be called an essay but a treatise. The word essay comes from the French *essai*, an attempt, an endeavor. So Francis Bacon, the first English essayist, said in the preface to his book: "To write just treatises requireth leisure in the writer and leisure in the reader, . . . which is the cause that hath made me choose to write certain brief notes, set down rather significantly than curiously, which I have called essays."

This gives us the second characteristic of the essay: it is brief, and does not attempt to treat a subject either completely or systematically. In fact, an essay is a sort of literary go-as-you-please. An essayist may, like Montaigne, announce as his subject "Coaches," and proceed to write about sneezing, the entertainments of Roman emperors, and the conquest of Mexico, with only a brief mention of coaches. And yet while the essayist

may seem to be careless how he begins or where he leaves
off his subject, there is one thing that he is always careful
about, his style. More than any other form of prose, the
essay demands mastery of style. How the thing is said
is as important—often more important, than what is
said. This style may take many forms, from the stately,
thought-weighted sentences of Bacon to the whimsical
turns of Charles Lamb; it may have the calm and beauty
of a Newman, or the passionate eloquence of Carlyle: in
each case we feel that the style is the perfect medium for
the thought.

In its lack of logical method, its freedom to stray hither
and thither, the essay is like good conversation. It is
like conversation again in its tone, which may be now
serious, now humorous, now merely playful. Some essayists, like Ruskin, are always serious; some, like Lamb,
are nearly always humorous; some, like Addison, are both
by turns. And the same essay may be partly serious,
partly humorous. As you read these essays, then, be on
the watch for a twinkle of the eye.

To sum up the characteristics of the essay, we may say
that it is a short piece of prose, not attempting to treat
its subject completely nor logically, but rather giving the
author's opinions upon it; opinions which may or may not
be serious, but which are set forth with a high degree of
literary art. It usually reveals more or less of the personality of the author, and in this respect corresponds
in prose to the lyric in poetry.

THE HISTORY OF THE ESSAY

The essay as a form in modern literature began with
a French writer, Michel de Montaigne, who in 1580
published two volumes entitled *Essais*. These dealt with
such subjects as Fortune, Cannibals, Names, Smells,

Liars, Virtue, and the like. The book was soon translated into English, and had a marked influence upon English writers. Francis Bacon, Lamb, Hazlitt, and Stevenson were readers of Montaigne, and acknowledge their debt to him.

The first English writer of essays was Francis Bacon, whose *Essays, or Counsels Civil and Moral* appeared in 1625. This little volume contained sixty essays, in length from two to ten pages; the subjects were all general, such as Studies, Riches, Love, Great Place. The tone of the essays was grave; one seems to hear the voice of the Lord Chief Justice of England delivering his wise verdicts upon human affairs. And of all Bacon's works, which number fifteen large volumes, dealing with science and philosophy, written by the wisest man of his time, only this slender book of essays survives to be read to-day.

From the time of Sir Francis Bacon to the beginning of the eighteenth century, occasional volumes of essays appeared. Such were the *Religio Medici* of Sir Thomas Browne; *Several Discourses by Way of Essays*, by Abraham Cowley, and the *Miscellanea* of Sir William Temple. But the great development of the essay came with the rise of periodical literature in England.

In our day, with the newspapers thrust into our hands twice a day, and with newsstands piled with weekly and monthly journals, it is hard to imagine a time when neither newspaper nor magazine existed. Yet in 1688 this was exactly the situation in England. Newspapers were the first to appear; then in 1691 came the first magazine, the *Athenian Gazette*, a little sheet made up chiefly of questions and answers. In 1704 Daniel Defoe, the author of *Robinson Crusoe*, began a journal called *A Weekly Review of the Affairs of France*, which contained, in addition to the news from Europe, a short essay or editorial. This idea was still further developed by Richard Steele, who in 1709 began the publication of the *Tatler*, a weekly paper consisting of a single large sheet printed on both sides, containing a paragraph of news and one or more essays. After a few numbers of the paper had appeared, Steele was aided by his friend Joseph Addison. The *Tatler* became popular; its editors saw an opportunity for improving it, and in 1711 they discontinued the *Tatler* and began the *Spectator*. This was published at first three times a week, then daily; it contained no news, merely a single essay, and a few advertisements. The essays covered a wide range of topics. They did not touch politics, but with this exception they treated almost every topic of interest to the Londoner of the day. There were papers on duelling, on the Italian opera, on fashionable slang, on style in women's dress, on the treatment of servants, on education, on courtship and marriage. And in practically all these essays the writers had the same aim as an editorial writer of to-day: to bring to public attention some wrong or folly that ought to be corrected. The editors did not deal with great public questions, or with crimes punishable by law, but with matters of behavior and the customs of the time. These papers thus show a new type of essay: that which is written to influence public opinion in some particular direction. This may be called the editorial essay.

The success of the *Spectator* led to many imitations. Dr. Johnson wrote the *Rambler* and the *Idler*. Oliver Goldsmith wrote a series of papers called *The Citizen of the World*, and there were hundreds of others. But none of them equalled the work of Addison and Steele, the founders of the type.

The next development of the essay was also a result of the development of periodical literature. The early journals were affairs of only a few pages. But with the beginning of the nineteenth century we have the appearance of magazines, published monthly or quarterly, of a size to permit the publication of long articles. The *Edinburgh Review* was established in 1802; the *Quarterly Review* in 1809, *Blackwood's Magazine* in 1817, the *London Magazine* in 1820. The rivalry between these journals led them to pay contributors liberally, and to allow much freedom to these writers. Hence such authors as Macaulay, Lamb, De Quincey, Hazlitt, and Hunt were stimulated to do their best. Macaulay, with his wide reading and his marvellous memory, could write for the *Edinburgh* a book review in which he discussed not only the book itself, and all the subjects mentioned in it, but other subjects which the author should have discussed, but did not. Charles Lamb, who by day was a bookkeeper, by night read his favorite authors, and wrote his whimsical essays for the *London Magazine*. Hazlitt and De Quincey, both great readers and famous as talkers, could pour out their talk on paper at the rate of a guinea a printed page. So with the advent of the modern magazine came the full development of the critical and descriptive and personal essays as we know them to-day. The magazine has continued to be the medium for the first publication of almost all essays. Carlyle published his *Sartor Resartus* in *Fraser's Magazine;* Thackeray's *Roundabout Papers* were written for the *Cornhill;* Stevenson's earlier essays appeared in the *Cornhill*, his later ones in *Scribner's;* Holmes's *Autocrat of the Breakfast-Table* was published in the *Atlantic*, and Van Dyke's essays in *Scribner's*.

THE TYPES OF ESSAYS

When we read Lamb's essay on Old China, we do not learn very much about porcelain, but we learn a good deal about Charles Lamb, his likes and dislikes. Such essays,

aiming primarily to entertain, and revealing the personality of the author, are called personal essays. To this
group belong the writings of Thackeray, of Hazlitt, and
most of Stevenson. As we read their essays we grow
better and better acquainted with the writers. Montaigne, who was the first to write essays of this type,
says in the introduction to his book, "It is myself I por-
tray." So the personal essay, or, as it is sometimes
called, the familiar essay, forms a distinct class, and includes some of the most noted essays in English literature.

The descriptive essay is self-explanatory. It may deal
with the larger aspects of nature, as Ruskin's description
of the sky, or with animals, as Thoreau's Brute Neighbors, or indeed with any created thing. It differs from
pure description in that you are always conscious of the
author: he tells what he thinks as well as what he sees.
Thus Thoreau begins by asking questions about nature,
and Ruskin closes with an appeal to let the beauty of the
sky strengthen our faith. Such touches mark the writing as belonging to the essay type.

The character sketch differs from the description in
that while the description deals with the outward appear-
ance, the character sketch deals with the inner man.
It may have as its subject an imaginary individual, as
Goldsmith's *Man in Black*, or real persons, as in Julian
Street's portrait of Theodore Roosevelt.

In the critical essay, the subject is usually a work of
art. It may be a book, a painting, an opera, a statue, or
an architectural work. When Macaulay wrote a review
of a new edition of the *Pilgrim's Progress*, or when a
critic of to-day writes an account of a new book or play,
each tells us something about the contents of the book,
and in addition gives his opinion, in the form of praise
or blame. Or the critical essay may be general, as when

Ruskin tells us how to choose books and how to read them.

Another type is the editorial essay, or that which is published in a periodical with the aim of influencing public opinion. It is necessary to distinguish between the editorial and the editorial essay. Most editorials are really brief arguments: they are plain in style, they aim at convincing their readers and nothing more. Such articles cannot be called essays. But the writers of the *Spectator* aimed to entertain their readers quite as much as to persuade them; they gave careful attention to their style, and they so imbued what they wrote with their own personality that it has power to charm us yet. There are occasional articles of the essay type on the editorial pages of our newspapers: sometimes a column regularly appears, such as the "Topics of the Times" in the New York *Times*, made up of brief papers which in mood and form are true essays.

The reflective essay differs from the others in two respects: its subjects are general, often abstract, and its tone is serious. Francis Bacon writing upon Studies, Emerson writing upon Self-Reliance, Carlyle writing upon the Influence of Books, John Galsworthy writing upon the differences between Americans and Englishmen, are examples of the reflective essay at its best. In each case the writer is a man with a philosophic mind, one who looks beneath the appearance of things to find realities; each has thought deeply upon an important subject, and in the essay gives his matured conclusions.

HOW TO STUDY THESE ESSAYS

First, do not expect to find a story. Short stories are delightful—and simple. Anybody can read them; a child can understand them. A taste for essays is like a taste for olives: it must be cultivated. An essay requires more attention to read than a story, and it repays you by giving you more to think about.

The essays in each group should be read with a different purpose. In the personal essays, ask yourself what each one shows about the man who wrote it. How many of these experiences are like your own? What bits of humor do you find? What ideas that are well expressed?

For the descriptive essays, read slowly and try to see with your imagination the pictures presented. Recall similar sights you have seen. Try to write something yourself in imitation of one of these descriptions.

In reading a character sketch, ask yourself such questions as these: What are the chief traits of the person portrayed? How are these made clear, by stating them or by giving instances to illustrate the point? Why did the writer choose this particular person as his subject? Does he give his opinion of the person directly, or does he let you infer it?

In the critical essays, note how fully the writers tell about the books they discuss. Few books are reviewed at such length as Professor Schapiro's review of Wells's *History*, and few are reviewed so well. What qualifications should one have to review a book? What should be his aim: to tell the contents of a book? to praise it so that it may sell? to attack it? to show his own cleverness? to point out its merits and faults without prejudice? Which of these aims is seen in Macaulay's review? in Schapiro's? Has either one an introduction? a conclusion? Point out the extent of each. Compare these reviews with other essays as regards logical arrangement.

For the editorial essays, state in a sentence the point which the writer wished to make. Why did he introduce imaginary characters? What subjects might engage the attention of the *Spectator* to-day? Try to treat one of them in the *Spectator* manner.

The reflective essay demands careful reading, sentence by sentence, to get its meaning. As you read, note sentences that contain ideas new to you, or particularly well expressed, and copy them into a note-book. Form the habit of making quotations from what you read. As you finish each essay, ask yourself what new ideas you have gained. What do essays give you that fiction does not?

The writers in this book represent the leading essayists of England and America. In the biographies of these authors, given in the notes, you will find the titles of various books of essays written by these men; other volumes of essays are given in the list at the end of the book. Some of these books you will read in the library, some of them you ought to own.

THE PERSONAL ESSAY

RICHARD STEELE

A DAY IN LONDON

Richard Steele (1672–1729) was born in Dublin. At twelve years of age he was sent to the Charterhouse School in London, where he met Joseph Addison and the two became fast friends. He entered Oxford, but left without a degree; soon afterward he entered the army. After some years Captain Steele of the Guards became interested in writing. Several of his plays were produced at the Drury Lane Theatre: the best of these was a comedy, *The Tender Husband*. Encouraged by success, Steele resigned from the army and devoted himself to literature. He knew Pope and Swift and most of the writers of the day, and still kept up his friendship with Addison. In 1709 he started a paper of his own, the *Tatler*, which was the beginning of the periodical essay. (See Introduction, p. x.) This was later followed by the *Spectator;* to both periodicals Addison was a frequent contributor, but the plan was Steele's and he first sketched the members of the famous Spectator Club. In the first volume of the *Tatler* Steele thus set forth its purpose:

"The general purpose of this paper is to expose the false arts of life, to pull off the disguises of cunning, vanity and affectation, and to recommend a general simplicity in our dress, our discourse and our behavior."

But Steele was not always bent upon reforming society. In the paper here quoted, as in many others, he writes to entertain his readers, and at the end he tries desperately to find a moral. This essay gives an account of a day of his own life: reading between the lines, we learn not a little about lively Dick Steele.

RICHARD STEELE

A DAY IN LONDON

(From the *Tatler*)

It is an inexpressible pleasure to know a little of the world, and be of no character or significancy in it.

To be ever unconcerned, and ever looking on new objects with an endless curiosity, is a delight known only to those who are turned for speculation: nay, they who enjoy it must value things only as they are the objects of speculation, without drawing any worldly advantage to themselves from them, but just as they are what contribute to their amusement, or the improvement of the mind. I lay one night last week at Richmond; and being restless, not out of dissatisfaction, but a certain busy inclination one sometimes has, I rose at four in the morning, and took boat for London, with a resolution to rove by boat and coach for the next four-and-twenty hours, till the many different objects I must needs meet with should tire my imagination, and give me an inclination to a repose more profound than I was at that time capable of. I beg people's pardon for an odd humor I am guilty of, and was often that day, which is saluting any person whom I like, whether I know him or not. This is a particularity which would be tolerated in me, if they considered that the greatest pleasure I know I receive at my eyes, and that I am obliged to an agreeable person for coming abroad into my view, as another is for a visit of conversation at their own houses.

3

The hours of the day and night are taken up in the cities of London and Westminster, by people as different from each other as those who are born in different centuries. Men of six o'clock give way to those of nine, they of nine to the generation of twelve; and they of twelve disappear, and make room for the fashionable world, who have made two o'clock the noon of the day.

When we first put off from shore, we soon fell in with a fleet of gardeners, bound for the several market ports of London; and it was the most pleasing scene imaginable to see the cheerfulness with which those industrious people plied their way to a certain sale of their goods. The banks on each side are as well peopled, and beautified with as agreeable plantations, as any spot on the earth; but the Thames itself, loaded with the product of each shore, added very much to the landscape. It was very easy to observe by their sailing, and the countenances of the ruddy virgins, who were supercargoes, the parts of the town to which they were bound. There was an air in the purveyors for Covent-garden, who frequently converse with morning rakes, very unlike the seeming sobriety of those bound for Stocks-market.

Nothing remarkable happened in our voyage; but I landed with ten sail of apricot-boats, at Strand-bridge, after having put in at Nine-Elms, and taken in melons, consigned by Mr. Cuffe, of that place, to Sarah Sewell and Company, at their stall in Covent-garden. We arrived at Strand-bridge at six of the clock, and were unloading, when the hackney-coachmen of the foregoing night took their leave of each other at the Darkhouse, to go to bed before the day was too far spent. Chimney-sweepers passed by us as we made up to the market, and some raillery happened between one of the fruit-wenches and those black men about the Devil and Eve, with allusion to their several professions. I could not believe any place more entertaining than Covent-garden; where I strolled from one fruit-shop to another, with crowds of agreeable young women around me, who were purchasing fruit for their respective families.

It was almost eight of the clock before I could leave that variety of objects. I took coach and followed a young lady, who tripped into another just before me, attended by her maid. I saw immediately she was of the family of the Vainloves. There are a set of these, who, of all things, affect the play of Blind-man's-buff, and leading men into love for they know not whom, who are fled they know not where. This sort of woman is usually a jaunty slattern; she hangs on her clothes, plays her head, varies her posture, and changes place incessantly, and all with an appearance of striving at the same time to hide herself, and yet give you to understand she is in humor to laugh at you. You must have often seen the coachmen make signs with their fingers, as they drive by each other, to intimate how much they have got that day. They can carry on that language to give intelligence where they are driving. In an instant my coachman took the wink to pursue; and the lady's driver gave the hint that he was going through Long-acre toward St. James's; while he whipped up James-street, we drove for King-street, to save the pass at St. Martin's-lane. The coachmen took care to meet, jostle, and threaten each other for way, and be entangled at the end of New-port-street and Long-acre. The fright, you must believe, brought down the lady's coach-door, and obliged her, with her mask off, to inquire into the bustle,—when she sees the man she would avoid. The tackle of the coach-window is so bad she cannot draw it up again, and she drives on sometimes wholly discovered, and sometimes half-escaped, according to the accident of carriages in her way. One of these ladies keeps her seat in a hackney-coach as well as the best rider does on a managed horse. The laced shoe on her left foot, with a careless gesture, just appearing on the opposite cushion, held her both firm, and in a proper attitude to receive the next jolt.

As she was an excellent coach-woman, many were the glances at each other which we had for an hour and a half, in all parts of the town, by the skill of our drivers; till at last my lady was conveniently lost, with notice from her coachman to ours to make off, and he should hear where she went. This chase was now at an end: and the fellow who drove her came to us, and discovered that he was ordered to come again in an hour, for that she was a silk-worm. I was surprised with this phrase, but found it was a cant among the hackney fraternity for their best customers, women who ramble twice or thrice a week from shop to shop, to turn over all the goods in town without buying anything. The silk-worms are, it seems, indulged by the tradesmen; for, though they never buy, they are ever talking of new silks, laces, and ribbons, and serve the owners in getting them customers, as their common dunners do in making them pay.

The day of people of fashion began now to break, and carts and hacks were mingled with equipages of show and vanity; when I resolved to walk it out of cheapness; but my unhappy curiosity is such, that I find it always my interest to take coach; for some odd adventure among beggars, ballad-singers, or the like, detains and throws me into expense. It happened so immediately: for at the corner of Warwick-street, as I was listening to a new ballad, a ragged rascal, a beggar who knew me, came up to me, and began to turn the eyes of the good company upon me, by telling me he was extremely poor, and should die in the street for want of drink, except I immediately would have the charity to give him sixpence to go into the next ale-house and save his life. He urged, with a melancholy face, that all his family had died of thirst. All the mob have humor, and two or three began to take the jest; by which Mr. Sturdy carried his point, and let me sneak off to a coach. As I drove along, it was a pleasing reflection to see the world so prettily checkered since I left Richmond, and the scene still filling with children of a new hour.

This satisfaction increased as I moved toward the city; and gay signs, well-disposed streets, magnificent public structures, and wealthy shops adorned with contented faces, made the joy still rising till we came into the centre of the city, and centre of the world of trade, the Exchange of London. As other men in the crowds about me were pleased with their hopes and bargains, I found my account in observing them, in attention to their several interests. I, indeed, looked upon myself as the richest man that walked the Exchange that day; for my benevolence made me share the gains of every bargain that was made. It was not the least of my satisfaction in my survey, to go upstairs, and pass the shops of agreeable females; to observe so many pretty hands busy in the folding of ribbons, and the utmost eagerness of agreeable faces in the sale of patches, pins, and wires, on each side of the counters, was an amusement in which I could longer have indulged myself, had not the dear creatures called to me, to ask what I wanted, when I could not answer, only "To look at you." I went to one of the windows which opened to the area below, where all the several voices lost their distinction, and rose up in a confused humming; which created in me a reflection that could not come into the mind of any but of one a little too studious; for I said to myself with a kind of pun in thought, "What nonsense is all the hurry of this world to those who are above it?" In these, or not much wiser thoughts, I had like to have lost my place at the chop-house, where every man, according to the natural bashfulness or sullenness of our nation, eats in a public room a mess of broth, or chop of meat, in dumb silence, as if they had no pretense to speak to each other on the foot of being men, except they were of each other's acquaintance.

I went afterward to Robin's, and saw people, who had dined with me at the five-penny ordinary just before, give bills for the value of large estates; and could not but behold with great pleasure, property lodged in, and transferred in a moment from, such as would never be masters of half as much as is seemingly in them, and given from them, every day they live. But before five in the afternoon I left the city, came to my common scene of Coventgarden, and passed the evening at Will's* in attending the discourses of several sets of people, who relieved each other within my hearing on the subjects of cards, dice, love, learning, and politics. The last subject kept me till I heard the streets in the possession of the bellman, who had now the world to himself, and cried, "Past two o'clock." This roused me from my seat; and I went to my lodgings, led by a light, whom I put into the discourse of his private economy, and made him give me an account of the charge, hazard, profit, and loss of a family that depended upon a link, with a design to end my trivial day with the generosity of sixpence, instead of a third part of that sum. When I came to my chambers, I writ down these minutes; but was at a loss what instruction I should propose to my reader from the enumeration of so many insignificant matters and occurrences; and I thought it of great use, if they could learn with me to keep their minds open to gratification, and ready to receive it from any thing it meets with. This one circum-

* Will's, a famous coffee-house in Russell Street, London, frequented by literary men.

stance will make every face you see give you the satisfaction you now take in beholding that of a friend; will make every object a pleasing one; will make all the good which arrives to any man, an increase of happiness to yourself.

CHARLES LAMB

A DISSERTATION UPON ROAST PIG

Charles Lamb (1775–1834) has been called the best loved of English writers. He was the son of a poor London clerk, and attended as a charity scholar the famous boys' school Christ's Hospital. Here he learned the Latin which he is fond of introducing in his essays; here he met Coleridge, and they became lifelong friends. When school-days ended, Coleridge went to the university, and Lamb became a bookkeeper in a London office. His work in this place is described in two essays, The South Sea House, and The Superannuated Man. He lived with his sister Mary, who appears in the essays as Bridget Elia. With her he wrote the *Tales from Shakespeare*, which have introduced the plays to many young readers. His chief work is the *Essays of Elia*. These were contributed to the *London Magazine*, over the signature of James Elia, a fellow-clerk in the office. Lamb's style is unique. He was a great reader of Elizabethan literature, especially plays, and frequently uses quaint old words from these books. He is fond of giving an unexpected turn to his sentences, and humor, a quiet, sly humor, peeps out everywhere.

In connection with the essay on Roast Pig, it is interesting to read this letter of Lamb's, addressed to a farmer and his wife:

Twelfth Day, '23.

The pig was above my feeble praise. It was a dear pigmy. There was some contention as to who should have the ears; but in spite of his obstinacy, (deaf as these little creatures are to advice) I contrived to get at one of them. . . .

He must have been the least of his race. His little foots would have gone into the silver slipper. I take him to have been a Chinese, and a female.

He crackled delicately.

I left a blank at the top of the page, not being determined which to address it to: so farmer and farmer's wife will please to divide our thanks. May your granaries be full, and your rats empty, and your chickens plump, and your envious neighbors lean, and your laborers busy, and you as idle and as happy as the day is long.

Yours truly,

C. LAMB.

CHARLES LAMB

A DISSERTATION UPON ROAST PIG

(From the *Essays of Elia*, First Series)

Mankind, says a Chinese manuscript, which my friend
M. was obliging enough to read and explain to me, for
the first seventy thousand ages ate their meat raw,
clawing or biting it from the living animal, just as they
do in Abyssinia to this day.   This period is not obscurely
hinted at by their great Confucius in the second chapter
of his Mundane Mutations, where he designates a kind
of golden age by the term Cho-fang, literally the Cooks'
Holiday.   The manuscript goes on to say, that the art
of roasting, or rather broiling (which I take to be the
elder brother) was accidentally discovered in the manner
following.   The swine-herd, Ho-ti, having gone out into
the woods one morning, as his manner was, to collect
mast for his hogs, left his cottage in the care of his eldest
son Bo-bo, a great lubberly boy, who being fond of playing with fire, as younkers of his age commonly are, let
some sparks escape into a bundle of straw, which kindling quickly, spread the conflagration over every part of
their poor mansion, till it was reduced to ashes.   Together
with the cottage (a sorry antediluvian makeshift of a
building, you may think it), what was of much more
importance, a fine litter of new-farrowed pigs, no less than
nine in number, perished.   China pigs have been esteemed
a luxury all over the East, from the remotest periods that
we read of.   Bo-bo was in the utmost consternation, as
you may think, not so much for the sake of the tenement,
which his father and he could easily build up again with

a few dry branches, and the labor of an hour or two, at any time, as for the loss of the pigs. While he was thinking what he should say to his father, and wringing his hands over the smoking remnants of one of those untimely sufferers, an odor assailed his nostrils, unlike any scent which he had before experienced. What could it proceed from?—not from the burnt cottage—he had smelt that smell before—indeed, this was by no means the first accident of the kind which had occurred through the negligence of this unlucky young firebrand. Much less did it resemble that of any known herb, weed, or flower. A premonitory moistening at the same time overflowed his nether lip. He knew not what to think. He next stooped down to feel the pig, if there were any signs of life in it. He burnt his fingers, and to cool them he applied them in his booby fashion to his mouth. Some of the crumbs of the scorched skin had come away with his fingers, and for the first time in his life (in the world's life indeed, for before him no man had known it) he tasted—*crackling!* Again he felt and fumbled at the pig. It did not burn him so much now, still he licked his fingers from a sort of habit. The truth at length broke into his slow understanding, that it was the pig that smelt so, and the pig that tasted so delicious; and surrendering himself up to the new-born pleasure, he fell to tearing up whole handfuls of the scorched skin with the flesh next it, and was cramming it down his throat in his beastly fashion, when his sire entered amid the smoking rafters, armed with retributory cudgel, and finding how affairs stood, began to rain blows upon the young rogue's shoulders, as thick as hailstones, which Bo-bo heeded not any more than if they had been flies. The tickling pleasure, which he experienced in his lower regions, had rendered him quite callous to any inconveniences he might feel in those remote quarters. His father might lay on, but he could

not beat him from his pig, till he had fairly made an end
of it, when, becoming a little more sensible of his situation, something like the following dialogue ensued.

"You graceless whelp, what have you got there de-
vouring? Is it not enough that you have burnt me down
three houses with your dog's tricks, and be hanged to
you! but you must be eating fire, and I know not what—
what have you got there, I say?"

"O father, the pig, the pig! do come and taste how nice
the burnt pig eats."

The ears of Ho-ti tingled with horror. He cursed his
son, and he cursed himself that ever he should beget a
son that should eat burnt pig.

Bo-bo, whose scent was wonderfully sharpened since
morning, soon raked out another pig, and fairly rend-
ing it asunder, thrust the lesser half by main force into
the fists of Ho-ti, still shouting out, "Eat, eat, eat the
burnt pig, father, only taste—O Lord!"—with such-like
barbarous ejaculations, cramming all the while as if he
would choke.

Ho-ti trembled in every joint while he grasped the
abominable thing, wavering whether he should not put
his son to death for an unnatural young monster, when
the crackling scorching his fingers, as it had done his
son's, and applying the same remedy to them, he in his
turn tasted some of its flavor, which, make what sour
mouths he would for a pretense, proved not altogether
displeasing to him. In conclusion (for the manuscript
here is a little tedious), both father and son fairly set down
to the mess, and never left off till they had despatched all
that remained of the litter.

Bo-bo was strictly enjoined not to let the secret escape,
for the neighbors would certainly have stoned them for
a couple of abominable wretches, who could think of improving upon the good meat which God had sent them.

Nevertheless, strange stories got about. It was observed that Ho-ti's cottage was burnt down now more frequently than ever. Nothing but fires from this time forward. Some would break out in broad day, others in the night-time. As often as the sow farrowed, so sure was the house of Ho-ti to be in a blaze; and Ho-ti himself, which was the more remarkable, instead of chastising his son, seemed to grow more indulgent to him than ever. At length they were watched, the terrible mystery discovered, and father and son summoned to take their trial at Pekin, then an inconsiderable assize town. Evidence was given, the obnoxious food itself produced in court, and verdict about to be pronounced, when the foreman of the jury begged that some of the burnt pig, of which the culprits stood accused, might be handed into the box. He handled it, and they all handled it; and burning their fingers, as Bo-bo and his father had done before them, and nature prompting to each of them the same remedy, against the face of all the facts, and the clearest charge which judge had ever given,—to the surprise of the whole court, townsfolk, strangers, reporters, and all present— without leaving the box, or any manner of consultation whatever, they brought in a simultaneous verdict of Not Guilty.

The judge, who was a shrewd fellow, winked at the manifest iniquity of the decision: and when the court was dismissed, went privily and bought up all the pigs that could be had for love or money. In a few days his lordship's town-house was observed to be on fire. The thing took wing, and now there was nothing to be seen but fires in every direction. Fuel and pigs grew enormously dear all over the district. The insurance-offices one and all shut up shop. People built slighter and slighter every day, until it was feared that the very science of architecture would in no long time be lost to the world. Thus this custom of firing houses continued, till in process of time, says my manuscript, a sage arose, like our Locke, who made a discovery that the flesh of swine, or indeed of any other animal, might be cooked (*burnt*, as they called it) without the necessity of consuming a whole house to dress it. Then first began the rude form of a gridiron. Roasting by the string or spit came in a century or two later, I forget in whose dynasty. By such slow degrees, concludes the manuscript, do the most useful, and seemingly the most obvious, arts make their way among mankind.

Without placing too implicit faith in the account above given, it must be agreed that if a worthy pretext for so dangerous an experiment as setting houses on fire (especially in these days) could be assigned in favor of any culinary object, that pretext and excuse might be found in ROAST PIG.

Of all the delicacies in the whole *mundus edibilis,** I will maintain it to be the most delicate—*princeps obsoniorum.*†

I speak not of your grown porkers—things between pig and pork—these hobbledehoys—but a young and tender suckling—under a moon old—guiltless as yet of the sty—with no original speck of the *amor immunditiæ,*‡ the hereditary failing of the first parent, yet manifest—his voice as yet not broken, but something between a childish treble and a grumble—the mild forerunner or *præludium*§ of a grunt.

He must be roasted. I am not ignorant that our ancestors ate them seethed, or boiled—but what a sacrifice of the exterior tegument!

* *Mundus edibilis,* world of eatables.
† *Princeps obsoniorum,* the chief of viands.
‡ *Amor immunditiæ,* the love of dirt.
§ *Præludium,* prelude.

There is no flavor comparable, I will contend, to that of the crisp, tawny, well-watched, not over-roasted, *crackling*, as it is well called—the very teeth are invited to their share of the pleasure at this banquet, in overcoming the coy, brittle resistance—with the adhesive oleaginous—O call it not fat! but an indefinable sweetness growing up to it—the tender blossoming of fat— fat cropped in the bud—taken in the shoot—in the first innocence—the cream and quintessence of the child-pig's yet pure food—the lean, no lean, but a kind of animal manna—or, rather, fat and lean (if it must be so) so blended and running into each other, that both together make but one ambrosian result or common substance.

Behold him while he is "doing"—it seemeth rather a refreshing warmth, than a scorching heat, that he is so passive to. How equably he twirleth round the string! Now he is just done. To see the extreme sensibility of that tender age! he hath wept out his pretty eyes—radiant jellies—shooting stars.—

See him in the dish, his second cradle, how meek he lieth!—wouldst thou have had this innocent grow up to the grossness and indocility which too often accompany maturer swinehood? Ten to one he would have proved a glutton, a sloven, an obstinate, disagreeable animal—wallowing in all manner of filthy conversation—from these sins he is happily snatched away—

> Ere sin could blight or sorrow fade,
> Death came with timely care,—

his memory is odoriferous—no clown curseth, while his stomach half rejecteth, the rank bacon—no coal-heaver bolteth him in reeking sausages—he hath a fair sepulchre in the grateful stomach of the judicious epicure—and for such a tomb might be content to die.

He is the best of sapors.* Pine-apple is great. She is indeed almost too transcendent—a delight, if not sinful, yet so like to sinning, that really a tender-conscienced person would do well to pause,—too ravishing for mortal taste, she woundeth and excoriateth the lips that approach her—like lovers' kisses, she biteth—she is a pleasure bordering on pain from the fierceness and insanity of her relish—but she stoppeth at the palate—she meddleth not with the appetite—and the coarsest hunger might barter her consistently for a mutton-chop.

Pig—let me speak his praise—is no less provocative of the appetite than he is satisfactory to the criticalness of the censorious palate. The strong man may batten on him, and the weakling refuseth not his mild juices.

Unlike to mankind's mixed characters, a bundle of virtues and vices, inexplicably intertwisted, and not to be unravelled without hazard, he is—good throughout. No part of him is better or worse than another. He helpeth, as far as his little means extend, all around. He is the least envious of banquets. He is all neighbors' fare.

I am one of those who freely and ungrudgingly impart a share of the good things of this life which fall to their lot (few as mine are in this kind) to a friend. I protest I take as great an interest in my friend's pleasures, his relishes, and proper satisfactions, as in mine own. "Presents," I often say, "endear Absents." Hares, pheasants, partridges, snipes, barn-door chickens (those "tame villatic fowl"), capons, plovers, brawn, barrels of oysters, I dispense as freely as I receive them. I love to taste them, as it were, upon the tongue of my friend. But a stop must be put somewhere. One would not, like Lear, "give everything." I make my stand upon pig. Methinks it is an ingratitude to the Giver of all good flavors to extra-domiciliate, or send out of the house slightingly

* Sapor, flavor, taste.

(under pretext of friendship, or I know not what) a blessing so particularly adapted, predestined, I may say, to
my individual palate.—It argues an insensibility.

I remember a touch of conscience in this kind at school.
My good old aunt, who never parted from me at the end
of a holiday without stuffing a sweetmeat, or some nice
thing, into my pocket, had dismissed me one evening
with a smoking plum-cake, fresh from the oven.   In my
way to school (it was over London Bridge) a gray-headed
old beggar saluted me (I have no doubt at this time of day,
that he was a counterfeit).   I had no pence to console
him with, and in the vanity of self-denial, and the very
coxcombry of charity, schoolboy like, I made him a present of—the whole cake!   I walked on a little, buoyed
up, as one is on such occasions, with a sweet soothing of
self-satisfaction; but, before I had got to the end of the
bridge, my better feelings returned, and I burst into
tears, thinking how ungrateful I had been to my good
aunt, to go and give her good gift away to a stranger that
I had never seen before, and who might be a bad man for
aught I knew; and then I thought of the pleasure my aunt
would be taking in thinking that I—I myself, and not
another—would eat her nice cake—and what should I
say to her the next time I saw her—how naughty I was
to part with her pretty present!—and the odor of that
spicy cake came back upon my recollection, and the pleasure and the curiosity I had taken in seeing her make it,
and her joy when she sent it to the oven, and how disappointed she would feel that I had never had a bit of it in
my mouth at last—and I blamed my impertinent spirit
of alms-giving, and out-of-place hypocrisy of goodness;
and above all I wished never to see the face again of that
insidious, good-for-nothing, old gray impostor.

Our ancestors were nice in their method of sacrificing
these tender victims.   We read of pigs whipped to death

with something of a shock, as we hear of any other obsolete custom. The age of discipline is gone by, or it would be curious to inquire (in a philosophical light merely) what effect this process might have toward intenerating and dulcifying a substance naturally so mild and dulcet as the flesh of young pigs. It looks like refining a violet. Yet we should be cautious, while we condemn the inhumanity, how we censure the wisdom of the practice. It might impart a gusto.—

I remember an hypothesis, argued upon by the young students, when I was at St. Omer's, and maintained with much learning and pleasantry on both sides, "Whether, supposing that the flavor of a pig who obtained his death by whipping (*per flagellationem extremam**) superadded a pleasure upon the palate of a man more intense than any possible suffering we can conceive in the animal, is man justified in using that method of putting the animal to death?" I forget the decision.

His sauce should be considered. Decidedly, a few bread crumbs, done up with his liver and brains, and a dash of mild sage. But banish, dear Mrs. Cook, I beseech you, the whole onion tribe. Barbecue your whole hogs to your palate, steep them in shalots, stuff them out with plantations of the rank and guilty garlic; you cannot poison them, or make them stronger than they are—but consider, he is a weakling—a flower.

* *Per flagellationem*, through capital punishment by whipping.

CHARLES LAMB

OLD CHINA

Few passages in the history of English literature are more touching than the story of Charles and Mary Lamb. She was ten years his senior; the mother was an invalid, so that as a child Charles was cared for by his sister. There was a trait of insanity in the family. When Charles was twenty-one, Mary, her mind affected by a long strain, became insane, and killed her mother. She was placed in an asylum, and although she regained her reason, she was only released upon the solemn pledge of her brother that he would watch over her. From time to time the affliction recurred, and the brother would take her to the asylum for a season. At other times she was an ideal companion, interested in books as Charles was, helping him to write his *Tales from Shakespeare*, making a pleasant home for him, where his friends Hazlitt, Coleridge, Godwin, Haydon the painter, and Wordsworth formed a famous group. Yet over all their life hung the shadow. Charles, faithful to his sister, never sought to marry. They had been very poor, but as Charles's literary work gradually won recognition, their circumstances became easier, even allowing a few luxuries. They were both intensely fond of the theatre, and numbered among their friends some of the best actors of the day. Such are the materials out of which Lamb made the essay on Old China. Mary appears there as Bridget; all their pleasures and the sweet intimacy of their lives are told, but the shadow is not there. Like Stevenson, Lamb resolutely carried his own burden; it might be heavy, but no whimper or groan escapes into his pages.

CHARLES LAMB

OLD CHINA

(From the *Essays of Elia*, Second Series)

I have an almost feminine partiality for old china.
When I go to see any great house, I inquire for the china-
closet, and next for the picture-gallery. I cannot defend the order of preference, but by saying that we have
all some taste or other, of too ancient a date to admit of
our remembering distinctly that it was an acquired one.
I can call to mind the first play, and the first exhibition,
that I was taken to; but I am not conscious of a time when
china jars and saucers were introduced into my imagination.

I had no repugnance then—why should I now have?
—to those little, lawless, azure-tinctured grotesques, that,
under the notion of men and women, float about, uncir-
cumscribed by any element, in that world before perspec-
tive—a china tea-cup.

I like to see my old friends—whom distance cannot
diminish—figuring up in the air (so they appear to our
optics), yet on *terra firma* still—for so we must in courtesy
interpret that speck of deeper blue, which the decorous
artist, to prevent absurdity, had made to spring up beneath their sandals.

I love the men with women's faces, and the women,
if possible, with still more womanish expressions.

Here is a young and courtly Mandarin, handing tea
to a lady from a salver—two miles off. See how distance
seems to set off respect! And here the same lady, or
another—for likeness is identity on tea-cups—is stepping

25

into a little fairy boat, moored on the hither side of this calm garden river, with a dainty mincing foot, which in a right angle of incidence (as angles go in our world) must infallibly land her in the midst of a flowery mead— a furlong off on the other side of the same strange stream!

Farther on—if far or near can be predicated of their world—see horses, trees, pagodas, dancing the hays.*

Here—a cow and rabbit couchant, and co-extensive— so objects show, seen through the lucid atmosphere of fine Cathay.

I was pointing out to my cousin last evening, over our Hyson (which we are old-fashioned enough to drink unmixed still of an afternoon), some of these *speciosa miracula†* upon a set of extraordinary old blue china (a recent purchase) which we were now for the first time using; and could not help remarking, how favorable circumstances had been to us of late years, that we could afford to please the eye sometimes with trifles of this sort— when a passing sentiment seemed to overshade the brows of my companion. I am quick at detecting these summer clouds in Bridget.

"I wish the good old times would come again," she said, "when we were not quite so rich. I do not mean that I want to be poor; but there was a middle state"— so she was pleased to ramble on,—"in which I am sure we were a great deal happier. A purchase is but a purchase, now that you have money enough and to spare. Formerly it used to be a triumph. When we coveted a cheap luxury (and, O! how much ado I had to get you to consent in those times!)—we were used to have a debate two or three days before, and to weigh the *for* and *against*, and think what we might spare it out of, and what saving we could hit upon, that should be an equivalent. A

* Hays, an old English dance, where the dancers stood in a ring.
† *Speciosa miracula*, beautiful marvels.

thing was worth buying then, when we felt the money that we paid for it.

"Do you remember the brown suit, which you made to hang upon you, till all your friends cried shame upon you, it grew so threadbare—and all because of that folio Beaumont and Fletcher, which you dragged home late at night from Barker's in Covent Garden? Do you remember how we eyed it for weeks before we could make up our minds to the purchase, and had not come to a determination till it was near ten o'clock of the Saturday night, when you set off from Islington, fearing you should be too late—and when the old bookseller with some grumbling opened his shop, and by the twinkling taper (for he was setting bedwards) lighted out the relic from his dusty treasures—and when you lugged it home, wishing it were twice as cumbersome—and when you presented it to me—and when we were exploring the perfectness of it (*collating*, you called it)—and while I was repairing some of the loose leaves with paste, which your impatience would not suffer to be left till daybreak—was there no pleasure in being a poor man? or can those neat black clothes which you wear now, and are so careful to keep brushed, since we have become rich and finical—give you half the honest vanity with which you flaunted it about in that overworn suit—your old corbeau*—for four or five weeks longer than you should have done to pacify your conscience for the mighty sum of fifteen— or sixteen shillings was it?—a great affair we thought it then—which you had lavished on the old folio. Now you can afford to buy any book that pleases you, but I do not see that you ever bring me home any nice old purchases now.

"When you came home with twenty apologies for laying out a less number of shillings upon that print

* Corbeau, a crow, a raven.

after Lionardo,* which we christened the 'Lady Blanch'; when you looked at the purchase, and thought of the money—and thought of the money, and looked again at the picture—was there no pleasure in being a poor man? Now, you have nothing to do but to walk into Colnaghi's, and buy a wilderness of Lionardos. Yet do you?

"Then, do you remember our pleasant walks to Enfield, and Potter's Bar, and Waltham, when we had a holiday —holidays and all other fun are gone now we are rich—and the little hand-basket in which I used to deposit our day's fare of savory cold lamb and salad—and how you would pry about at noontide for some decent house, where we might go in and produce our store—only paying for the ale that you must call for—and speculate upon the looks of the landlady, and whether she was likely to allow us a tablecloth—and wish for such another honest hostess as Izaak Walton has described many a one on the pleasant banks of the Lea, when he went a-fishing—and sometimes they would prove obliging enough, and sometimes they would look grudgingly upon us— but we had cheerful looks still for one another, and would eat our plain food savorily, scarcely grudging Piscator† his Trout Hall? Now—when we go out a day's pleasuring, which is seldom, moreover, we *ride* part of the way, and go into a fine inn, and order the best of dinners, never debating the expense—which, after all, never has half the relish of those chance country snaps, when we were at the mercy of uncertain usage, and a precarious welcome.

"You are too proud to see a play anywhere now but in the pit. Do you remember where it was we used to sit, when we saw the *Battle of Hexham*, and the *Surrender*

* Lionardo, Leonardo da Vinci; perhaps the picture referred to is the "Mona Lisa."

† Piscator, the name of the fisherman in Walton's *Compleat Angler*.

of Calais, and Bannister and Mrs. Bland in the *Children in the Wood*—when we squeezed out our shillings apiece to sit three or four times in a season in the one-shilling gallery—where you felt all the time that you ought not to have brought me—and more strongly I felt obligation to you for having brought me—and the pleasure was the better for a little shame—and when the curtain drew up, what cared we for our place in the house, or what mattered it where we were sitting, when our thoughts were with Rosalind in Arden, or with Viola at the Court of Illyria? You used to say that the gallery was the best place of all for enjoying a play socially—that the relish of such exhibitions must be in proportion to the infrequency of going—that the company we met there, not being in general readers of plays, were obliged to attend the more, and did attend, to what was going on, on the stage—because a word lost would have been a chasm which it was impossible for them to fill up. With such reflections we consoled our pride then—and I appeal to you whether, as a woman, I met generally with less attention and accommodation than I have done since in more expensive situations in the house? The getting in, indeed, and the crowding up those inconvenient staircases, was bad enough—but there was still a law of civility to woman recognized to quite as great an extent as we ever found in the other passages—and how a little difficulty overcome heightened the snug seat and the play, afterwards! Now we can only pay our money and walk in. You cannot see, you say, in the galleries now. I am sure we saw, and heard too, well enough then—but sight, and all, I think, is gone with our poverty.

"There was pleasure in eating strawberries, before they became quite common—in the first dish of peas, while they were yet dear—to have them for a nice supper, a treat. What treat can we have now? If we were to treat ourselves now—that is, to have dainties a little above our means, it would be selfish and wicked. It is the very little more that we allow ourselves beyond what the actual poor can get at, that makes what I call a treat—when two people, living together as we have done, now and then indulge themselves in a cheap luxury, which both like; while each apologizes, and is willing to take both halves of the blame to his single share. I see no harm in people making much of themselves, in that sense of the word. It may give them a hint how to make much of others. But now—what I mean by the word—we never *do* make much of ourselves. None but the poor can do it. I do not mean the veriest poor of all, but persons as we were, just above poverty.

"I know what you were going to say, that it is mighty pleasant at the end of the year to make all meet,—and much ado we used to have every Thirty-first Night of December to account for our exceedings—many a long face did you make over your puzzled accounts, and in contriving to make it out how we had spent so much—or that we had not spent so much—or that it was impossible we should spend so much next year—and still we found our slender capital decreasing—but then,—betwixt ways, and projects, and compromises of one sort or another, and talk of curtailing this charge, and doing without that for the future—and the hope that youth brings, and laughing spirits (in which you were never poor till now), we pocketed up our loss, and in conclusion, with 'lusty brimmers' (as you used to quote it out of *hearty cheerful Mr. Cotton*, as you called him), we used to welcome in the 'coming guest.' Now we have no reckoning at all at the end of the old year—no flattering promises about the new year doing better for us."

Bridget is so sparing of her speech on most occasions, that when she gets into a rhetorical vein, I am careful

how I interrupt it. I could not help, however, smiling
at the phantom of wealth which her dear imagination
had conjured up out of a clear income of poor —— hundred pounds a year. "It is true we were happier when
we were poorer, but we were also younger, my cousin.
I am afraid we must put up with the excess, for if we were
to shake the superflux into the sea, we should not much
mend ourselves. That we had much to struggle with,
as we grew up together, we have reason to be most thankful. It strengthened and knit our compact closer. We
could never have been what we have been to each other,
if we had always had the sufficiency which you now complain of. The resisting power—those natural dilations
of the youthful spirit, which circumstances cannot
straiten—with us are long since passed away. Com-
petence to age is supplementary youth, a sorry supplement indeed, but I fear the best that is to be had. We
must ride where we formerly walked: live better and lie
softer—and shall be wise to do so—than we had means
to do in those good old days you speak of. Yet could
those days return—could you and I once more walk our
thirty miles a day—could Bannister and Mrs. Bland
again be young, and you and I be young to see them—
could the good old one-shilling gallery days return—they
are dreams, my cousin, now—but could you and I at
this moment, instead of this quiet argument, by our
well-carpeted fireside, sitting on this luxurious sofa—be
once more struggling up those inconvenient staircases,
pushed about and squeezed, and elbowed by the poorest
rabble of poor gallery scramblers—could I once more
hear those anxious shrieks of yours—and the delicious
Thank God, we are safe, which always followed when the
topmost stair, conquered, let in the first light of the whole
cheerful theatre down beneath us—I know not the fathom
line that ever touched a descent so deep as I would be

willing to bury more wealth in than Crœsus had, or
the great Jew R—— is supposed to have, to purchase it.
And now do just look at that merry little Chinese waiter
holding an umbrella, big enough for a bed-tester, over the
head of that pretty insipid half Madonna-ish chit of a
lady in that very blue summer-house."

WILLIAM HAZLITT

MY FIRST ACQUAINTANCE WITH POETS

William Hazlitt (1778–1830) was the son of an English clergyman, and was himself educated for the ministry, but declined to enter it. An elder brother was a portrait-painter; William tried for four years to learn the art, but without success. He went to London, where he became theatrical critic for a newspaper. Leigh Hunt, who was then editing the *Examiner*, asked him to write some essays for it. The result was *The Round Table*, a series of papers on books, manners, and social customs, written in a style of singular clearness and charm. Stevenson says in one of his essays, "We are fine fellows, but we cannot write like Hazlitt."

A course of lectures on literature which Hazlitt delivered was later published in three volumes, *English Comic Writers*, *English Poetry*, and *Dramatic Literature of the Age of Elizabeth*. These contain some admirable literary criticism. But his chief fame rests upon his volumes of essays, which include *Table Talk*, *The Round Table*, *The Plain Speaker*, *Sketches and Essays*, and *Winterslow*. Hazlitt was the friend of interesting people like Coleridge, Lamb, and Wordsworth; he was himself an interesting character, strong in his likes and dislikes, very apt to quarrel with his friends. In this essay he shows himself as a true hero-worshipper. It was published in 1823, twenty-five years after the events which it relates. Note the frequency with which he quotes from his beloved poets; the ease of the style, and the vividness with which he describes the appearance of Coleridge, and the impression made by him.

WILLIAM HAZLITT

MY FIRST ACQUAINTANCE WITH POETS

(From *Winterslow*, a collection of Hazlitt's essays
published after his death)

My father was a Dissenting minister, at Wem, in
Shropshire; and in the year 1798 (the figures that compose the date are to me like the "dreaded name of Demogorgon" *) Mr. Coleridge came to Shrewsbury, to succeed Mr. Rowe in the spiritual charge of a Unitarian
congregation there. He did not come till late on the
Saturday afternoon before he was to preach; and Mr.
Rowe, who himself went down to the coach, in a state
of anxiety and expectation, to look for the arrival of
his successor, could find no one at all answering the description but a round-faced man, in a short black coat
(like a shooting jacket) which hardly seemed to have
been made for him, but who seemed to be talking at a
great rate to his fellow passengers. Mr. Rowe had scarce
returned to give an account of his disappointment when
the round-faced man in black entered, and dissipated all
doubts on the subject by beginning to talk. He did not
cease while he stayed; nor has he since, that I know of.
He held the good town of Shrewsbury in delightful suspense for three weeks that he remained there, "flutter-
ing the *proud Salopians*,† like an eagle in a dove-cote";
and the Welsh mountains that skirt the horizon with
their tempestuous confusion, agree to have heard no such
mystic sounds since the days of

"High-born Hoel's harp or soft Llewellyn's lay." ‡

* Demogorgon, one of the fallen angels in Milton's *Paradise Lost.*
† *Salopians*, inhabitants of Salop, an old name for Shropshire.
‡ Quoted from Gray's "The Bard."

As we passed along between Wem and Shrewsbury, and I eyed their blue tops seen through the wintry branches, or the red rustling leaves of the sturdy oak-trees by the roadside, a sound was in my ears as of a Siren's song; I was stunned, startled with it, as from deep sleep; but I had no notion then that I should ever be able to express my admiration to others in motley imagery or quaint allusion, till the light of his genius shone into my soul like the sun's rays glittering in the puddles of the road. I was at that time dumb, inarticulate, help-less, like a worm by the wayside, crushed, bleeding, life-less; but now, bursting the deadly bands that "bound them,

"With Styx nine times round them," *

my ideas float on winged words, and as they expand their plumes, catch the golden light of other years. My soul has indeed remained in its original bondage, dark, ob-scure, with longings infinite and unsatisfied; my heart, shut up in the prison-house of this rude clay, has never found, nor will it ever find, a heart to speak to; but that my understanding also did not remain dumb and brutish, or at length found a language to express itself, I owe to Coleridge. But this is not to my purpose.

My father lived ten miles from Shrewsbury, and was in the habit of exchanging visits with Mr. Rowe, and with Mr. Jenkins of Whitchurch (nine miles farther on), according to the custom of Dissenting ministers in each other's neighborhood. A line of communication is thus established, by which the flame of civil and religious liberty is kept alive, and nourishes its smouldering fire unquenchable, like the fires in the *Agamemnon* of Æschy-lus, placed at different stations, that waited for ten long years to announce with their blazing pyramids the de-

* From Pope's "Ode for St. Cecilia's Day."

struction of Troy. Coleridge had agreed to come over and see my father, according to the courtesy of the country, as Mr. Rowe's probable successor; but in the meantime, I had gone to hear him preach the Sunday after his arrival. A poet and a philosopher getting up into a Unitarian pulpit to preach the gospel, was a romance in these degenerate days, a sort of revival of the primitive spirit of Christianity, which was not to be resisted.

It was in January of 1798, that I rose one morning before daylight, to walk ten miles in the mud, to hear this celebrated person preach. Never, the longest day I have to live, shall I have such another walk as this cold, raw, comfortless one, in the winter of the year 1798. *Il y a des impressions que ni le temps ni les circonstances peuvent effacer. Dusse-je vivre des siècles entiers, le doux temps de ma jeunesse ne peut renaître pour moi, ni s'effacer jamais dans ma mémoire.** When I got there, the organ was playing the hundredth Psalm, and when it was done, Mr. Coleridge rose and gave out his text, "And he went up into the mountain to pray, *himself, alone.*" As he gave out this text, his voice "rose like a steam of rich distilled perfumes," † and when he came to the two last words, which he pronounced loud, deep, and distinct, it seemed to me, who was then young, as if the sounds had echoed from the bottom of the human heart, and as if that prayer might have floated in solemn silence through the universe. The idea of St. John came into my mind, "of one crying in the wilderness, who had his loins girt about, and whose food was locusts and wild honey."

---

* *Il y a*, etc. "There are impressions which neither time nor circumstances can efface. If I should live whole ages, the sweet days of my youth could never return to me, nor ever be effaced from my memory."—Rousseau's *Confessions*.

† Quoted from Milton's "Comus."

The preacher then launched into his subject, like an
eagle dallying with the wind. The sermon was upon
peace and war; upon church and state—not their alli-
ance but their separation—on the spirit of the world and
the spirit of Christianity, not as the same, but as opposed
to one another. He talked of those who had "inscribed
the cross of Christ on banners dripping with human
gore." He made a poetical and pastoral excursion—
and to show the fatal effects of war, drew a striking contrast between the simple shepherd-boy, driving his team
afield, or sitting under the hawthorn, piping to his flock,
"as though he should never be old," and the same poor
country lad, crimped,* kidnapped, brought into town,
made drunk at an ale-house, turned into a wretched
drummer boy, with his hair sticking on end with
powder and pomatum, a long cue at his back, and
tricked out in the loathsome finery of the profession
of blood:

"Such were the notes our once-loved poet sung."†

And for myself, I could not have been more delighted if
I had heard the music of the spheres. Poetry and Philosophy had met together. Truth and Genius had em-
braced, under the eye and with the sanction of Religion.
This was even beyond my hopes. I returned home well
satisfied. The sun that was still laboring pale and wan
through the sky, obscured by thick mists, seemed an
emblem of the *good cause;* and the cold dank drops of
dew, that hung half melted on the beard of the thistle,
had something genial and refreshing in them; for there
was a spirit of hope and youth in all nature, that turned

* Crimped, entrapped in order to be forced into military or naval
service.

† From Pope's "Epistle to Oxford."

everything into good. The face of nature had not then the brand of *Jus Divinum** on it:

> "Like to that sanguine flower inscrib'd with woe."†

On the Tuesday following, the half-inspired speaker came. I was called down into the room where he was, and went half hoping, half afraid. He received me very graciously, and I listened for a long time without uttering a word. I did not suffer in his opinion by my silence. "For those two hours," he afterward was pleased to say, "he was conversing with William Hazlitt's forehead"! His appearance was different from what I had anticipated from seeing him before. At a distance, and in the dim light of the chapel, there was to me a strange wildness in his aspect, a dusky obscurity, and I thought him pitted with the smallpox. His complexion was at that time clear, and even bright—

> "As are the children of yon azure sheen." ‡

His forehead was broad and high, light as if built of ivory, with large projecting eyebrows, and his eyes rolling beneath them, like a sea with darkened lustre. "A certain tender bloom his face o'erspread," a purple tinge as we see it in the pale thoughtful complexions of the Spanish portrait-painters, Murillo and Velasquez. His mouth was gross, voluptuous, open, eloquent; his chin good-humored and round; but his nose, the rudder of the face, the index of the will, was small, feeble, nothing, —like what he has done. It might seem that the genius of his face as from a height surveyed and projected him (with sufficient capacity and huge aspiration) into the

---

* *Jus Divinum*, the doctrine of the divine right of kings, *i. e.*, that kings enjoyed their power by the sanction of God.

† From Milton's "Lycidas."

‡ From Thomson's "Castle of Indolence."

world unknown of thought and imagination, with nothing to support or guide his veering purpose, as if Columbus had launched his adventurous course for the New World in a scallop, without oars or compass. So, at least, I comment on it after the event. Coleridge, in his person, was rather above the common size, inclining to the corpulent, or like Lord Hamlet, "somewhat fat and pursy." His hair (now, alas! gray) was then black and glossy as the raven's, and fell in smooth masses over his forehead. This long pendulous hair is peculiar to enthusiasts, to those whose minds tend heavenward; and is traditionally inseparable (though of a different color) from the pictures of Christ. It ought to belong, as a character, to all who preach *Christ crucified*, and Coleridge was at that time one of those!

It was curious to observe the contrast between him and my father, who was a veteran in the cause, and then declining into the vale of years. He had been a poor Irish lad, carefully brought up by his parents, and sent to the University of Glasgow (where he studied under Adam Smith*) to prepare him for his future destination. It was his mother's proudest wish to see her son a Dissenting minister. So, if we look back to past generations (as far as eye can reach), we see the same hopes, fears, wishes, followed by the same disappointments, throbbing in the human heart; and so we may see them (if we look forward) rising up forever, and disappearing, like vaporish bubbles, in the human breast! After being tossed about from congregation to congregation in the heats of the Unitarian controversy, and squabbles about the American war, he had been relegated to an obscure village, where he was to spend the last thirty years of his life, far from the only converse that he loved, the talk about

---

* Adam Smith, author of the *Wealth of Nations*, one of the most notable books on political economy.

disputed texts of Scripture, and the cause of civil and religious liberty. Here he passed his days, repining, but resigned, in the study of the Bible, and the perusal of the commentators—huge folios, not easily got through, one of which would outlast a winter! Why did he pore on these from morn to night (with the exception of a walk in the fields or a turn in the garden to gather broccoli-plants or kidney-beans of his own rearing, with no small degree of pride and pleasure)? Here were "no figures nor no fantasies"—neither poetry nor philosophy —nothing to dazzle, nothing to excite modern curiosity; but to his lack-lustre eyes there appeared within the pages of the ponderous, unwieldy, neglected tomes, the sacred name of JEHOVAH in Hebrew capitals: pressed down by the weight of the style, worn to the last fading thinness of the understanding, there were glimpses, glimmering notions of the patriarchal wanderings, with palm-trees hovering in the horizon, and processions of camels at the distance of three thousand years; there was Moses with the Burning Bush, the number of the Twelve Tribes, types, shadows, glosses on the law and the prophets; there were discussions (dull enough) on the age of Methuselah, a mighty speculation! there were outlines, rude guesses at the shape of Noah's Ark and of the riches of Solomon's Temple; questions as to the date of the creation, predictions of the end of all things; the great lapses of time, the strange mutations of the globe were unfolded with the voluminous leaf, as it turned over; and though the soul might slumber with an hieroglyphic veil of inscrutable mysteries drawn over it, yet it was in a slumber ill exchanged for all the sharpened realities of sense, wit, fancy, or reason. My father's life was comparatively a dream; but it was a dream of infinity and eternity, of death, the resurrection, and a judgment to come!

No two individuals were ever more unlike than were the host and his guest. A poet was to my father a sort of nondescript; yet whatever added grace to the Unitarian cause was to him welcome. He could hardly have been more surprised or pleased, if our visitor had worn wings. Indeed, his thoughts had wings: and as the silken sounds rustled round our little wainscoted parlor, my father threw back his spectacles over his forehead, his white hairs mixing with its sanguine hue; and a smile of delight beamed across his rugged, cordial face, to think that Truth had found a new ally in Fancy! * Besides, Coleridge seemed to take considerable notice of me, and that of itself was enough.

He talked very familiarly, but agreeably, and glanced over a variety of subjects. At dinner time he grew more animated, and dilated in a very edifying manner on Mary Wollstonecraft† and Mackintosh. The last, he said, he considered (on my father's speaking of his *Vindiciæ Gallicæ* as a capital performance) as a clever, scholastic man —a master of the topics—or, as the ready warehouseman of letters, who knew exactly where to lay his hand on what he wanted, though the goods were not his own. He thought him no match for Burke, either in style or matter. Burke was a metaphysician, Mackintosh a mere logician. Burke was an orator (almost a poet) who reasoned in figures, because he had an eye for nature: Mackintosh, on the other hand, was a rhetorician, who had only an

---

* My father was one of those who mistook his talent, after all. He used to be very much dissatisfied that I preferred his *Letters* to his *Sermons*. The last were forced and dry; the first came naturally from him. For ease, half-plays on words, and a supine, monkish, indolent pleasantry, I have never seen them equalled. (Hazlitt's note.)

† Mary Wollstonecraft was the author of the *Vindication of the Rights of Women*, published in 1792. James Mackintosh's *Vindiciæ Gallicæ* was a defense of the French Revolution. Both books were regarded as very radical in their day.

eye to commonplaces. On this I ventured to say that I had always entertained a great opinion of Burke, and that (as far as I could find) the speaking of him with contempt might be made the test of a vulgar, democratical mind. This was the first observation I ever made to Coleridge, and he said it was a very just and striking one. I remember the leg of Welsh mutton and the turnips on the table that day had the finest flavor imaginable. Coleridge added that Mackintosh and Tom Wedgewood* (of whom, however, he spoke highly) had expressed a very indifferent opinion of his friend Mr. Wordsworth, on which he remarked to them—"He strides on so far before you, that he dwindles in the distance!" Godwin had once boasted to him of having carried on an argument with Mackintosh for three hours with dubious success; Coleridge told him—"If there had been a man of genius in the room he would have settled the question in five minutes." He asked me if I had ever seen Mary Wollstonecraft, and I said, I had once for a few moments, and that she seemed to me to turn off Godwin's objections to something she advanced with quite a playful, easy air. He replied, that "this was only one instance of the ascendancy which people of imagination exercised over those of mere intellect." He did not rate Godwin very high† (this was caprice or prejudice, real or affected), but he had a great idea of Mrs. Wollstonecraft's powers of conversation; none at all of her talent for book-making. We talked a little about Holcroft. He had been asked if

---

* Thomas Wedgewood was a famous maker of pottery. The works he established at Burslem grew into the Five Towns described in Arnold Bennett's novels.

† He complained in particular of the presumption of his attempting to establish the future immortality of man, "without" (as he said) "knowing what Death was or what Life was"—and the tone in which he pronounced these two words seemed to convey a complete image of both. (Hazlitt's note.)

he was not much struck *with* him, and he said, he thought himself in more danger of being struck *by* him. I complained that he would not let me get on at all, for he required a definition of every the commonest word, exclaiming, "What do you mean by a *sensation,* Sir? What do you mean by an *idea?*" This, Coleridge said, was barricading the road to truth; it was setting up a turnpike-gate at every step we took. I forget a great number of things, many more than I remember; but the day passed off pleasantly, and the next morning Mr. Coleridge was to return to Shrewsbury.

When I came down to breakfast, I found that he had just received a letter from his friend, T. Wedgewood, making him an offer of 150 *l.* a year if he chose to waive his present pursuit, and devote himself entirely to the study of poetry and philosophy. Coleridge seemed to make up his mind to close with this proposal in the act of tying on one of his shoes. It threw an additional damp on his departure. It took the wayward enthusiast quite from us to cast him into Deva's winding vales, or by the shores of old romance. Instead of living at ten miles' distance, of being the pastor of a Dissenting congregation at Shrewsbury, he was henceforth to inhabit the Hill of Parnassus, to be a Shepherd on the Delectable Mountains.* Alas! I knew not the way thither, and felt very little gratitude for Mr. Wedgewood's bounty. I was presently relieved from this dilemma, for Mr. Coleridge, asking for a pen and ink, and going to a table to write something on a bit of card, advanced toward me with undulating step, and giving me the precious document, said that that was his address, *Mr. Coleridge, Nether Stowey, Somersetshire;* and that he should be glad to see me there in a few weeks' time, and, if I chose, would

* Delectable Mountains, described in Bunyan's *Pilgrim's Progress* as a place from which one may see the Celestial City.

come half-way to meet me. I was not less surprised than the shepherd-boy (this simile is to be found in *Cassandra*), when he sees a thunderbolt fall close at his feet. I stammered out my acknowledgments and acceptance of this offer (I thought Mr. Wedgewood's annuity a trifle to it) as well as I could; and this mighty business being settled, the poet-preacher took leave, and I accompanied him six miles on the road.

It was a fine morning in the middle of winter, and he talked the whole way. The scholar in Chaucer is described as going

       ——"sounding on his way."

So Coleridge went on his. In digressing, in dilating, in passing from subject to subject, he appeared to me to float in air, to slide on ice. He told me in confidence (going along) that he should have preached two sermons before he accepted the situation at Shrewsbury, one on Infant Baptism, the other on the Lord's Supper, showing that he could not administer either, which would have effectually disqualified him for the object in view. I observed that he continually crossed me on the way by shifting from one side of the footpath to the other. This struck me as an odd movement; but I did not at that time connect it with any instability of purpose or involuntary change of principle, as I have done since. He seemed unable to keep on in a straight line. He spoke slightingly of Hume (whose *Essay on Miracles* he said was stolen from an objection started in one of South's sermons—*Credat Judæus Appella!* *) I was not very much pleased at this account of Hume, for I had just been reading, with infinite relish, that completest of all metaphysical *chokepears*, his *Treatise on Human Nature*,

---

* *Credat*, etc. "Let the Jew Appella believe it, I will not!" Quoted from Horace.

to which the *Essays* in point of scholastic subtlety and close reasoning, are mere elegant trifling, light summer reading. Coleridge even denied the excellence of Hume's general style, which I think betrayed a want of taste or candor. He however made me amends by the manner in which he spoke of Berkeley. He dwelt particularly on his *Essay on Vision* as a masterpiece of analytical reasoning. So it undoubtedly is. He was exceedingly angry with Dr. Johnson for striking the stone with his foot, in allusion to this author's theory of matter and spirit, and saying, "Thus I confute him, Sir." Coleridge drew a parallel (I don't know how he brought about the connection) between Bishop Berkeley and Tom Paine. He said the one was an instance of a subtle, the other of an acute mind, than which no two things could be more distinct. The one was a shop-boy's quality, the other the characteristic of a philosopher. He considered Bishop Butler as a true philosopher, a profound and conscientious thinker, a genuine reader of nature and his own mind. He did not speak of his *Analogy*, but of his *Sermons at the Rolls' Chapel*, of which I had never heard. Coleridge somehow always contrived to prefer the *unknown* to the *known*. In this instance he was right. The *Analogy* is a tissue of sophistry, of wire-drawn, theological special-pleading; the *Sermons* (with the preface to them) are in a fine vein of deep, matured reflection, a candid appeal to our observation of human nature, without pedantry and without bias. I told Coleridge I had written a few remarks, and was sometimes foolish enough to believe that I had made a discovery on the same subject (the *Natural Disinterestedness of the Human Mind*)—and I tried to explain my view of it to Coleridge, who listened with great willingness, but I did not succeed in making myself understood.

I sat down to the task shortly afterward for the twentieth time, got new pens and paper, determined to make clear work of it, wrote a few meagre sentences in the skeleton style of a mathematical demonstration, stopped halfway down the second page; and, after trying in vain to pump up any words, images, notions, apprehensions, facts, or observations, from that gulf of abstraction in which I had plunged myself for four or five years preceding, gave up the attempt as labor in vain, and shed tears of helpless despondency on the blank, unfinished paper. I can write fast enough now. Am I better than I was then? Oh no! One truth discovered, one pang of regret at not being able to express it, is better than all the fluency and flippancy in the world. Would that I could go back to what I then was! Why can we not revive past times as we can revisit old places? If I had the quaint Muse of Sir Philip Sidney to assist me, I would write a *Sonnet to the Road between Wem and Shrewsbury*, and immortalize every step of it by some fond enigmatical conceit. I would swear that the very milestones had ears, and that Harmer-hill stooped with all its pines, to listen to a poet, as he passed! I remember but one other topic of discourse in this walk. He mentioned Paley, praised the naturalness and clearness of his style, but condemned his sentiments, thought him a mere time-serving casuist, and said that "the fact of his work on Moral and Political Philosophy being made a text-book in our universities was a disgrace to the national character."

We parted at the six-mile stone; and I returned homeward, pensive, but much pleased. I had met with unexpected notice from a person whom I believed to have been prejudiced against me. "Kind and affable to me had been his condescension, and should be honored ever with suitable regard." He was the first poet I had known, and he certainly answered to that inspired name. I had heard a great deal of his powers of conversation and was not disappointed. In fact, I never met with anything at all like them, either before or since. I could easily credit the accounts which were circulated of his holding forth to a large party of ladies and gentlemen, an evening or two before, on the Berkeleian Theory, when he made the whole material universe look like a transparency of fine words; and another story (which I believe he has somewhere told himself) of his being asked to a party at Birmingham, of his smoking tobacco and going to sleep after dinner on a sofa, where the company found him, to their no small surprise, which was increased to wonder when he started up of a sudden, and rubbing his eyes, looked about him, and launched into a three hours' description of the third heaven, of which he had had a dream, very different from Mr. Southey's *Vision of Judgment*, and also from that other "Vision of Judgment,"* which Mr. Murray, the Secretary of the Bridge-street Junta, took into his especial keeping.

On my way back I had a sound in my ears—it was the voice of Fancy; I had a light before me—it was the face of Poetry. The one still lingers there, the other has not quitted my side! Coleridge, in truth, met me half-way on the ground of philosophy, or I should not have been won over to his imaginative creed. I had an uneasy, pleasurable sensation all the time, till I was to visit him. During those months the chill breath of winter gave me a welcoming; the vernal air was balm and inspiration to me. The golden sunsets, the silver star of evening, lighted me on my way to new hopes and prospects. *I was to visit Coleridge in the spring.* This circumstance was never absent from my thoughts, and mingled with

---

* "Vision of Judgment," by Byron. This poem, which satirized George the Third, was sent to Byron's publisher, Murray, who refused to print it.

all my feelings. I wrote to him at the time proposed, and received an answer postponing my intended visit for a week or two, but very cordially urging me to complete my promise then. This delay did not damp, but rather increased my ardor. In the meantime, I went to Llangollen Vale, by way of initiating myself in the mysteries of natural scenery; and I must say I was enchanted with it. I had been reading Coleridge's description of England in his fine *Ode on the Departing Year*, and I applied it, *con amore*,* to the objects before me. That valley was to me (in a manner) the cradle of a new existence: in the river that winds through it, my spirit was baptized in the waters of Helicon!

I returned home, and soon after set out on my journey with unworn heart, and untired feet. My way lay through Worcester and Gloucester, and by Upton, where I thought of Tom Jones† and the adventure of the muff. I remember getting completely wet through one day, and stopping at an inn (I think it was at Tewkesbury) where I sat up all night to read *Paul and Virginia*.‡ Sweet were the showers in early youth that drenched my body, and sweet the drops of pity that fell upon the books I read! I recollect a remark of Coleridge's upon this very book that nothing could show the gross indelicacy of French manners and the entire corruption of their imagination more strongly than the behavior of the heroine in the last fatal scene, who turns away from a person on board the sinking vessel, that offers to save her life, because he has thrown off his clothes to assist him in swimming. Was this a time to think of such a circumstance? I once hinted to Wordsworth, as we were

---

* *Con amore*, earnestly, with love.

† Tom Jones, the hero of the novel of that name, by Henry Fielding. It was a great favorite of Hazlitt's.

‡ *Paul and Virginia*, a novel by Bernardin St. Pierre.

sailing in his boat on Grasmere lake, that I thought he
had borrowed the idea of his *Poems on the Naming of
Places* from the local inscriptions of the same kind in
Paul and Virginia. He did not own the obligation, and
stated some distinction without a difference in defense
to his claim to originality. Any, the slightest varia-
tion, would be sufficient for this purpose in his mind;
for whatever *he* added or altered would inevitably be
worth all that any one else had done, and contain the
marrow of the sentiment. I was still two days before the
time fixed for my arrival, for I had taken care to set out
early enough. I stopped these two days at Bridgewater;
and when I was tired of sauntering on the banks of its
muddy river, returned to the inn and read *Camilla.**   So
have I loitered my life away, reading books, looking at
pictures, going to plays, hearing, thinking, writing on
what pleased me best. I have wanted only one thing
to make me happy; but wanting that have wanted everything!

I arrived, and was well received. The country about
Nether Stowey is beautiful, green and hilly, and near the
seashore. I saw it but the other day, after an interval
of twenty years, from a hill near Taunton. How was
the map of my life spread out before me, as the map of
the country lay at my feet! In the afternoon, Coleridge
took me over to Alfoxden, a romantic old family mansion
of the St. Aubins, where Wordsworth lived. It was then
in the possession of a friend of the poet's, who gave him
the free use of it. Somehow, that period (the time just
after the French Revolution) was not a time when *nothing was given for nothing.* The mind opened and a softness might be perceived coming over the heart of individuals, beneath "the scales that fence" our self-interest.

* *Camilla*, a novel by Madame D'Arblay, better known as Fanny
Burney.

Wordsworth himself was from home, but his sister kept
house, and set before us a frugal repast; and we had free
access to her brother's poems, the *Lyrical Ballads*, which
were still in manuscript, or in the form of *Sybilline Leaves*.
I dipped into a few of these with great satisfaction, and
with the faith of a novice. I slept that night in an old
room with blue hangings, and covered with the round-
faced family portraits of the age of George I. and II.,
and from the wooded declivity of the adjoining park
that overlooked my window, at the dawn of day, could

————"hear the loud stag speak."

In the outset of life (and particularly at this time I
felt it so) our imagination has a body to it. We are in a
state between sleeping and waking, and have indistinct
but glorious glimpses of strange shapes, and there is
always something to come better than what we see. As
in our dreams the fulness of the blood gives warmth and
reality to the coinage of the brain, so in youth our ideas
are clothed, and fed, and pampered with our good spirits;
we breathe thick with thoughtless happiness, the weight
of future years presses on the strong pulses of the heart,
and we repose with undisturbed faith in truth and good.
As we advance, we exhaust our fund of enjoyment and
of hope. We are no longer wrapped in *lamb's-wool*,
lulled in Elysium. As we taste the pleasures of life,
their spirit evaporates, the sense palls; and nothing is left
but the phantoms, the lifeless shadows of what *has been!*

That morning, as soon as breakfast was over, we
strolled out into the park, and seating ourselves on the
trunk of an old ash-tree that stretched along the ground,
Coleridge read aloud with a sonorous and musical voice,
the ballad of "Betty Foy."* I was not critically or

* "Betty Foy" and the other poems here mentioned are by Wordsworth.

sceptically inclined. I saw touches of truth and nature, and took the rest for granted. But in the "Thorn," the "Mad Mother," and the "Complaint of a Poor Indian Woman," I felt that deeper power and pathos which have been since acknowledged,

"In spite of pride, in erring reason's spite," *

as the characteristics of this author; and the sense of a new style and a new spirit in poetry came over me. It had to me something of the effect that arises from the turning up of the fresh soil, or of the first welcome breath of Spring:

"While yet the trembling year is unconfirmed." †

Coleridge and myself walked back to Stowey that evening, and his voice sounded high

"Of Providence, foreknowledge, will, and fate,
Fix'd fate, free-will, foreknowledge absolute," ‡

as we passed through echoing grove, by fairy stream or waterfall, gleaming in the summer moonlight! He lamented that Wordsworth was not prone enough to believe in the traditional superstitions of the place, and that there was a something corporeal, a *matter-of-factness*, a clinging to the palpable, or often to the petty, in his poetry, in consequence. His genius was not a spirit that descended to him through the air; it sprung out of the ground like a flower, or unfolded itself from a green spray, on which the goldfinch sang. He said, however (if I remember right), that this objection must be confined to his descriptive pieces, that his philosophic poetry had a grand and comprehensive spirit in it, so that his

* From Pope's *Essay on Man*.   † From Thomson's *Seasons*.
‡ From Milton's *Paradise Lost*.

soul seemed to inhabit the universe like a palace, and to discover truth by intuition, rather than by deduction.

The next day Wordsworth arrived from Bristol at Coleridge's cottage. I think I see him now. He answered in some degree to his friend's description of him, but was more gaunt and Don Quixote-like. He was quaintly dressed (according to the costume of that unconstrained period) in a brown fustian jacket and striped pantaloons. There was something of a roll, a lounge in his gait, not unlike his own *Peter Bell*. There was a severe, worn pressure of thought about his temples, a fire in his eye (as if he saw something in objects more than the outward appearance), an intense, high, narrow forehead, a Roman nose, cheeks furrowed by strong purpose and feeling, and a convulsive inclination to laughter about the mouth, a good deal at variance with the solemn, stately expression of the rest of his face. Chantrey's bust wants the marking traits; but he was teased into making it regular and heavy: Haydon's head of him, introduced into the *Entrance of Christ into Jerusalem*, is the most like his drooping weight of thought and expression. He sat down and talked very naturally and freely, with a mixture of clear, gushing accents in his voice, a deep guttural intonation, and a strong tincture of the northern *burr*, like the crust on wine. He instantly began to make havoc of the half of a Cheshire cheese on the table, and said, triumphantly, that "his marriage with experience had not been so productive as Mr. Southey's in teaching him a knowledge of the good things of this life." He had been to see the *Castle Specter* by Monk Lewis, while at Bristol, and described it very well. He said "it fitted the taste of the audience like a glove." This *ad captandum* * merit was however by no means a recommendation of it, according to the severe

* *Ad captandum*, to catch the crowd.

principles of the new school, which reject rather than court popular effect. Wordsworth, looking out of the low, latticed window, said, "How beautifully the sun sets on that yellow bank!" I thought within myself, "With what eyes these poets see nature!" and ever after, when I saw the sunset stream upon the objects facing it, conceived I had made a discovery, or thanked Mr. Wordsworth for having made one for me!

We went over to Alfoxden again the day following, and Wordsworth read us the story of *Peter Bell* in the open air; and the comment upon it by his face and voice was very different from that of some later critics! Whatever might be thought of the poem, "his face was as a book where men might read strange matters," * and he announced the fate of his hero in prophetic tones. There is a *chaunt* in the recitation both of Coleridge and Wordsworth, which acts as a spell upon the hearer, and disarms the judgment. Perhaps they have deceived themselves by making habitual use of this ambiguous accompaniment. Coleridge's manner is more full, animated, and varied; Wordsworth's more equable, sustained, and internal. The one might be termed more *dramatic*, the other more *lyrical*. Coleridge has told me that he himself liked to compose in walking over uneven ground, or breaking through the straggling branches of a copse wood; whereas Wordsworth always wrote (if he could) walking up and down a straight gravel walk, or in some spot where the continuity of his verse met with no collateral interruption. Returning that same evening, I got into a metaphysical argument with Wordsworth, while Coleridge was explaining the different notes of the nightingale to his sister, in which we neither of us succeeded in making ourselves perfectly clear and intelligible. Thus I passed three weeks at Nether Stowey and

* From *Macbeth*, I, v, 63.

in the neighborhood, generally devoting the afternoons to a delightful chat in an arbor made of bark by the poet's friend Tom Poole, sitting under two fine elm-trees, and listening to the bees humming round us while we quaffed our flip.

It was agreed, among other things, that we should make a jaunt down the Bristol Channel, as far as Linton. We set off together on foot, Coleridge, John Chester, and I. This Chester was a native of Nether Stowey, one of those who were attracted to Coleridge's discourse as flies are to honey, or bees in swarming-time to the sound of a brass pan. He "followed in the chase like a dog who hunts, not like one that made up the cry." * He had on a brown cloth coat, boots, and corduroy breeches, was low in stature, bow-legged, had a drag in his walk like a drover, which he assisted by a hazel switch, and kept on a sort of trot by the side of Coleridge, like a running footman by a state coach, that he might not lose a syllable or sound that fell from Coleridge's lips. He told me his private opinion, that Coleridge was a wonderful man. He scarcely opened his lips, much less offered an opinion the whole way: yet of the three, had I to choose during that journey, I would be John Chester. He afterward followed Coleridge into Germany, where the Kantean philosophers were puzzled how to bring him under any of their categories. When he sat down at table with his idol, John's felicity was complete; Sir Walter Scott's, or Mr. Blackwood's, when they sat down at the same table with the king, was not more so. We passed Dunster on our right, a small town between the brow of a hill and the sea. I remember eying it wistfully as it lay below us: contrasted with the woody scene around, it looked as clear, as pure, as *embrowned* and ideal as any landscape I have seen since, of Gaspar Poussin's or Domenichino's.

* From *Othello*, II, iii, 370.

We had a long day's march (our feet kept time to the echoes of Coleridge's tongue) through Minehead and by the Blue Anchor, and on to Linton, which we did not reach till near midnight, and where we had some difficulty in making a lodgment. We, however, knocked the people of the house up at last, and we were repaid for our apprehensions and fatigue by some excellent rashers of fried bacon and eggs. The view in coming along had been splendid. We walked for miles and miles on dark brown heaths overlooking the Channel, with the Welsh hills beyond, and at times descended into little sheltered valleys close by the seaside, with a smuggler's face scowling by us, and then had to ascend conical hills with a path winding up through a coppice to a barren top, like a monk's shaven crown, from one of which I pointed out to Coleridge's notice the bare masts of a vessel on the very edge of the horizon, and within the red-orbed disk of the setting sun, like his own spectre-ship in the *Ancient Mariner*.

At Linton the character of the seacoast becomes more marked and rugged. There is a place called the *Valley of Rocks* (I suspect this was only the poetical name for it), bedded among precipices overhanging the sea, with rocky caverns beneath, into which the waves dash, and where the sea-gull forever wheels its screaming flight. On the tops of these are huge stones thrown transverse, as if an earthquake had tossed them there, and behind these is a fretwork of perpendicular rocks, something like the Giant's Causeway. A thunder-storm came on while we were at the inn, and Coleridge was running out bareheaded to enjoy the commotion of the elements in the *Valley of Rocks*, but as if in spite, the clouds only muttered a few angry sounds, and let fall a few refreshing drops. Coleridge told me that he and Wordsworth were to have made this place the scene of a prose-tale, which was to have been in the manner of, but far superior to, the *Death of Abel*, but they had relinquished the design. In the morning of the second day, we breakfasted luxuriously in an old-fashioned parlor on tea, toast, eggs, and honey, in the very sight of the beehives from which it had been taken, and a garden full of thyme and wild flowers that had produced it.

On this occasion Coleridge spoke of Virgil's *Georgics*, but not well. I do not think he had much feeling for the classical or elegant.* It was in this room that we found a little worn-out copy of the *Seasons*, lying in a window-seat, on which Coleridge exclaimed, "*That* is true fame!" He said Thomson was a great poet, rather than a good one; his style was as meretricious as his thoughts were natural. He spoke of Cowper as the best modern poet. He said the *Lyrical Ballads* were an experiment about to be tried by him and Wordsworth, to see how far the public taste would endure poetry written in a more natural and simple style than had hitherto been attempted; totally discarding the artifices of poetical diction, and making use only of such words as had probably been common in the most ordinary language since the days of Henry II. Some comparison was introduced between Shakespeare and Milton. He said "he hardly knew which to prefer. Shakespeare appeared to him a mere stripling in the art; he was as tall and as strong, with infinitely more activity than Milton, but he never appeared to have come to man's estate; or if he had, he

---

* He had no idea of pictures, of Claude or Raphael, and at this time I had as little as he. He sometimes gives a striking account at present of the Cartoons at Pisa by Buffamalco and others; of one in particular, where Death is seen in the air brandishing his scythe, and the great and mighty of the earth shudder at his approach, while the beggars and the wretched kneel to him as their deliverer. He would, of course, understand so broad and fine a moral as this at any time. (Hazlitt's note.)

would not have been a man, but a monster." He spoke with contempt of Gray, and with intolerance of Pope. He did not like the versification of the latter. He observed that "the ears of these couplet writers might be charged with having short memories, that could not retain the harmony of whole passages." He thought little of Junius as a writer; he had a dislike of Dr. Johnson; and a much higher opinion of Burke as an orator and politician, than of Fox or Pitt. He, however, thought him very inferior in richness of style and imagery to some of our elder prose-writers, particularly Jeremy Taylor. He liked Richardson, but not Fielding; nor could I get him to enter into the merits of *Caleb Williams*.* In short, he was profound and discriminating with respect to those authors whom he liked, and where he gave his judgment fair play; capricious, preverse, and prejudiced in his antipathies and distastes.

We loitered on the "ribbed sea sands," in such talk as this a whole morning, and, I recollect, met with a curious seaweed, of which John Chester told us the country name! A fisherman gave Coleridge an account of a boy that had been drowned the day before, and that they had tried to save him at the risk of their own lives. He said "he did not know how it was that they ventured, but, Sir, we have a *nature* toward one another." This expression, Coleridge remarked to me, was a fine illustration of that theory of disinterestedness which I (in common with Butler) had adopted. I broached to him an argument of mine to prove that *likeness* was not mere association of ideas. I said that the mark in the sand put one in mind of a man's foot, not because it was part of a former impression of a man's foot (for it was quite new), but because it was like the shape of a man's foot. He assented to the justness of this distinction (which I have explained

* *Caleb Williams*, a political novel by Godwin, famous in its day.

at length elsewhere, for the benefit of the curious) and
John Chester listened; not from any interest in the subject, but because he was astonished that I should be able
to suggest anything to Coleridge that he did not already
know. We returned on the third morning, and Coleridge
remarked the silent cottage-smoke curling up the valleys
where, a few evenings before, we had seen the lights
gleaming through the dark.

In a day or two after we arrived at Stowey, we set
out, I on my return home, and he for Germany. It
was a Sunday morning, and he was to preach that day
for Dr. Toulmin of Taunton. I asked him if he had prepared anything for the occasion? He said he had not
even thought of the text, but should as soon as we parted.
I did not go to hear him—this was a fault—but we met
in the evening at Bridgewater. The next day we had a
long day's walk to Bristol, and sat down, I recollect, by a
well side on the road, to cool ourselves and satisfy our
thirst, when Coleridge repeated to me some descriptive
lines of his tragedy of *Remorse;* which I must say became
his mouth and that occasion better than they, some years
after, did Mr. Elliston's and the Drury-lane * boards—

"Oh memory! shield me from the world's poor strife,
And give those scenes thine everlasting life."

I saw no more of him for a year or two, during which
period he had been wandering in the Hartz Forest, in
Germany; and his return was cometary, meteorous, unlike his setting out. It was not till some time after that
I knew his friends Lamb and Southey. The last always
appears to me (as I first saw him) with a commonplace
book under his arm, and the first with a *bon mot* in his
mouth. It was at Godwin's that I met him with Holcroft and Coleridge, where they were disputing fiercely

* Drury Lane, a famous London theatre. Elliston acted there.

which was the best—*Man as he was, or man as he is to be.*
"Give me," says Lamb, "man as he is *not* to be." This
saying was the beginning of a friendship between us which
I believe still continues. Enough of this for the present.

> "But there is matter for another rime,
> And I to this may add a second tale."

LEIGH HUNT

ON GETTING UP ON COLD MORNINGS

Leigh Hunt (1784–1859) was a London boy; he received his early education in the Christ's Hospital School, as did Charles Lamb. He very early began to write verse, which his father published under the title, *A Collection of Poems Written between the Ages of Twelve and Sixteen.* In 1808 Leigh and his brother John started a newspaper called the *Examiner.* For certain articles in this criticising the Prince Regent, the editors were prosecuted and imprisoned for two years. Here they continued their writing and entertained their friends; Thomas Moore, Byron, and John Keats came to see them. After Hunt's release he continued his literary work, writing criticism, book reviews, essays, plays, and poems. In 1822 he went to Italy to edit *The Liberal,* at a safe distance from England. Charles Dickens in *Bleak House* caricatured Hunt as Harold Skimpole, magnifying some of his weaknesses. Hunt's best-known works are his *Autobiography,* an interesting book, and the volumes of essays entitled, *Men, Women, and Books* and *Table Talk.* While he does not rank among the greater English essayists, his writing has a freedom and spontaneity that make it very pleasant reading.

LEIGH HUNT

ON GETTING UP ON COLD MORNINGS

(From the *Examiner*)

An Italian author—Giulio Cordara, a Jesuit—has written a poem upon insects, which he begins by insisting, that those troublesome and abominable little animals were created for our annoyance, and that they were certainly not inhabitants of Paradise. We of the north may dispute this piece of theology; but on the other hand, it is as clear as the snow on the housetops, that Adam was not under the necessity of shaving; and that when Eve walked out of her delicious bower, she did not step upon ice three inches thick.

Some people say it is a very easy thing to get up of a cold morning. You have only, they tell you, to take the resolution; and the thing is done. This may be very true; just as a boy at school has only to take a flogging, and the thing is over. But we have not at all made up our minds upon it; and we find it a very pleasant exercise to discuss the matter, candidly, before we get up. This, at least, is not idling, though it may be lying. It affords an excellent answer to those who ask how lying in bed can be indulged in by a reasoning being,—a rational creature. How? Why, with the argument calmly at work in one's head, and the clothes over one's shoulder. Oh— it is a fine way of spending a sensible, impartial half-hour.

If these people would be more charitable they would get on with their argument better. But they are apt to reason so ill, and to assert so dogmatically, that one could wish to have them stand round one's bed, of a bitter morning, and *lie* before their faces. They ought to hear both sides of the bed, the inside and out. If they cannot entertain themselves with their own thoughts for half an hour or so, it is not the fault of those who can.

Candid inquiries into one's decumbency, besides the greater or less privileges to be allowed a man in proportion to his ability of keeping early hours, the work given his faculties, etc., will at least concede their due merits to such representations as the following. In the first place, says the injured but calm appealer, I have been warm all night, and find my system in a state perfectly suitable to a warm-blooded animal. To get out of this state into the cold, besides the inharmonious and uncritical abruptness of the transition, is so unnatural to such a creature, that the poets, refining upon the tortures of the damned, make one of their greatest agonies consist in being suddenly transported from heat to cold,—from fire to ice. They are "haled" out of their "beds," says Milton, by "harpy-footed furies,"—fellows who come to call them. On my first movement toward the anticipation of getting up I find that such parts of the sheets and bolster as are exposed to the air of the room are stone-cold. On opening my eyes, the first thing that meets them is my own breath rolling forth, as if in the open air, like smoke out of a chimney. Think of this symptom. Then I turn my eyes sideways and see the window all frozen over. Think of that. Then the servant comes in. "It is very cold this morning, is it not?"—"Very cold, sir."—"Very cold indeed, isn't it?" —"Very cold indeed, sir."—"More than usually so, isn't it, even for this weather?" (Here the servant's wit and good nature are put to a considerable test, and the inquirer lies on thorns for the answer.) "Why, sir . . . I think it *is*." (Good creature! There is not a better or more truth-telling servant going.) "I must rise, however—get me some warm water."—Here comes a fine interval between the departure of the servant and the arrival of the hot water; during which, of course, it is of "no use" to get up. The hot water comes. "Is it quite hot?"—"Yes, sir."—"Perhaps too hot for shaving; I must wait a little?"—"No, sir; it will just do." (There is an overnice propriety sometimes, an officious zeal of virtue, a little troublesome.) "Oh—the shirt—you must air my clean shirt;—linen gets very damp this weather." —"Yes, sir." Here another delicious five minutes. A knock at the door. "Oh, the shirt—very well. My stockings—I think the stockings had better be aired too." —"Very well, sir." Here another interval. At length everything is ready, except myself.

I now, continues our incumbent (a happy word, by the by, for a country vicar)—I now cannot help thinking a good deal—who can?—upon the unnecessary and villainous custom of shaving: it is a thing so unmanly (here I nestle closer)—so effeminate (here I recoil from an unlucky step into the colder part of the bed).—No wonder that the Queen of France took part with the rebels against that degenerate king, her husband, who first affronted her smooth visage with a face like her own. The Emperor Julian never showed the luxuriancy of his genius to better advantage than in reviving the flowing beard. Look at Cardinal Bembo's picture—at Michael Angelo's —at Titian's—at Shakespeare's—at Fletcher's—at Spenser's—at Chaucer's—at Alfred's—at Plato's—I could name a great man for every tick of my watch.—Look at the Turks, a grave and otiose people.—Think of Haroun Al Raschid and Bed-ridden Hassan.—Think of Wortley Montague, the worthy son of his mother, above the prejudice of his time.—Look at the Persian gentlemen, whom one is ashamed of meeting about the suburbs, their dress and appearance are so much finer than our own.—Lastly,

think of the razor itself—how totally opposed to every
sensation of bed—how cold, how edgy, how hard! how
utterly different from anything like the warm and circling
amplitude, which

> Sweetly recommends itself
> Unto our gentle senses.*

Add to this, benumbed fingers, which may help you to
cut yourself, a quivering body, a frozen towel, and a ewer
full of ice; and he that says there is nothing to oppose
in all this, only shows that he has no merit in opposing
it.

Thomson the poet, who exclaims in his *Seasons*—

> Falsely luxurious! Will not man awake?

used to lie in bed till noon, because he said he had no
motive in getting up. He could imagine the good of
rising; but then he could also imagine the good of lying
still; and his exclamation, it must be allowed, was made
upon summer-time, not winter. We must proportion
the argument to the individual character. A money-
getter may be drawn out of his bed by three or four pence;
but this will not suffice for a student. A proud man may
say, "What shall I think of myself, if I don't get up?"
but the more humble one will be content to waive this
prodigious notion of himself, out of respect to his kindly
bed. The mechanical man shall get up without any ado
at all; and so shall the barometer. An ingenious lier in
bed will find hard matter of discussion even on the score
of health and longevity. He will ask us for our proofs
and precedents of the ill effects of lying later in cold
weather; and sophisticate much on the advantages of an
even temperature of body; of the natural propensity
(pretty universal) to have one's way; and of the animals

* From *Macbeth*, I, vi, 3,

that roll themselves up and sleep all the winter. As to longevity, he will ask whether the longest is of necessity the best; and whether Holborn is the handsomest street in London.

WILLIAM MAKEPEACE THACKERAY

ON A LAZY IDLE BOY

William Makepeace Thackeray (1811–1863) one of the leading writers of the Victorian age, was born in Calcutta; at six he was sent to England to be educated. He entered the Charterhouse school in London, a place that appears as Greyfriars in his novel *Pendennis*. He attended Trinity College, Cambridge, but did not graduate. He spent some years abroad, partly in rambling over Europe, partly in studying art in Paris. His ability in this direction was shown later in the illustrations he made for his own books. He learned German at Weimar; the essay *On a Lazy Idle Boy*, contains a reminiscence of this period. On his return to England he became a contributor to various magazines, writing sketches of Paris and Irish life. His first novel, *The Great Hoggarty Diamond*, appeared in 1841, but it was not until the publication of *Vanity Fair* (1847) that he became famous as a novelist. He delivered a course of lectures on English history; his success in this field led him to make lecture tours to America in 1852 and 1855. His lectures were later published in two volumes, *English Humorists of the Eighteenth Century* and *The Four Georges*. He was the first editor of the *Cornhill Magazine*, and contributed to it a series of essays entitled *The Roundabout Papers*. These reveal the personality of a man whom Thomas Carlyle—a man not given to sentiment—always called "dear old Thackeray." Easy in style, yet never undignified; worldly-wise, yet not cynical; shrewd, but not sarcastic, the essays are the best talk of one of the best of gentlemen.

WILLIAM MAKEPEACE THACKERAY

ON A LAZY IDLE BOY

(From the *Roundabout Papers*)

I had occasion to pass a week in the autumn in the little old town of Coire or Chur, in the Grisons,* where lies buried that very ancient British king, saint, and martyr, Lucius,† who founded the Church of St. Peter, on Cornhill. Few people note the church nowadays, and fewer ever heard of the saint. In the cathedral at Chur, his statue appears surrounded by other sainted persons of his family. With tight red breeches, a Roman habit, a curly brown beard, and a neat little gilt crown and sceptre, he stands, a very comely and cheerful image: and from what I may call his peculiar position with regard to Cornhill, I beheld this figure of St. Lucius with more interest than I should have bestowed upon personages who, hierarchically, are, I dare say, his superiors.

The pretty little city stands, so to speak, at the end of the world—of the world of to-day, the world of rapid motion, and rushing railways, and the commerce and intercourse of men. From the northern gate, the iron road stretches away to Zürich, to Basle, to Paris, to home. From the old southern barriers, before which a

---

* Grisons, a canton of Switzerland. Chur is the capital.

† Stow quotes the inscription still extant "from the table fast chained in St. Peter's Church, Cornhill"; and says, "he was after some chronicle buried at London, and after some chronicle buried at Glowcester"—but, oh! these incorrect chroniclers! when Alban Butler, in the *Lives of the Saints*, v. 12, and Murray's *Handbook*, and the sacristan at Chur, all say Lucius was killed there, and I saw his tomb with my own eyes. (Thackeray's note.)

little river rushes, and around which stretch the crumbling battlements of the ancient town, the road bears the slow diligence or lagging vetturino * by the shallow Rhine, through the awful gorges of the Via Mala, and presently over the Splügen to the shores of Como.

I have seldom seen a place more quaint, pretty, calm, and pastoral, than this remote little Chur. What need have the inhabitants for walls and ramparts, except to build summer-houses, to trail vines, and hang clothes to dry on them? No enemies approach the great mouldering gates: only at morn and even the cows come lowing past them, the village maidens chatter merrily round the fountains, and babble like the ever-voluble stream that flows under the old walls. The schoolboys, with book and satchel, in smart uniforms, march up to the gymnasium,† and return thence at their stated time. There is one coffee-house in the town, and I see one old gentleman goes to it. There are shops with no customers seemingly, and the lazy tradesmen look out of their little windows at the single stranger sauntering by. There is a stall with baskets of queer little black grapes and apples, and a pretty brisk trade with half-a-dozen urchins standing round. But, beyond this, there is scarce any talk or movement in the street. There's nobody at the book-shop. "If you will have the goodness to come again in an hour," says the banker, with his mouth full of dinner at one o'clock, "you can have the money." There is nobody at the hotel, save the good landlady, the kind waiters, the brisk young cook who ministers to you. Nobody is in the Protestant church—(Oh! strange sight, the two confessions are here at peace!)—nobody in the Catholic church: until the sacristan, from his snug abode in the cathedral close, espies the traveller eying the monsters

* Vetturino, a four-wheeled carriage.
† Gymnasium, a school which prepares for the university.

and pillars before the old shark-toothed arch of his cathedral, and comes out (with a view to remuneration possibly) and opens the gate, and shows you the venerable church, and the queer old relics in the sacristy, and the ancient vestments (a black velvet cope, amongst other robes, as fresh as yesterday, and presented by that notorious "pervert," Henry of Navarre and France), and the statue of St. Lucius who built St. Peter's Church, on Cornhill.

What a quiet, kind, quaint, pleasant, pretty old town! Has it been asleep these hundreds and hundreds of years, and is the brisk young Prince of the Sidereal Realms in his screaming car drawn by his snorting steel elephant coming to waken it? Time was when there must have been life and bustle and commerce here. Those vast, venerable walls were not made to keep out cows, but men-at-arms, led by fierce captains, who prowled about the gates, and robbed the traders as they passed in and out with their bales, their goods, their pack-horses, and their wains. Is the place so dead that even the clergy of the different denominations can't quarrel? Why, seven or eight, or a dozen, or fifteen hundred years ago (they haven't the register of St. Peter's up to that remote period. I dare say it was burned in the fire of London)—a dozen hundred years ago, when there was some life in the town, St. Lucius was stoned here on account of theological differences, after founding our church in Cornhill.

There was a sweet pretty river walk we used to take in the evening and mark the mountains round glooming with a deeper purple; the shades creeping up the golden walls; the river brawling, the cattle calling, the maids and chatterboxes round the fountains babbling and bawling; and several times in the course of our sober walks we overtook a lazy slouching boy, or hobbledehoy, with a rusty coat, and trousers not too long, and big feet trailing lazily one after the other, and large lazy hands dawdling from out the tight sleeves, and in the lazy hands a little book, which my lad held up to his face, and which I dare say so charmed and ravished him, that he was blind to the beautiful sights around him; unmindful, I would venture to lay any wager, of the lessons he had to learn for to-morrow; forgetful of mother waiting supper, and father preparing a scolding;—absorbed utterly and entirely in his book.

What was it that so fascinated the young student, as he stood by the river shore? Not the *Pons Asinorum*.* What book so delighted him, and blinded him to all the rest of the world, so that he did not care to see the apple-woman with her fruit, or (more tempting still to sons of Eve) the pretty girls with their apple-cheeks, who laughed and prattled round the fountain! What was the book? Do you suppose it was Livy, or the Greek grammar? No; it was a NOVEL that you were reading, you lazy, not very clean, good-for-nothing, sensible boy! It was D'Artagnan locking up General Monk in a box, or almost succeeding in keeping Charles the First's head on. It was the prisoner of the Château d'If cutting himself out of the sack fifty feet under water (I mention the novels I like best myself—novels without love or talking, or any of that sort of nonsense, but containing plenty of fight-ing, escaping, robbery, and rescuing)—cutting himself out of the sack, and swimming to the island of Monte Cristo. O Dumas! O thou brave, kind, gallant old Alexandre! I hereby offer thee homage, and give thee thanks for many pleasant hours. I have read thee (being sick in bed) for thirteen hours of a happy day,

---

* *Pons Asinorum*, literally "bridge of asses," an old name for the proposition in geometry which sets forth that if a triangle has two sides of equal length the angles opposite those sides are also equal. This is the first difficult proposition in geometry, hence its name.

and had the ladies of the house fighting for the volumes. Be assured that lazy boy was reading Dumas (or I will go so far as to let the reader here pronounce the eulogium, or insert the name of his favorite author); and as for the anger, or it may be, the reverberations of his schoolmaster, or the remonstrances of his father, or the tender pleadings of his mother that he should not let the supper grow cold—I don't believe the scapegrace cared one fig. No! figs are sweet, but fictions are sweeter.

Have you ever seen a score of white-bearded, white-robed warriors, or grave seniors of the city, seated at the gate of Jaffa or Beyrout, and listening to the story-teller reciting his marvels out of *Antar* or the *Arabian Nights?* I was once present when a young gentleman at the table put a tart away from him, and said to his neighbor, the Younger Son (with rather a fatuous air): "I never eat sweets."

"Not eat sweets! and do you know why?" says T.

"Because I am past that kind of thing," says the young gentleman.

"Because you are a glutton and a sot!" cries the Elder (and Juvenis winces a little). "All people who have natural, healthy appetites, love sweets; all children, all women, all Eastern people, whose tastes are not corrupted by gluttony and strong drink." And a plateful of raspberries and cream disappeared before the philosopher.

You take the allegory? Novels are sweets. All people with healthy literary appetites love them—almost all women;—a vast number of clever, hardheaded men. Why, one of the most learned physicians in England said to me only yesterday, "I have just read *So-and-So* for the second time" (naming one of Jones's exquisite fictions). Judges, bishops, chancellors, mathematicians, are notorious novel-readers; as well as young boys and sweet girls, and their kind tender mothers. Who has not read about Eldon, and how he cried over novels every night when he was not at whist?

As for that lazy naughty boy at Chur, I doubt whether *he* will like novels when he is thirty years of age. He is taking too great a glut of them now. He is eating jelly until he will be sick. He will know most plots by the time he is twenty, so that *he* will never be surprised when the Stranger turns out to be the rightful earl,—when the old Waterman, throwing off his beggarly gabardine, shows his stars and the collars of his various orders, and clasping Antonia to his bosom, proves himself to be the prince, her long-lost father. He will recognize the novelist's same characters, though they appear in red-heeled pumps and *ailes-de-pigeon*, or the garb of the nineteenth century. He will get weary of sweets, as boys of private schools grow (or used to grow, for I have done growing some little time myself, and the practice may have ended too)— as private schoolboys used to grow tired of the pudding before their mutton at dinner.

And pray what is the moral of this apologue? The moral I take to be this: the appetite for novels extending to the end of the world; far away in the frozen deep, the sailors reading them to one another during the endless night;—far away under the Syrian stars, the solemn sheiks and elders hearkening to the poet as he recites his tales; far away in the Indian camps, where the soldiers listen to ——'s tales, or ——'s, after the hot day's march; far away in little Chur yonder where the lazy boy pores over the fond volume, and drinks it in with all his eyes:— the demand being what we know it is, the merchant must supply it, as he will supply saddles and pale ale for Bombay or Calcutta.

But as surely as the cadet drinks too much pale ale, it will disagree with him; and so surely, dear youth, will too much novels cloy on thee. I wonder, do novel-writers themselves read many novels? If you go into Gunter's you don't see those charming young ladies (to whom I present my most respectful compliments) eating tarts and ices, but at the proper eventide they have good plain wholesome tea and bread and butter. Can anybody tell me does the author of the *Tale of Two Cities* read novels? does the author of the *Tower of London* devour romances? does the dashing *Harry Lorrequer* delight in *Plain or Ringlets* or *Spunge's Sporting Tour?* Does the veteran, from whose flowing pen we had the books which delighted our young days, *Darnley,* and *Richelieu,* and *Delorme,** relish the works of Alexandre the Great, and thrill over the *Three Musqueteers?* Does the accomplished author of *The Caxtons* read the other tales in *Blackwood?* (For example, that ghost-story printed last August, and which for my part, though I read it in the public reading-room at the "Pavilion Hotel" at Folkestone, I protest frightened me so that I scarce dared look over my shoulder.) Does *Uncle Tom* admire *Adam Bede;* and does the author of the *Vicar of Wrexhill* laugh over *The Warden* and the *Three Clerks?* Dear youth of ingenuous countenance and ingenuous pudor !† I make no doubt that the eminent parties above named all partake of novels in moderation—eat jellies— but mainly nourish themselves upon wholesome roast and boiled.

Here, dear youth aforesaid! our *Cornhill Magazine* owners strive to provide thee with facts as well as fiction; and though it does not become them to brag of their

---

* By the way, what a strange fate is that which befell the veteran novelist! He was appointed her Majesty's Consul-General in Venice, the only city in Europe where the famous "Two Cavaliers" cannot by any possibility be seen riding together. (Thackeray's note.) The reference is to G. P. R. James, whose romantic novels usually opened with a description of two cavaliers riding together.

† Pudor (Lat.), shyness, modesty.

Ordinary, at least they invite thee to a table where thou
shalt sit in good company.* That story of the *Fox* † was
written by one of the gallant seamen who sought for poor
Franklin under the awful Arctic Night: that account of
China‡ is told by the man of all the empire most likely
to know of what he speaks: those pages regarding Volun-
teers§ come from an honored hand that has borne the
sword in a hundred famous fields, and pointed the British
guns in the greatest siege in the world.

Shall we point out others? We are fellow-travellers,
and shall make acquaintance as the voyage proceeds
In the Atlantic steamers, on the first day out (and on
high and holy days subsequently), the jellies set down on
table are richly ornamented; *medioque in fonte leporum* ‖
rise the American and British flags nobly emblazoned in
tin. As the passengers remark this pleasing phenomenon,
the Captain no doubt improves the occasion by expressing
a hope, to his right and left, that the flag of Mr. Bull
and his younger Brother may always float side by side
in friendly emulation. Novels having been previously
compared to jellies—here are two (one perhaps not entirely saccharine, and flavored with an *amari aliquid*¶
very distasteful to some palates)—two novels** under two
flags, the one that ancient ensign which has hung before

---

* This essay appeared in the first issue of the *Cornhill Magazine*,
of which Thackeray was editor. In the following sentences he men-
tions the chief articles in that number of the magazine.

† *The Search for Sir John Franklin*. (From the Private Journal
of an Officer of the *Fox*.)

‡ *The Chinese and the Outer Barbarians*. By Sir John Bowring.
§ *Our Volunteers*. By Sir John Burgoyne.

‖ In the midst of this abundance of attractive things.

¶ *Amari aliquid*, something bitter, referring to the occasional
satire in Thackeray's novels.

** In this issue of the *Cornhill* appeared the opening chapters of
Thackeray's *Lovel the Widower* and of Anthony Trollope's *Framley
Parsonage*.

the well-known booth of *Vanity Fair;* the other that fresh and handsome standard which has lately been hoisted on *Barchester Towers.* Pray, sir, or madam, to which dish will you be helped?

So have I seen my friends Captain Lang and Captain Comstock press their guests to partake of the fare on that memorable "First day out," when there is no man, I think, who sits down but asks a blessing on his voyage, and the good ship dips over the bar, and bounds away into the blue water.

ROBERT LOUIS STEVENSON

A COLLEGE MAGAZINE

Robert Louis Stevenson (1850–1894), one of the best-known English novelists, was born in Edinburgh. His father was a builder of lighthouses and wished his son to follow his profession, but the boy's health forbade this. He attended Edinburgh University, where he was not a very diligent student but a tremendous reader. He began the study of law, although his heart was not in it; as he tells us in this essay, he desired of all things to become a writer. In this he was handicapped by his poor health; an inherited tendency to consumption made him an invalid practically all his life. In search of health he went to the south of France, to Switzerland, to the Adirondacks, and finally to the South Sea islands, where he died in 1894.

The beginning of his literary work is told in this essay. He made a canoe trip through Holland and Belgium, and described it in *An Inland Voyage;* a walking tour in France gave material for *Travels with a Donkey.* Then followed two volumes of essays, *Virginibus Puerisque* (*To Girls and Boys*), and *Familiar Studies of Men and Books.* His first novel, *Treasure Island,* published in 1883, made him famous. It has taken its place beside *Robinson Crusoe* as one of the best boys' books ever written. Other novels of his are *Kidnapped, David Balfour, The Master of Ballantrae,* and *The Weir of Hermiston.* He wrote a number of notable short stories, of which the best known is *Dr. Jekyll and Mr. Hyde;* also a volume of poems, *A Child's Garden of Verses.*

In his essays Stevenson shows himself one of the great masters of style. Clear, flexible, musical, it is a perfect medium for conveying his thought. How he acquired this style is told in the paper *A College Magazine.*

ROBERT LOUIS STEVENSON

A COLLEGE MAGAZINE

(From *Memories and Portraits*)

I

All through my boyhood and youth, I was known and pointed out for the pattern of an idler; and yet I was always busy on my own private end, which was to learn to write. I kept always two books in my pocket, one to read, one to write in. As I walked, my mind was busy fitting what I saw with appropriate words; when I sat by the roadside, I would either read, or a pencil and a penny version-book would be in my hand, to note down the features of the scene or commemorate some halting stanzas. Thus I lived with words. And what I thus wrote was for no ulterior use, it was written consciously for practice. It was not so much that I wished to be an author (though I wished that too) as that I had vowed that I would learn to write. That was a proficiency that tempted me; and I practised to acquire it, as men learn to whittle, in a wager with myself. Description was the principal field of my exercise; for to any one with senses there is always something worth describing, and town and country are but one continuous subject. But I worked in other ways also; often accompanied my walks with dramatic dialogues, in which I played many parts; and often exercised myself in writing down conversations from memory.

This was all excellent, no doubt; so were the diaries I sometimes tried to keep, but always and very speedily discarded, finding them a school of posturing and melancholy self-deception. And yet this was not the most efficient part of my training. Good though it was, it only taught me (so far as I have learned them at all) the lower and less intellectual elements of the art, the choice of the essential note and the right word: things that to a happier constitution had perhaps come by nature. And regarded as training, it had one grave defect; for it set me no standard of achievement. So that there was perhaps more profit, as there was certainly more effort, in my secret labors at home. Whenever I read a book or a passage that particularly pleased me, in which a thing was said or an effect rendered with propriety, in which there was either some conspicuous force or some happy distinction in the style, I must sit down at once and set myself to ape that quality. I was unsuccessful, and I knew it; and tried again, and was again unsuccessful and always unsuccessful; but at least in these vain bouts, I got some practice in rhythm, in harmony, in construction, and in the co-ordination of parts. I have thus played the sedulous ape to Hazlitt, to Lamb, to Wordsworth, to Sir Thomas Browne, to Defoe, to Hawthorne, to Montaigne, to Baudelaire, and to Obermann. I remember one of these monkey tricks, which was called *The Vanity of Morals*: it was to have had a second part, *The Vanity of Knowledge;* and as I had neither morality nor scholarship, the names were apt; but the second part was never attempted, and the first part was written (which is my reason for recalling it, ghostlike, from its ashes) no less than three times: first in the manner of Hazlitt, second in the manner of Ruskin, who had cast on me a passing spell, and third, in a laborious pasticcio * of Sir Thomas Browne. So with

* *Pasticcio,* a term used in painting to denote a picture painted in direct imitation of the style of another artist.

my other works: *Cain*, an epic, was (save the mark!) an imitation of *Sordello*; *Robin Hood*, a tale in verse, took an eclectic middle course among the fields of Keats, Chaucer, and Morris; in *Monmouth*, a tragedy, I reclined on the bosom of Mr. Swinburne; in my innumerable gouty-footed lyrics, I followed many masters; in the first draft of *The King's Pardon*, a tragedy, I was on the trail of no lesser man than John Webster; in the second draft of the same piece, with staggering versatility, I had shifted my allegiance to Congreve, and of course conceived my fable in a less serious vein—for it was not Congreve's verse, it was his exquisite prose, that I admired and sought to copy. Even at the age of thirteen I had tried to do justice to the inhabitants of the famous city of Peebles in the style of the *Book of Snobs*. So I might go on forever, through all my abortive novels, and down to my later plays, of which I think more tenderly, for they were not only conceived at first under the bracing influence of old Dumas, but have met with resurrections: one, strangely bettered by another hand, came on the stage itself and was played by bodily actors; the other, originally known as *Semiramis: a Tragedy*, I have observed on book-stalls under the *alias* of *Prince Otto*. But enough has been said to show by what arts of impersonation, and in what purely ventriloquial efforts I first saw my words on paper.

That, like it or not, is the way to learn to write; whether I have profited or not, that is the way. It was so Keats learned, and there was never a finer temperament for literature than Keats's; it was so, if we could trace it out, that all men have learned; and that is why a revival of letters is always accompanied or heralded by a cast back to earlier and fresher models. Perhaps I hear some one cry out: But this is not the way to be original! It is not; nor is there any way but to be born so. Nor yet, if you are born original, is there anything in this training that shall clip the wings of your originality. There can be none more original than Montaigne, neither could any be more unlike Cicero; yet no craftsman can fail to see how much the one must have tried in his time to imitate the other. Burns is the very type of a prime force in letters: he was of all men the most imitative. Shakespeare himself, the imperial, proceeds directly from a school. It is only from a school that we can expect to have good writers; it is almost invariably from a school that great writers, these lawless exceptions, issue. Nor is there anything here that should astonish the considerate. Before he can tell what cadences he truly prefers, the student should have tried all that are possible; before he can choose and preserve a fitting key of words, he should long have practised the literary scales; and it is only after years of such gymnastic that he can sit down at last, legions of words swarming to his call, dozens of turns of phrase simultaneously bidding for his choice, and he himself knowing what he wants to do and (within the narrow limit of a man's ability) able to do it.

And it is the great point of these imitations that there still shines beyond the student's reach his inimitable model. Let him try as he please, he is still sure of failure; and it is a very old and a very true saying that failure is the only highroad to success. I must have had some disposition to learn; for I clear-sightedly condemned my own performances. I liked doing them indeed; but when they were done, I could see they were rubbish. In consequence, I very rarely showed them even to my friends; and such friends as I chose to be my confidants I must have chosen well, for they had the friendliness to be quite plain with me. "Padding," said one. Another wrote: "I cannot understand why you do lyrics so badly." No more could I! Thrice I put myself in the way of a more authoritative rebuff, by sending a paper to a magazine. These were returned; and I was not surprised nor even pained. If they had not been looked at, as (like all amateurs) I suspected was the case, there was no good in repeating the experiment; if they had been looked at—well, then I had not yet learned to write, and I must keep on learning and living. Lastly, I had a piece of good fortune, which is the occasion of this paper, and by which I was able to see my literature in print, and to measure experimentally how far I stood from the favor of the public.

II

The Speculative Society is a body of some antiquity, and has counted among its members Scott, Brougham, Jeffrey, Horner, Benjamin Constant, Robert Emmet, and many a legal and local celebrity besides. By an accident, variously explained, it has its rooms in the very buildings of the University of Edinburgh: a hall, Turkey-carpeted, hung with pictures, looking, when lighted up at night with fire and candle, like some goodly dining-room; a passage-like library, walled with books in their wire cages; and a corridor with a fireplace, benches, a table, many prints of famous members, and a mural tablet to the virtues of a former secretary. Here a member can warm himself and loaf and read; here, in defiance of Senatus-consults, he can smoke. The Senatus looks askance at these privileges; looks even with a somewhat vinegar aspect on the whole society; which argues a lack of proportion in the learned mind, for the world, we may be sure, will prize far higher this haunt of dead lions than all the living dogs of the professorate.

I sat one December morning in the library of the Speculative; a very humble-minded youth, though it was a virtue I never had much credit for; yet proud of my privileges as a member of the Spec.; proud of the pipe I was smoking in the teeth of the Senatus; and in particular, proud of being in the next room to three very distinguished students, who were then conversing beside the corridor fire. One of these has now his name on the back of several volumes, and his voice, I learn, is influential in the law courts. Of the death of the second, you have just been reading what I had to say.* And the third also has escaped out of that battle of life in which he fought so hard, it may be so unwisely. They were all three, as I have said, notable students; but this was the most conspicuous. Wealthy, handsome, ambitious, adventurous, diplomatic, a reader of Balzac, and of all men that I have known, the most like to one of Balzac's characters, he led a life, and was attended by an ill fortune, that could be properly set forth only in the *Comédie Humaine*. He had then his eye on Parliament; and soon after the time of which I write, he made a showy speech at a political dinner, was cried up to heaven next day in the *Courant*, and the day after was dashed lower than earth with a charge of plagiarism in the *Scotsman*. Report would have it (I dare say, very wrongly) that he was betrayed by one in whom he particularly trusted, and that the author of the charge had learned its truth from his own lips. Thus, at least, he was up one day on a pinnacle, admired and envied by all; and the next, though still but a boy, he was publicly disgraced. The blow would have broken a less finely tempered spirit; and even him I suppose it rendered reckless; for he took flight to London, and there, in a fast club, disposed of the bulk of his considerable patrimony in the space of one winter. For years thereafter he lived I know not

* The reference is to the essay "Old Mortality," which precedes this essay in the volume *Memories and Portraits*.

how; always well dressed, always in good hotels and good society, always with empty pockets. The charm of his manner may have stood him in good stead; but though my own manners are very agreeable, I have never found in them a source of livelihood; and to explain the miracle of his continued existence, I must fall back upon the theory of the philosopher, that in his case, as in all of the same kind, "there was a suffering relative in the background." From this genteel eclipse he reappeared upon the scene, and presently sought me out in the character of a generous editor. It is in this part that I best remember him; tall, slender, with a not ungraceful stoop; looking quite like a refined gentleman, and quite like an urbane adventurer; smiling with an engaging ambiguity; cocking at you one peaked eyebrow with a great appearance of finesse; speaking low and sweet and thick, with a touch of burr; telling strange tales with singular deliberation and, to a patient listener, excellent effect. After all these ups and downs, he seemed still, like the rich student that he was of yore, to breathe of money; seemed still perfectly sure of himself and certain of his end. Yet he was then upon the brink of his last overthrow. He had set himself to found the strangest thing in our society: one of those periodical sheets from which men suppose themselves to learn opinions; in which young gentlemen from the universities are encouraged, at so much a line, to garble facts, insult foreign nations, and calumniate private individuals; and which are now the source of glory, so that if a man's name be often enough printed there, he becomes a kind of demigod; and people will pardon him when he talks back and forth, as they do for Mr. Gladstone; and crowd him to suffocation on railway platforms, as they did the other day to General Boulanger; and buy his literary works, as I hope you have just done for me. Our fathers, when they were

upon some great enterprise, would sacrifice a life; building, it may be, a favorite slave into the foundations of
their palace.   It was with his own life that my companion
disarmed the envy of the gods.   He fought his paper
single-handed; trusting no one, for he was something of
a cynic; up early and down late, for he was nothing of a
sluggard; daily ear-wigging influential men, for he was
a master of ingratiation.   In that slender and silken
fellow there must have been a rare vein of courage, that
he should thus have died at his employment; and doubtless ambition spoke loudly in his ear, and doubtless love
also, for it seems there was a marriage in his view had he
succeeded.   But he died, and his paper died after him;
and of all this grace, and tact, and courage, it must seem
to our blind eyes as if there had come literally nothing.

These three students sat, as I was saying, in the corridor, under the mural tablet that records the virtues of
Macbean, the former secretary.   We would often smile
at that ineloquent memorial, and thought it a poor thing
to come into the world at all and leave no more behind
one than Macbean.   And yet of these three, two are gone
and have left less; and this book, perhaps, when it is
old and foxy, and some one picks it up in a corner of a
book-shop, and glances through it, smiling at the old,
graceless turns of speech, and perhaps for the love of
Alma Mater (which may be still extant and flourishing)
buys it, not without haggling, for some pence—this book
may alone preserve a memory of James Walter Ferrier
and Robert Glasgow Brown.

Their thoughts ran very differently on that December
morning; they were all on fire with ambition; and when
they had called me in to them, and made me a sharer in
their design, I too became drunken with pride and hope.
We were to found a University magazine.   A pair of
little, active brothers—Livingstone by name, great

skippers on the foot, great rubbers of the hands, who kept a book-shop over against the University building—had been debauched to play the part of publishers. We four were to be conjunct editors and, what was the main point of the concern, to print our own works; while, by every rule of arithmetic—that flatterer of credulity—the adventure must succeed and bring great profit. Well, well: it was a bright vision. I went home that morning walking upon air. To have been chosen by these three distinguished students was to me the most unspeakable advance; it was my first draught of consideration; it reconciled me to myself and to my fellow men; and as I steered round the railings at the Tron, I could not withhold my lips from smiling publicly. Yet, in the bottom of my heart, I knew that magazine would be a grim fiasco; I knew it would not be worth reading; I knew, even if it were, that nobody would read it; and I kept wondering how I should be able, upon my compact income of twelve pounds per annum, payable monthly, to meet my share in the expense. It was a comfortable thought to me that I had a father.

The magazine appeared, in a yellow cover which was the best part of it, for at least it was unassuming; it ran four months in undisturbed obscurity, and died without a gasp. The first number was edited by all four of us with prodigious bustle; the second fell principally into the hands of Ferrier and me; the third I edited alone; and it has long been a solemn question who it was that edited the fourth. It would perhaps be still more difficult to say who read it. Poor yellow sheet, that looked so hopefully in the Livingstones' window! Poor, harmless paper, that might have gone to print a *Shakespeare* on, and was instead so clumsily defaced with nonsense! And, shall I say, Poor Editors? I cannot pity myself, to whom it was all pure gain. It was no news to me, but only the wholesome confirmation of my judgment, when the magazine struggled into half-birth, and instantly sickened and subsided into night. I had sent a copy to the lady with whom my heart was at that time somewhat engaged, and who did all that in her lay to break it; and she, with some tact, passed over the gift and my cherished contributions in silence. I will not say that I was pleased at this; but I will tell her now, if by any chance she takes up the work of her former servant, that I thought the better of her taste. I cleared the decks after this lost engagement; had the necessary interview with my father, which passed off not amiss; paid over my share of the expense to the two little, active brothers, who rubbed their hands as much, but methought skipped rather less than formerly, having perhaps, these two also, embarked upon the enterprise with some graceful illusions; and then, reviewing the whole episode, I told myself that the time was not yet ripe, nor the man ready; and to work I went again with my penny version-books, having fallen back in one day from the printed author to the manuscript student.

OLIVER WENDELL HOLMES

MY LAST WALK WITH THE SCHOOLMISTRESS

Oliver Wendell Holmes (1809–1894) was a member of the famous Cambridge group of writers, including also Longfellow and Lowell. He was born in Cambridge, Mass., and educated at Phillips Andover Academy and Harvard College, where Wendell Phillips the orator and John Lothrop Motley the historian were his classmates. He wrote verse for the college magazine, and an early poem, "Old Ironsides," was copied in newspapers all over the country. He studied medicine, and practised in Boston, besides being a professor in the Harvard Medical School. In the moments that he could spare from his profession he wrote several books that are a permanent addition to American literature. When the *Atlantic Monthly* was projected, it was Holmes who suggested its name, and in the first number appeared the opening pages of *The Autocrat of the Breakfast-Table*. The novelty of the form, a sort of conversational essay, the sparkling wit, the keen comments on life, the apt turns of phrase,—all these made the Autocrat a joy to his readers. Two later volumes, *The Professor at the Breakfast-Table* and *The Poet at the Breakfast-Table* continued the same vein. Holmes's other works include a novel, *Elsie Venner;* a volume of poems, and biographies of Emerson and Motley. The selection here given is from *The Autocrat of the Breakfast-Table*. While a thread of narrative runs through it, nearly all of the article is in the essay vein; the story is merely an opportunity for the writer to express his opinions on a variety of subjects.

OLIVER WENDELL HOLMES

MY LAST WALK WITH THE SCHOOLMISTRESS *

(From *The Autocrat of the Breakfast-Table*)

(*A Parenthesis*)

I can't say just how many walks she and I had taken together before this one. I found the effect of going out every morning was decidedly favorable on her health. Two pleasing dimples, the places for which were just marked when she came, played, shadowy, in her freshening cheeks when she smiled and nodded good morning to me from the schoolhouse steps.

I am afraid I did the greater part of the talking. At any rate, if I should try to report all that I said during the first half-dozen walks we took together, I fear that I might receive a gentle hint from my friends the publishers that a separate volume, at my own risk and expense, would be the proper method of bringing them before the public.

—I would have a woman as true as Death. At the first real lie which works from the heart outward, she should be tenderly chloroformed into a better world, where she can have an angel for a governess, and feed on strange fruits which will make her all over again, even to her bones and marrow.—Whether gifted with the accident of beauty or not, she should have been moulded in the rose-red clay of Love, before the breath of life made a moving mortal of her. Love-capacity is

* Used by permission of Houghton, Mifflin Company, the authorized publishers of Holmes's works.

a congenital endowment; and I think, after a while, one gets to know the warm-hued natures it belongs to from the pretty pipe-clay counterfeits of them.—Proud she may be, in the sense of respecting herself; but pride, in the sense of contemning others less gifted than herself, deserves the two lowest circles of a vulgar woman's Inferno, where the punishments are Smallpox and Bankruptcy.—She who nips off the end of a brittle courtesy, as one breaks the tip of an icicle, to bestow upon those whom she ought cordially and kindly to recognize, proclaims the fact that she comes not merely of low blood, but of bad blood. Consciousness of unquestioned position makes people gracious in proper measure to all; but if a woman put on airs with her real equals, she had something about herself or her family she is ashamed of, or ought to be. Middle, and more than middle-aged people, who know family histories, generally see through it. An official of standing was rude to me once. Oh, that is the maternal grandfather,—said a wise old friend to me,—he was a boor.—Better too few words, from the woman we love, than too many: while she is silent, Nature is working for her; while she talks, she is working for herself.—Love is sparingly soluble in the words of men; therefore they speak much of it; but one syllable of woman's speech can dissolve more of it than a man's heart can hold.

—Whether I said any or all of these things to the schoolmistress, or not,—whether I stole them out of Lord Bacon,—whether I cribbed them from Balzac, —whether I dipped them from the ocean of Tupperian * wisdom,—or whether I have just found them in my head, laid there by that solemn fowl, Experience (who, according to my observation, cackles oftener than she drops

* *Tupperian,* a reference to Martin F. Tupper, author of *Proverbial Philosophy,* a book of precepts and advice in verse.

real live eggs), I cannot say. Wise men have said more
foolish things,—and foolish men, I don't doubt, have
said as wise things. Anyhow, the schoolmistress and I
had pleasant walks and long talks, all of which I do not
feel bound to report.

—You are a stranger to me, Ma'am.—I don't doubt
you would like to know all I said to the schoolmistress.—
I sha'n't do it;—I had rather get the publishers to return
the money you have invested in these pages. Besides,
I have forgotten a good deal of it. I shall tell only what
I like of what I remember.

—My idea was, in the first place, to search out the
picturesque spots which the city affords a sight of, to
those who have eyes. I know a good many, and it was a
pleasure to look at them in company with my young
friend. There were the shrubs and flowers in the Frank-
lin-Place front yards or borders: Commerce is just putting
his granite foot upon them. Then there are certain small
seraglio gardens, into which one can get a peep through
the crevices of high fences,—one in Myrtle Street, or at
the back of it,—here and there one at the North and
South ends. Then the great elms in Essex Street. Then
the stately horse-chestnuts in that vacant lot in Chambers
Street, which hold their outspread hands over your head
(as I said in my poem the other day), and look as if they
were whispering, "May grace, mercy, and peace be with
you!"—and the rest of that benediction. Nay, there
are certain patches of ground, which, having lain neglected for a time, Nature, who always has her pockets
full of seeds, and holes in all her pockets, has covered
with hungry plebeian growths, which fight for life with
each other, until some of them get broad-leaved and
succulent, and you have a coarse vegetable tapestry
which Raphael would not have disdained to spread over
the foreground of his masterpiece. The Professor pre-

tends that he found such a one in Charles Street, which, in its dare-devil impudence of rough-and-tumble vegetation, beat the pretty-behaved flower-beds of the Public Garden as ignominiously as a group of young tatterdemalions playing pitch-and-toss beats a row of Sunday-school boys with their teacher at their head.

But then the Professor had one of his burrows in that region, and puts everything in high colors relating to it. That is his way about everything.—I hold any man cheap,—he said,—of whom nothing stronger can be uttered than that all his geese are swans.—How is that, Professor?—said I;—I should have set you down for one of that sort.—Sir,—said he,—I am proud to say, that Nature has so far enriched me, that I cannot own so much as a *duck* without seeing in it as pretty a swan as ever swam the basin in the garden of Luxembourg. And the Professor showed the whites of his eyes devoutly, like one returning thanks after a dinner of many courses.

I don't know anything sweeter than this leaking in of Nature through all the cracks in the walls and floors of cities. You heap up a million tons of hewn rocks on a square mile or two of earth which was green once. The trees look down from the hillsides and ask each other, as they stand on tiptoe,—"What are these people about?" And the small herbs at their feet look up and whisper back,—"We will go and see." So the small herbs pack themselves up in the least possible bundles, and wait until the wind steals to them at night and whispers,—"Come with me." Then they go softly with it into the great city,—one to a cleft in the pavement, one to a spout on the roof, one to a seam in the marbles over a rich gentleman's bones, and one to the grave without a stone where nothing but a man is buried,—and there they grow, looking down on the generations of men from mouldy roofs, looking up from between the less-trodden pavements, looking out through iron cemetery-railings. Listen to them, when there is only a light breath stirring, and you will hear them saying to each other,—"Wait awhile!" The words run along the telegraph of those narrow green lines that border the roads leading from the city, until they reach the slope of the hills, and the trees repeat in low murmurs to each other,—"Wait awhile!" By and by the flow of life in the streets ebbs, and the old leafy inhabitants—the smaller tribes always in front—saunter in, one by one, very careless seemingly, but very tenacious, until they swarm so that the great stones gape from each other with the crowding of their roots, and the feldspar begins to be picked out of the granite to find them food. At last the trees take up their solemn line of march, and never rest until they have encamped in the market-place. Wait long enough and you will find an old doting oak hugging a huge worn block in its yellow underground arms; that was the corner-stone of the State-House. Oh, so patient she is, this imperturbable Nature!

—Let us cry!—

But all this has nothing to do with my walks and talks with the schoolmistress. I did not say that I would not tell you something about them. Let me alone, and I shall talk to you more than I ought to, probably. We never tell our secrets to people that pump for them.

Books we talked about, and education. It was her duty to know something of these, and of course she did. Perhaps I was somewhat more learned than she, but I found that the difference between her reading and mine was like that of a man's and a woman's dusting a library. The man flaps about with a bunch of feathers; the woman goes to work softly with a cloth. She does not raise half the dust, nor fill her own eyes and mouth with it,—but she goes into all the corners and attends to the leaves as much as to the covers.—Books are the *negative* pictures of thought, and the more sensitive the mind that receives their images, the more nicely the finest lines are reproduced. A woman (of the right kind), reading after a man, follows him as Ruth followed the reapers of Boaz, and her gleanings are often the finest of the wheat.

But it was in talking of Life that we came most nearly together. I thought I knew something about that,—that I could speak or write about it somewhat to the purpose.

To take up this fluid earthly being of ours as a sponge sucks up water,—to be steeped and soaked in its realities as a hide fills its pores lying seven years in a tan-pit,—to have winnowed every wave of it as a mill-wheel works up the stream that runs through the flume upon its float-boards,—to have curled up in the keenest spasms and flattened out in the laxest languors of this breathing sickness, which keeps certain parcels of matter uneasy for three or four score years,—to have fought all the devils and clasped all the angels of its delirium,—and then, just at the point when the white-hot passions have cooled down to cherry-red, plunge our experience into the ice-cold stream of some human language or other, one might think would end in a rhapsody with something of spring and temper in it All this I thought my power and province.

The schoolmistress had tried life, too. Once in a while one meets with a single soul greater than all the living pageant which passes before it. As the pale astronomer sits in his study with sunken eyes and thin fingers, and weighs Uranus or Neptune as in a balance, so there are meek, slight women who have weighed all which this planetary life can offer, and hold it like a bauble in the palm of their slender hands. This was one of them. Fortune had left her, sorrow had baptized her; the routine of labor and the loneliness of almost friendless city life were before her. Yet, as I looked upon her tranquil face, gradually regaining a cheerfulness which was often sprightly, as she became interested in the various matters we talked about and places we visited, I saw that eye and lip and every shifting lineament were made for love,— unconscious of their sweet office as yet, and meeting the cold aspect of Duty with the natural graces which were meant for the reward of nothing less than the Great Passion.

—I never addressed one word of love to the school-mistress in the course of these pleasant walks. It seemed to me that we talked of everything but love on that particular morning. There was, perhaps, a little more timidity and hesitancy on my part than I have commonly shown among our people at the boarding-house. In fact, I considered myself the master at the breakfast-table; but, somehow, I could not command myself just then so well as usual. The truth is, I had secured a passage to Liverpool in the steamer which was to leave at noon,—with the condition, however, of being released in case circumstances occurred to detain me. The school-mistress knew nothing about all this, of course, as yet.

It was on the Common that we were walking. The *mall*, or boulevard of our Common, you know, has various branches leading from it in different directions. One of these runs down from opposite Joy Street southward across the whole length of the Common to Boylston Street. We called it the long path, and were fond of it.

I felt very weak indeed (though of a tolerably robust habit) as we came opposite the head of this path on that morning. I think I tried to speak twice without making myself distinctly audible. At last I got out the question, —Will you take the long path with me?—Certainly,— said the schoolmistress,—with much pleasure.—Think,—

I said,—before you answer: if you take the long path with me now, I shall interpret it that we are to part no more!— The schoolmistress stepped back with a sudden movement, as if an arrow had struck her.

One of the long granite blocks used as seats was hard by, the one you may still see close by the Gingko-tree.— Pray, sit down,—I said.—No, no, she answered, softly,— I will walk the *long path* with you!

—The old gentleman who sits opposite met us walking, arm in arm, about the middle of the long path, and said, very charmingly,—"Good morning, my dears!"

THE DESCRIPTIVE ESSAY

JOHN RUSKIN

THE SKY

John Ruskin (1819–1900), eminent as author, art critic, and social reformer, was the son of a wealthy English merchant. His father was a lover of pictures, and took the boy to see the great collections in public and private galleries in England. His mother read to him daily from the Bible, and to this Ruskin attributed the clearness and beauty of his style. He was educated at Oxford. His first intellectual interest was in art, and his first book was *Modern Painters*. Later volumes were *Stones of Venice*, and *Seven Lamps of Architecture*. These established his position as one of the great art critics of his time, and as a master of English prose. He next turned his attention to social and economic questions. It was his belief that no nation could produce great art unless it had moral and spiritual greatness as a foundation. He saw the English people in their great industrial development, forgetful of higher things. He wrote books and delivered lectures untiringly in the effort to arouse the nation to a sense of its wrong aims. Nor did he stop at writing. The death of his father left him a fortune of nearly a million dollars: he spent practically all of this in various projects for bettering the condition of the working people of England. He built model tenements, established co-operative associations, started schools for workers. Many of the reform movements of to-day owe their origin to John Ruskin.

He wrote a great number of books, dealing mainly with the three great interests of his life, painting, architecture, and political economy. The selection "The Sky" illustrates Ruskin's wonderful descriptive power, and his gift of writing prose that has the beauty and music of poetry.

JOHN RUSKIN

THE SKY

(From *Modern Painters*)

It is a strange thing how little in general people know about the sky. It is the part of creation in which Nature has done more for the sake of pleasing man—more for the sole and evident purpose of talking to him, and teaching him—than in any other of her works; and it is just the part in which we least attend to her. There are not many of her other works in which some more material or essential purpose than the mere pleasing of man is not answered by every part of their organization; but every essential purpose of the sky might, so far as we know, be answered if once in three days, or thereabouts, a great, ugly, black rain-cloud were brought up over the blue, and everything well watered, and so all left blue again till next time, with perhaps a film of morning and evening mist for dew—and instead of this, there is not a moment of any day of our lives, when Nature is not producing scene after scene, picture after picture, glory after glory, and working still upon such exquisite and constant principles of the most perfect beauty, that it is quite certain it is all done for us, and intended for our perpetual pleasure. And every man, wherever placed, however far from other sources of interest of or beauty, has this doing for him constantly. The noblest scenes of the earth can be seen and known but by few; it is not intended that man should live always in the midst of them; he injures

them by his presence, he ceases to feel them if he is always
with them; but the sky is for all: bright as it is, it is not

> "too bright nor good
> For human nature's daily food;"*

it is fitted in all its functions for the perpetual comfort
and exalting of the heart,—for soothing it, and purifying
it from its dross and dust.   Sometimes gentle, sometimes
capricious, sometimes awful—never the same for two
moments together; almost human in its passions, almost
spiritual in its tenderness, almost divine in its infinity,
its appeal to what is immortal in us is as distinct as its
ministry of chastisement or of blessing to what is mortal
is essential.

And yet we never attend to it, we never make it a subject of thought, but as it has to do with our animal sensa-
tions; we look upon all by which it speaks to us more
clearly than to brutes, upon all which bears witness to
the intention of the Supreme that we are to receive more
from the covering vault than the light and the dew which
we share with the weed and the worm, only as a succession of meaningless and monotonous accident, too common and too vain to be worthy of a moment of watch-
fulness, or a glance of admiration.   If in our moments
of utter idleness and insipidity, we turn to the sky as
a last resource, which of its phenomena do we speak
of?   One says, it has been wet; and another, it has been
windy, and another, it has been warm.   Who among the
whole chattering crowd can tell one of the forms and the
precipices of the chain of tall white mountains that girded
the horizon at noon yesterday?   Who saw the narrow
sunbeam that came out of the south, and smote upon their
summits until they melted and mouldered away in the

* Quoted from Wordsworth's "She was a Phantom of Delight."

dust of blue rain? Who saw the dance of the dead clouds where the sunlight left them last night, and the west wind blew them before it like withered leaves? All has passed unregretted as unseen; or if the apathy be ever shaken off even for an instant, it is only by what is gross, or what is extraordinary. And yet it is not in the broad and fierce manifestations of the elemental energies, nor in the clash of the hail, nor the drift of the whirl-wind, that the highest characters of the sublime are de-veloped. God is not in the earthquake, nor in the fire, but in the still small voice. They are but the blunt and the low faculties of our nature, which can only be addressed through lamp-black and lightning. It is in quiet and unsubdued passages of unobtrusive majesty, the deep and the calm, and the perpetual; that which must be sought ere it is seen, and loved ere it is under-stood; things which the angels work out for us daily, and yet vary eternally; which are never wanting, and never repeated, which are to be found always, yet each found but once; it is through these that the lesson of devotion is chiefly taught, and the blessing of beauty given.

We habitually think of the rain-cloud only as dark and gray; not knowing that we owe to it perhaps the fairest, though not the most dazzling, of the hues of heaven. Often in our English mornings, the rain-clouds in the dawn form soft, level fields, which melt imperceptibly into the blue; or, when of less extent, gather into apparent bars, crossing the sheets of broader clouds above; and all these bathed throughout in an unspeakable light of pure rose-color, and purple, and amber, and blue; not shining, but misty-soft; the barred masses, when seen nearer, composed of clusters or tresses of cloud, like floss silk; looking as if each knot were a little swathe or sheaf of lighted rain.

Has the reader any distinct idea of what clouds are?

That mist which lies in the morning so softly in the valley, level and white, through which the tops of the trees rise as if through an inundation—why is *it* so heavy, and why does it lie so low, being yet so thin and frail that it will melt away utterly into splendor of morning when the sun has shone on it but a few moments more? Those colossal pyramids, huge and firm, with outlines as of rocks, and strength to bear the beating of the high sun full on their fiery flanks,—why are *they* so light, their bases high over our heads, high over the heads of Alps? Why will these melt away, not as the sun *rises*, but as he *descends*, and leave the stars of twilight clear; while the valley vapor gains again upon the earth, like a shroud? Or that ghost of a cloud, which steals by yonder clump of pines; nay, which does *not* steal by them, but haunts them, wreathing yet round them, and yet,—and yet,— slowly; now falling in a fair waved line like a woman's veil; now fading, now gone; we look away for an instant, and look back, and it is again there. What has it to do with that clump of pines, that it broods by them, and waves itself among their branches, to and fro? Has it hidden a cloudy treasure among the moss at their roots, which it watches thus? Or has some strong enchanter charmed it into fond returning, or bound it fast within those bars of bough? And yonder filmy crescent, bent like an archer's bow above the snowy summit, the highest of all the hills—that white arch which never forms but over the supreme crest,—how it is stayed there, repelled apparently from the snow,—nowhere touching it, the clear sky seen between it and the mountain edge, yet never leaving it—poised as a white bird hovers over its nest! Or those war clouds that gather on the horizon, dragon-crested, tongued with fire,—how is their barbed strength bridled? What bits are those they are champing with their vaporous lips, flinging off flakes of black foam? Leagued leviathans of the Sea and Heaven,—out of their nostrils goeth smoke, and their eyes are like the eyelids of the morning; the sword of him that layeth at them cannot hold the spear, the dart, nor the habergeon. Where ride the captains of their armies? Where are set the measures of their march? Fierce murmurers, answering each other from morning until evening—what rebuke is this which has awed them into peace;—what hand has reined them back by the way in which they came?

I know not if the reader will think at first that questions like these are easily answered. So far from it, I rather believe that some of the mysteries of the clouds never will be understood by us at all. "Knowest thou the balancing of the clouds?" Is the answer ever to be one of pride? The wondrous works of Him, which is perfect in knowledge! Is *our* knowledge ever to be so? . . .

On some isolated mountain at daybreak, when the night mists first rise from off the plain, watch their white and lake-like fields, as they float in level bays, and winding gulfs about the islanded summits of the lower hills, untouched yet by more than dawn, colder and more quiet than a windless sea under the moon of midnight; watch when the first sunbeam is sent upon the silver channels, how the foam of their undulating surface parts, and passes away, and down under their depths the glittering city and green pasture lie like Atlantis, between the white paths of winding rivers; the flakes of light falling every moment faster and broader among the starry spires, as the wreathed surges break and vanish above them, and the confused crests and ridges of the dark hills shorten their gray shadows upon the plain. Wait a little longer, and you shall see those scattered mists rallying in the ravines, and floating up toward you, along the winding valleys, till they couch in quiet masses, iridescent with the morning light, upon the broad breasts of the higher hills, whose leagues of massy undulation will melt back,

back into that robe of material light, until they fade away, and set in its lustre, to appear again above in the serene heaven like a wild, bright, impossible dream, foundation-less, and inaccessible, their very base vanishing in the unsubstantial, and making blue of the deep lake below.

Wait yet a little longer, and you shall see those mists gather themselves into white towers, and stand like for-tresses along the promontories, massy and motionless, only piled with every instant higher and higher into the sky, and casting longer shadows athwart the rocks; and out of the pale blue of the horizon you will see forming and advancing a troop of narrow, dark, pointed vapors, which will cover the sky, inch by inch, with their gray network, and take the light off the landscape with an eclipse which will stop the singing of the birds, and the motion of the leaves, together;—and then you will see horizontal bars of black shadow forming under them, and lurid wreaths create themselves, you know not how, among the shoulders of the hills; you never see them form, but when you look back to a place which was clear an instant ago, there is a cloud on it, hanging by the precipice as a hawk pauses over his prey;—and then you will hear the sudden rush of the awakened wind, and you will see those watch-towers of vapor swept away from their foun-dations, and waving curtains of opaque rain let down to the valley, swinging from the burdened clouds in black bending fringes, or, pacing in pale columns along the lake level, grazing its surface into foam as they go. And then as the sun sinks you shall see the storm drift for an instant from off the hills, leaving their broad sides smok-ing and loaded yet with snow-white, torn, steam-like rags of capricious vapor, now gone, now gathered again,—while the smouldering sun, seeming not far away, but burning like a red-hot ball beside you, and as if you could reach it, plunges through the rushing wind and rolling cloud with headlong fall, as if it meant to rise no more, dyeing all the air about it with blood;—and then you shall hear the fainting tempest die in the hollow of the night, and you shall see a green halo kindling on the summit of the eastern hills, brighter, brighter yet, till the large white circle of the slow moon is lifted up among the barred clouds, step by step, line by line; star after star she quenches with her kindling light, setting in their stead an army of pale, penetrable fleecy wreaths in the heaven, to give light upon the earth, which move together hand in hand, company by company, troop by troop, so measured in their unity of motion that the whole heaven seems to roll with them, and the earth to reel under them.

And then wait yet for one hour, until the east again becomes purple, and the heaving mountains, rolling against it in darkness, like waves of a wild sea, are drowned one by one in the glory of its burning; watch the white glaciers blaze in their winding paths about the mountains, like mighty serpents with scales of fire: watch the columnar peaks of solitary snow, kindling downward chasm by chasm, each in itself a new morning—their long avalanches cast down in keen streams brighter than the lightning, sending each his tribute of driven snow, like altar-smoke up to heaven, the rose-light of their silent domes flushing that heaven about them, and above them, piercing with purer light through its purple lines of lifted cloud, casting a new glory on every wreath, as it passes by, until the whole heaven, one scarlet canopy, is interwoven with a roof of waving flame, and tossing vault beyond vault, as with the drifted wings of many companies of angels: and then when you can look no more for gladness, and when you are bowed down with fear and love of the Maker and Doer of this, tell me who has best delivered this His message unto men!

JOHN HENRY NEWMAN

THE SITE OF A UNIVERSITY

John Henry Newman (1801–1890), often called Cardinal Newman, belonged to the writers of the Victorian group. He was the son of a London banker. He early showed his bent to literature, writing verses at nine and a drama at twelve. Later he entered Oxford, where he won a fellowship. His life was spent as a clergyman, first in the Church of England, later in the Roman Catholic faith; the reasons for his change of belief are told in his *Apologia pro Vita Sua* (Apology for His Life). He was rector of the Catholic University at Dublin from 1854 to 1858; he was made a cardinal in 1879. Most of his life was spent at Birmingham, England. His writings include two novels, *Loss and Gain* and *Callista;* a number of poems, including the well-known hymn "Lead, Kindly Light"; and a volume of essays entitled *The Idea of a University*, written while he was at Dublin University.

Newman is considered one of the great masters of English prose. He took the greatest pains with his work, often writing whole chapters over and over again, besides making innumerable corrections. But in the finished work there is no trace of labor; his essays have the clearness and beauty of a statue. The description of Athens, in the selection here given, is one of the finest examples of Newman's style.

JOHN HENRY NEWMAN

THE SITE OF A UNIVERSITY

(From *Historical Sketches*, vol. III)

If we would know what a University is, considered in its elementary idea, we must betake ourselves to the first and most celebrated home of European literature and source of European civilization, to the bright and beautiful Athens,—Athens, whose schools drew to her bosom, and then sent back again to the business of life, the youth of the Western World for a long thousand years. Seated on the verge of the continent, the city seemed hardly suited for the duties of a central metropolis of knowledge; yet what it lost in convenience of approach, it gained in its neighborhood to the traditions of the mysterious East, and in the loveliness of the region in which it lay. Hither, then, as to a sort of ideal land, where all archetypes of the great and the fair were found in substantial being, and all departments of truth explored, and all diversities of intellectual power exhibited, where taste and philosophy were majestically enthroned as in a royal court, where there was no sovereignty but that of mind, and nobility but that of genius, where professors were rulers, and princes did homage, hither flocked continually from the very corners of the *orbis terrarum*,* the many-tongued generation, just rising, or just risen into manhood, in order to gain wisdom.

Pisistratus had in an early age discovered and nursed the infant genius of his people, and Cimon, after the Persian war, had given it a home. That war had established the naval supremacy of Athens; she had become

* *Orbis terrarum*, the circle of the world.

an imperial state; and the Ionians, bound to her by the double chain of kindred and of subjection, were importing into her both their merchandise and their civilization. The arts and philosophy of the Asiatic coast were easily carried across the sea, and there was Cimon, as I have said, with his ample fortune, ready to receive them with due honors. Not content with patronizing their professors, he built the first of those noble porticos, of which we hear so much in Athens, and he formed the groves, which in process of time became the celebrated Academy. Planting is one of the most graceful, as in Athens it was one of the most beneficent, of employments. Cimon took in hand the wild wood, pruned and dressed it, and laid it out with handsome walks and welcome fountains. Nor, while hospitable to the authors of the city's civilization, was he ungrateful to the instruments of her prosperity. His trees extended their cool, umbrageous branches over the merchants who assembled in the Agora, for many generations.

Those merchants certainly had deserved that act of bounty; for all the while their ships had been carrying forth the intellectual fame of Athens to the western world. Then commenced what may be called her University existence. Pericles, who succeeded Cimon both in the government and in the patronage of art, is said by Plutarch to have entertained the idea of making Athens the capital of federated Greece: in this he failed, but his encouragement of such men as Phidias and Anaxagoras led the way to her acquiring a far more lasting sovereignty over a far wider empire. Little understanding the sources of her own greatness, Athens would go to war: peace is the interest of a seat of commerce and the arts; but to war she went; yet to her, whether peace or war, it mattered not. The political power of Athens waned and disappeared; kingdoms rose and fell; centuries rolled away,—they did but bring fresh triumphs to the city of the poet and the sage. There at length the swarthy Moor and Spaniard were seen to meet the blue-eyed Gaul; and the Cappadocian, late subject of Mithridates, gazed without alarm at the haughty conquering Roman. Revolution after revolution passed over the face of Europe, as well as of Greece, but still she was there,— Athens, the city of mind,—as radiant, as splendid, as delicate, as young as ever she had been.

Many a more fruitful coast or isle is washed by the blue Ægean, many a spot is there more beautiful or sublime to see, many a territory more ample; but there was one charm in Attica, which in the same perfection was nowhere else. The deep pastures of Arcadia, the plain of Argos, the Thessalian vale, these had not the gift; Bœotia, which lay to its immediate north, was notorious for its very want of it. The heavy atmosphere of that Bœotia might be good for vegetation, but it was associated in popular belief with the dulness of the Bœotian intellect: on the contrary, the special purity, elasticity, clearness, and salubrity of the air of Attica, fit concomitant and emblem of its genius, did that for it which earth did not;— it brought out every bright hue and tender shade of the landscape over which it was spread, and would have illuminated the face even of a more bare and rugged country.

A confined triangle, perhaps fifty miles its greatest length, and thirty its greatest breadth; two elevated rocky barriers, meeting at an angle; three prominent mountains, commanding the plain,—Parnes, Pentelicus, and Hymettus; an unsatisfactory soil; some streams, not always full;—such is about the report which the agent of a London company would have made of Attica. He would report that the climate was mild; the hills were limestone; there was plenty of good marble; more pastureland than at first survey might have been expected, sufficient certainly for sheep and goats; fisheries productive; silver-mines once, but long since worked out; figs fair; oil first-rate; olives in profusion. But what he would not think of noting down, was, that that olive-tree was so choice in nature and so noble in shape, that it excited a religious veneration; and that it took so kindly to the light soil, as to expand into woods upon the open plain, and to climb up and fringe the hills. He would not think of writing word to his employers, how that clear air, of which I have spoken, brought out, yet blended and subdued, the colors on the marble, till they had a softness and harmony, for all their richness, which in a picture looks exaggerated, yet is after all within the truth. He would not tell, how that same delicate and brilliant atmosphere freshened up the pale olive, till the olive forgot its monotony, and its cheek glowed like the arbutus or beech of the Umbrian hills. He would say nothing of the thyme and thousand fragrant herbs which carpeted Hymettus; he would hear nothing of the hum of its bees; nor take much account of the rare flavor of its honey, since Gozo and Minorca were sufficient for the English demand. He would look over the Ægean from the height he had ascended: he would follow with his eye the chain of islands, which, starting from the Sunian headland, seemed to offer the fabled divinities of Attica, when they would visit their Ionian cousins, a sort of viaduct thereto across the sea: but that fancy would not occur to him, nor any admiration of the dark violet billows with their white edges down below; nor of those graceful, fan-like jets of silver upon the rocks, which slowly rise aloft like water spirits from the deep, then shiver, and break, and spread, and shroud themselves, and disappear, in a soft mist of foam; nor of the gentle, incessant heaving and panting of the whole liquid plain;

nor of the long waves, keeping steady time, like a line of soldiery, as they resound upon the hollow shore,—he would not deign to notice that restless living element at all, except to bless his stars that he was not upon it. Nor the distinct detail, nor the refined coloring, nor the graceful outline and roseate golden hue of the jutting crags, nor the bold shadows cast from Otus or Laurium by the declining sun;—our agent of a mercantile firm would not value these matters even at a low figure. Rather we must turn for the sympathy we seek to yon pilgrim student come from a semi-barbarous land to that small corner of the earth, as to a shrine, where he might take his fill of gazing on those emblems and coruscations of invisible unoriginate perfection. It was the stranger from a remote province, from Britain or from Mauritania, who in a scene so different from that of his chilly, woody swamps, or of his fiery choking sands, learned at once what a real University must be, by coming to understand the sort of country which was its suitable home.

Nor was this all that a University required, and found in Athens. No one, even there, could live on poetry. If the students at that famous place had nothing better than bright hues and soothing sounds, they would not have been able or disposed to turn their residence there to much account. Of course they must have the means of living, nay, in a certain sense, of enjoyment, if Athens was to be an Alma Mater at the time, or to remain afterward a pleasant thought in their memory. And so they had: be it recollected Athens was a port, and a mart of trade, perhaps the first in Greece; and this was very much to the point, when a number of strangers were ever flocking to it, whose combat was to be with intellectual, not physical difficulties, and who claimed to have their bodily wants supplied, that they might be at leisure to set about furnishing their minds. Now, barren as was the soil of Attica, and bare the face of the country, yet it had only too many resources for an elegant, nay luxurious abode there. So abundant were the imports of the place, that it was a common saying, that the productions, which were found singly elsewhere, were brought all together in Athens. Corn and wine, the staple of subsistence in such a climate, came from the isles of the Ægean; fine wool and carpeting from Asia Minor; slaves, as now, from the Euxine, and timber too; and iron and brass from the coasts of the Mediterranean. The Athenian did not condescend to manufactures himself, but encouraged them in others; and a population of foreigners caught at the lucrative occupation both for home consumption and for exportation. Their cloth, and other textures for dress and furniture, and their hardware—for instance, armor—were in great request. Labor was cheap; stone and marble in plenty; and the taste and skill, which at first were devoted to public buildings, as temples and porticos, were in course of time applied to the mansions of public men. If nature did much for Athens, it is undeniable that art did much more.

Here some one will interrupt me with the remark: "by the by, where are we, and whither are we going?— what has all this to do with a University? at least what has it to do with education? It is instructive doubtless; but still how much has it to do with your subject?" Now I beg to assure the reader that I am most conscientiously employed upon my subject; and I should have thought every one would have seen this: however, since the objection is made, I may be allowed to pause awhile, and show distinctly the drift of what I have been saying, before I go farther. *What* has this to do with my subject! why, the question of the *site* is the very first that comes into consideration, when a *Studium Generale* * is contemplated; for that site should be a liberal and noble one;

* *Studium Generale*, a course of study embracing all subjects.

who will deny it? All authorities agree in this, and very little reflection will be sufficient to make it clear. I recollect a conversation I once had on this very subject with a very eminent man. I was a youth of eighteen, and was leaving my University for the Long Vacation, when I found myself in company in a public conveyance with a middle-aged person, whose face was strange to me. However, it was the great academical luminary of the day, whom afterward I knew very well. Luckily for me, I did not suspect it; and luckily too, it was a fancy of his, as his friends knew, to make himself on easy terms especially with stage-coach companions. So, what with my flippancy and his condescension, I managed to hear many things which were novel to me at the time; and one point which he was strong upon, and was evidently fond of urging, was the material pomp and circumstance which should environ a great seat of learning. He considered it was worth the consideration of the government, whether Oxford should not stand in a domain of its own. An ample range, say four miles in diameter, should be turned into wood and meadow, and the University should be approached on all sides by a magnificent park, with fine trees in groups and groves and avenues, and with glimpses and views of the fair city, as the traveller drew near it. There is nothing surely absurd in the idea, though it would cost a round sum to realize it. What has a better claim to the purest and fairest possessions of nature, than the seat of wisdom? So thought my coach companion; and he did but express the tradition of ages and the instinct of mankind.

For instance, take the great University of Paris. That famous school engrossed as its territory the whole south bank of the Seine, and occupied one half, and that the pleasanter half, of the city. King Louis had the island pretty well as his own,—it was scarcely more than a fortification; and the north of the river was given over to the nobles and citizens to do what they could with its marshes; but the eligible south, rising from the stream, which swept around its base, to the fair summit of St. Genevieve, with its broad meadows, its vineyards and its gardens, and with the sacred elevation of Montmartre confronting it, all this was the inheritance of the University. There was that pleasant Pratum, stretching along the river's bank, in which the students for centuries took their recreation, which Alcuin seems to mention in his farewell verses to Paris, and which has given a name to the great Abbey of St. Germain-des-Prés. For long years it was devoted to the purposes of innocent and healthy enjoyment; but evil times came on the University; disorder arose within its precincts, and the fair meadow became the scene of party brawls; heresy stalked through Europe, and Germany and England no longer sending their contingent of students, a heavy debt was the consequence to the academical body. To let their land was the only resource left to them: buildings rose upon it, and spread along the green sod, and the country at length became town. Great was the grief and indignation of the doctors and masters, when this catastrophe occurred. "A wretched sight," said the Proctor of the German nation, "a wretched sight, to witness the sale of that ancient manor, whither the Muses were wont to wander for retirement and pleasure. Whither shall the youthful student now betake himself, what relief will he find for his eyes, wearied with intense reading, now that the pleasant stream is taken from him?" Two centuries and more have passed since this complaint was uttered; and time has shown that the outward calamity, which it recorded, was but the emblem of the great moral revolution, which was to follow; till the institution itself has followed its green meadows, into the region of things which once were and now are not.

ROBERT LOUIS STEVENSON

THE SEA FOGS

While Robert Louis Stevenson was living in an art colony near Paris he met Mrs. Fanny Osbourne, and fell in love with her. She returned to her home in California; Stevenson heard that she was ill and in trouble, and rushed to her assistance. His means were so scanty that he crossed as a steerage passenger, and travelled from New York to San Francisco in an emigrant train. The experience nearly cost him his life, but Mrs. Osbourne nursed him through his illness, and in the spring of 1880 they were married. The honeymoon was spent in an abandoned mining camp in the California mountains: the record of these weeks is given in the book *The Silverado Squatters*. They had chosen a lofty spot to be out of the fogs; in the following essay Stevenson describes how he was almost overtaken by them. One can imagine the frail, eager half-invalid, his own danger forgotten in the transport of gazing upon the wonderful spectacle, and perhaps even as he looked, fitting words to the scene.

ROBERT LOUIS STEVENSON

THE SEA FOGS

(From *The Silverado Squatters*)

A change in the color of the light usually called me in the morning. By a certain hour, the long, vertical chinks in our western gable, where the boards had shrunk and separated, flashed suddenly into my eyes as stripes of dazzling blue, at once so dark and splendid that I used to marvel how the qualities could be combined. At an earlier hour, the heavens in that quarter were still quietly colored, but the shoulder of the mountain which shuts in the canyon already glowed with sunlight in a wonderful compound of gold and rose and green; and this too would kindle, although more mildly and with rainbow tints, the fissures of our crazy gable. If I were sleeping heavily, it was the bold blue that struck me awake; if more lightly, then I would come to myself in that earlier and fairer light.

One Sunday morning, about five, the first brightness called me. I rose and turned to the east, not for my devotions, but for air. The night had been very still. The little private gale that blew every evening in our canyon, for ten minutes or perhaps a quarter of an hour, had swiftly blown itself out; in the hours that followed not a sigh of wind had shaken the tree tops; and our barrack, for all its breaches, was less fresh that morning than of wont. But I had no sooner reached the window than I forgot all else in the sight that met my eyes, and I made but two bounds into my clothes, and down the crazy plank to the platform.

125

The sun was still concealed below the opposite hill-tops, though it was shining already, not twenty feet above my head, on our own mountain slope. But the scene, beyond a few near features, was entirely changed. Napa Valley was gone; gone were all the lower slopes and woody foot-hills of the range; and in their place, not a thousand feet below me, rolled a great level ocean. It was as though I had gone to bed the night before, safe in a nook of inland mountains, and had awakened in a bay upon the coast. I had seen these inundations from below; at Calistoga I had risen and gone abroad in the early morning, coughing and sneezing, under fathoms on fathoms of gray sea vapor, like a cloudy sky—a dull sight for the artist, and a painful experience for the invalid. But to sit aloft one's self in the pure air and under the unclouded dome of heaven, and thus look down on the submergence of the valley, was strangely different and even delightful to the eyes. Far away were hill-tops like little islands. Nearer, a smoky surf beat about the foot of precipices and poured into all the coves of these rough mountains. The color of that fog ocean was a thing never to be forgotten. For an instant, among the Hebrides and just about sundown, I have seen something like it on the sea itself. But the white was not so opaline; nor was there, what surprisingly increased the effect, that breathless, crystal stillness over all. Even in its gentlest moods the salt sea travails, moaning among the weeds or lisping on the sand; but that vast fog ocean lay in a trance of silence, nor did the sweet air of the morning tremble with a sound.

As I continued to sit upon the dump, I began to observe that this sea was not so level as at first sight it appeared to be. Away in the extreme south, a little hill of fog arose against the sky above the general surface, and as it had already caught the sun, it shone on the horizon like the topsails of some giant ship. There were huge waves, stationary, as it seemed, like waves in a frozen sea; and yet, as I looked again, I was not sure but they were moving after all, with a slow and august advance. And while I was yet doubting, a promontory of the hills some four or five miles away, conspicuous by a bouquet of tall pines, was in a single instant overtaken and swallowed up. It reappeared in a little, with its pines, but this time as an islet, and only to be swallowed up once more and then for good. This set me looking nearer, and I saw that in every cove along the line of mountains the fog was being piled in higher and higher, as though by some wind that was inaudible to me. I could trace its progress, one pine-tree first growing hazy and then disappearing after another; although sometimes there was none of this forerunning haze, but the whole opaque white ocean gave a start and swallowed a piece of mountain at a gulp. It was to flee these poisonous fogs that I had left the seaboard, and climbed so high among the mountains. And now, behold, here came the fog to besiege me in my chosen altitudes, and yet came so beautifully that my first thought was of welcome.

The sun had now gotten much higher, and through all the gaps of the hills it cast long bars of gold across that white ocean. An eagle, or some other very great bird of the mountain, came wheeling over the nearer pine tops, and hung, poised and something sideways, as if to look abroad on that unwonted desolation, spying, perhaps with terror, for the aeries of her comrades. Then, with a long cry, she disappeared again toward Lake County and the clearer air. At length it seemed to me as if the flood were beginning to subside. The old landmarks, by whose disappearance I had measured its advance, here a crag, there a brave pine-tree, now began, in the inverse order, to make their reappearance into daylight. I judged all danger of the fog was over. This was not Noah's flood; it was but a morning spring, and would now drift out seaward whence it came. So, mightily relieved, and a good deal exhilarated by the sight, I went into the house to light the fire.

I suppose it was nearly seven when I once more mounted the platform to look abroad. The fog ocean had swelled up enormously since last I saw it; and a few hundred feet below me, in the deep gap where the Toll House stands and the road runs through into Lake County, it had already topped the slope, and was pouring over and down the other side like driving smoke. The wind had climbed along with it; and though I was still in calm air, I could see the trees tossing below me, and their long, strident sighing mounted to me where I stood.

Half an hour later, the fog had surmounted all the ridge on the opposite side of the gap, though a shoulder of the mountain still warded it out of our canyon. Napa Valley and its bounding hills were now utterly blotted out. The fog, sunny-white in the sunshine, was pouring over into Lake County in a huge, ragged cataract, tossing tree tops appearing and disappearing in the spray. The air struck with a little chill, and set me coughing. It smelled strong of the fog, like the smell of a washing-house, but with a shrewd tang of the sea salt.

Had it not been for two things—the sheltering spur which answered as a dike, and the great valley on the other side which rapidly engulfed whatever mounted— our own little platform in the canyon must have been already buried a hundred feet in salt and poisonous air. As it was, the interest of the scene entirely occupied our minds. We were set just out of the wind, and but just above the fog; we could listen to the voice of the one as to music on the stage; we could plunge our eyes down into the other, as into some flowing stream from over the parapet of a bridge; thus we looked on upon a strange, impetuous, silent, shifting exhibition of the powers of nature, and saw the familiar landscape changing from moment to moment like figures in a dream.

The imagination loves to trifle with what is not. Had this been indeed the deluge, I should have felt more strongly, but the emotion would have been similar in kind. I played with the idea, as the child flees in delighted terror from the creations of his fancy. The look of the thing helped me. And when at last I began to flee up the mountain, it was indeed partly to escape from the raw air that kept me coughing, but it was also part in play.

As I ascended the mountainside, I came once more to overlook the upper surface of the fog; but it wore a different appearance from what I had beheld at daybreak. For, first, the sun now fell on it from high overhead, and its surface shone and undulated like a great nor'land moor country, sheeted with untrodden morning snow. And next the new level must have been a thousand or fifteen hundred feet higher than the old, so that only five or six points of all the broken country below me, still stood out. Napa Valley was now one with Sonoma on the west. On the hither side, only a thin scattered fringe of bluffs was unsubmerged; and through all the gaps the fog was pouring over, like an ocean, into the blue clear sunny country on the east. There it was soon lost; for it fell instantly into the bottom of the valleys, following the watershed; and the hilltops in that quarter were still clear cut upon the eastern sky.

Through the Toll House gap and over the near ridges on the other side, the deluge was immense. A spray of thin vapor was thrown high above it, rising and falling, and blown into fantastic shapes. The speed of its course was like a mountain torrent. Here and there a few tree tops were discovered and then whelmed again; and for one second, the bough of a dead pine beckoned out of the spray like the arm of a drowning man. But still the imagination was dissatisfied, still the ear waited for something more. Had this indeed been water (as it seemed so, to the eye), with what a plunge of reverberating thunder would it have rolled upon its course, disembowelling mountains and deracinating pines! And yet water it was, and sea-water at that—true Pacific billows, only somewhat rarefied, rolling in mid air among the hilltops.

I climbed still higher, among the red rattling gravel and dwarf underwood of Mount Saint Helena, until I could look right down upon Silverado, and admire the favored nook in which it lay. The sunny plain of fog was several hundred feet higher; behind the protecting spur a gigantic accumulation of cottony vapor threatened, with every second, to blow over and submerge our homestead; but the vortex setting past the Toll House was too strong; and there lay our little platform, in the arms of the deluge, but still enjoying its unbroken sunshine. About eleven, however, thin spray came flying over the friendly buttress, and I began to think the fog had hunted out its Jonah after all. But it was the last effort. The wind veered while we were at dinner, and began to blow squally from the mountain summit; and by half-past one, all that world of sea fogs was utterly routed and flying here and there into the south in little rags of cloud. And instead of a lone sea beach, we found ourselves once more inhabiting a high mountainside, with the clear green country far below us, and the light smoke of Calistoga blowing in the air.

This was the great Russian campaign for that season. Now and then, in the early morning, a little white lakelet of fog would be seen far down in Napa Valley; but the heights were not again assailed, nor was the surrounding world again shut off from Silverado.

HENRY D. THOREAU

BRUTE NEIGHBORS

Henry David Thoreau (1817–1862) was one of the most original figures in American literature. He was born at Concord, Mass., a neighbor of Emerson's, and educated at Harvard. His father was a manufacturer of lead-pencils. Henry worked with him, and so improved the process that he turned out a better pencil than had ever been produced before. His neighbors congratulated him, telling him that his fortune was made. But he said that he would never make another pencil. "Why should I? I would not do again what I have done once." The remark was characteristic of Thoreau; he was not concerned with making money, but with living according to his own ideas. He had some skill as a carpenter and as a surveyor; he would work at these occupations occasionally—the rest of his days he spent in reading, writing, and observing nature. Wishing to spend some time in solitude, he built a hut on the shore of Walden pond, near Concord, and lived there alone for two years. The record of this experience is given in *Walden, or Life in the Woods*, from which the chapter here printed is taken. In addition to *Walden*, he wrote *A Week on the Concord and Merrimac Rivers; Excursions;* and *Cape Cod*. His *Journals* have been published in several volumes. All of his books are made up of descriptions of what he saw, observed with the trained eye of a naturalist, and set down with the pen of a poet. To these descriptions he adds his own reflections upon men and things.

HENRY D. THOREAU

BRUTE NEIGHBORS

(From *Walden, or Life in the Woods*)

Why do precisely these objects which we behold make a world? Why has man just these species of animals for his neighbors; as if nothing but a mouse could have filled this crevice? I suspect that Pilpay* and Co. have put animals to their best use, for they are all beasts of burden, in a sense, made to carry some portion of our thoughts.

The mice which haunted my house were not the common ones, which are said to have been introduced into the country, but a wild native kind not found in the village. I sent one to a distinguished naturalist, and it interested him much. When I was building, one of these had its nest underneath the house, and before I had laid the second floor, and swept out the shavings, would come out regularly at lunch time and pick up the crumbs at my feet. It probably had never seen a man before; and it soon became quite familiar, and would run over my shoes and up my clothes. It could readily ascend the sides of the room by short impulses, like a squirrel, which it resembled in its motions. At length, as I leaned with my elbow on the bench one day, it ran up my clothes, and along my sleeve, and round and round the paper which held my dinner, while I kept the latter close, and dodged and played at bo-peep with it; and when at last I held still a piece of cheese between my thumb and finger,

* Pilpay. The *Fables of Pilpay* is an ancient work, originally written in Sanskrit. It is a series of stories about animals, each story teaching a lesson.

it came and nibbled it, sitting in my hand, and afterward cleaned its face and paws, like a fly, and walked away.

A phœbe soon built in my shed, and a robin for protection in a pine which grew against the house. In June the partridge (*Tetrao umbellus*), which is so shy a bird, led her brood past my windows, from the woods in the rear to the front of my house, clucking and calling to them like a hen, and in all her behavior proving herself the hen of the woods. The young suddenly disperse on your approach, at a signal from the mother, as if a whirlwind had swept them away, and they so exactly resemble the dried leaves and twigs that many a traveller has placed his foot in the midst of a brood, and heard the whirr of the old bird as she flew off, and her anxious calls and mewing, or seen her trail her wings to attract his attention, without suspecting their neighborhood. The parent will sometimes roll and spin round before you in such a dishabille, that you cannot, for a few moments, detect what kind of a creature it is. The young squat still and flat, often running their heads under a leaf, and mind only their mother's directions given from a distance, nor will your approach make them run again and betray themselves. You may even tread on them, or have your eyes on them for a minute, without discovering them. I have held them in my open hand at such a time, and still their only care, obedient to their mother and their instinct, was to squat there without fear or trembling. So perfect is this instinct, that once, when I had laid them on the leaves again, and one accidentally fell on its side, it was found with the rest in exactly the same position ten minutes afterward. They are not callow like the young of most birds, but more perfectly developed and precocious even than chickens.

The remarkably adult yet innocent expression of their open and serene eyes is very memorable. All intelligence

seems reflected in them. They suggest not merely the
purity of infancy, but a wisdom clarified by experience.
Such an eye was not born when the bird was, but is coeval
with the sky it reflects. The woods do not yield another
such a gem. The traveller does not often look into such
a limpid well. The ignorant or reckless sportsman often
shoots the parent at such a time, and leaves these inno-
cents to fall a prey to some prowling beast or bird, or
gradually mingle with the decaying leaves which they
so much resemble. It is said that when hatched by a
hen they will directly disperse on some alarm, and so are
lost, for they never hear the mother's call which gathers
them again. These were my hens and chickens.

It is remarkable how many creatures live wild and free
though secret in the woods, and still sustain themselves
in the neighborhood of towns, suspected by hunters only.
How retired the otto manages to live here! He grows
to be four feet long, as big as a small boy, perhaps without any human being getting a glimpse of him. I formerly saw the raccoon in the woods behind where my
house is built, and probably still heard their whinnering
at night. Commonly I rested an hour or two in the
shade at noon, after planting, and ate my lunch, and read
a little by a spring which was the source of a swamp and
of a brook, oozing from under Brister's Hill, half a mile
from my field. The approach to this was through a succession of descending grassy hollows, full of young pitch-
pines, into a larger wood about the swamp. There, in a
very secluded and shaded spot, under a spreading white
pine, there was yet a clean firm sward to sit on. I had
dug out the spring, and made a well of clear gray water,
where I could dip up a pailful without roiling it, and
thither I went for this purpose almost every day in mid-
summer, when the pond was warmest. Thither too the
woodcock led her brood, to probe the mud for worms,

flying but a foot above them down the bank, while they ran in a troop beneath; but at last, spying me, she would leave her young and circle round and round me, nearer and nearer till within four or five feet, pretending broken wings and legs, to attract my attention, and get off her young, who would already have taken up their march, with faint wiry peep, single file through the swamp, as she directed. Or I heard the peep of the young when I could not see the parent bird. There too the turtle-doves sat over the spring, or fluttered from bough to bough of the soft white pines over my head; or the red squirrel, coursing down the nearest bough, was particularly familiar and inquisitive. You only need sit still long enough in some attractive spot in the woods that all its inhabitants may exhibit themselves to you by turns.

I was witness to events of a less peaceful character. One day when I went out to my wood-pile, or rather my pile of stumps, I observed two large ants, the one red, the other much larger, nearly half an inch long, and black, fiercely contending with one another. Having once got hold they never let go, but struggled and wrestled and rolled on the chips incessantly. Looking farther, I was surprised to find that the chips were covered with such combatants, that it was not a *duellum*, but a *bellum*, a war between two races of ants, the red always pitted against the black, and frequently two red ones to one black. The legions of these Myrmidons covered all the hills and vales in my wood-yard, and the ground was already strewn with the dead and dying, both red and black. It was the only battle which I have ever witnessed, the only battle-field I ever trod while the battle was raging; internecine war; the red republicans on the one hand, and the black imperialists on the other. On every side they were engaged in deadly combat, yet without any noise that I could hear, and human soldiers never

fought so resolutely. I watched a couple that were fast
locked in each other's embraces, in a little sunny valley
amid the chips, now at noonday prepared to fight till
the sun went down, or life went out. The smaller red
champion had fastened himself like a vise to his adversary's front, and through all the tumblings on that field
never for an instant ceased to gnaw at one of his feelers
near the root, having already caused the other to go by
the board; while the stronger black one dashed him from
side to side, and as I saw on looking nearer, had already
divested him of several of his members. They fought
with more pertinacity than bulldogs. Neither mani-
fested the least disposition to retreat. It was evident
that their battle-cry was Conquer or die.

In the meanwhile there came along a single red ant on
the hillside of this valley, evidently full of excitement,
who either had despatched his foe, or had not yet taken
part in the battle; probably the latter, for he had lost none
of his limbs; whose mother had charged him to return
with his shield or upon it. Or perchance he was some
Achilles, who had nourished his wrath apart, and had
now come to avenge or rescue his Patroclus. He saw
this unequal combat from afar—for the blacks were nearly
twice the size of the red—he drew near with rapid pace
till he stood on his guard within half an inch of the combatants; then, watching his opportunity, he sprang upon
the black warrior, and commenced his operations near
the root of his right fore-leg, leaving the foe to select
among his own members; and so there were three united
for life, as if a new kind of attraction had been invented
which put all other locks and cements to shame. I should
not have wondered by this time to find that they had
their respective musical bands stationed on some eminent chip, and playing their national airs the while, to
excite the slow and cheer the dying combatants. I was

myself excited somewhat even as if they had been men.
The more you think of it, the less the difference. And
certainly there is not a fight recorded in Concord history,
at least, if in the history of America, that will bear a moment's comparison with this, whether for the numbers
engaged in it, or for the patriotism and heroism displayed.
For numbers and for carnage it was an Austerlitz or Dres-
den. Concord Fight! Two killed on the patriots' side,
and Luther Blanchard wounded! Why here every ant
was a Buttrick,—"Fire! for God's sake, fire!"—and thousands shared the fate of Davis and Hosmer. There was
not one hireling there. I have no doubt that it was a
principle they fought for, as much as our ancestors, and
not to avoid a three-penny tax on their tea; and the re-
sults of this battle will be as important and memorable
to those whom it concerns as those of the battle of Bun-
ker Hill, at least.

I took up the chip on which the three I have particularly described were struggling, carried it into my house,
and placed it under a tumbler on my window-sill, in order
to see the issue. Holding a microscope to the first-
mentioned red ant, I saw that, though he was assiduously
gnawing at the near fore-leg of his enemy, having severed
his remaining feeler, his own breast was all torn away,
exposing what vitals he had there to the jaws of the black
warrior, whose breastplate was apparently too thick for
him to pierce; and the dark carbuncles of the sufferer's
eyes shone with ferocity such as war only could excite.
They struggled half an hour longer under the tumbler,
and when I looked again the black soldier had severed
the heads of his foes from their bodies, and the still living
heads were hanging on either side of him like ghastly
trophies at his saddle-bow, still apparently as firmly
fastened as ever, and he was endeavoring with feeble
struggles, being without feelers and with only the remnant

of a leg, and I know not how many other wounds, to divest himself of them; which at length, after half an hour more, he accomplished. I raised the glass, and he went off over the window-sill in that crippled state. Whether he finally survived that combat, and spent the remainder of his days in some Hôtel des Invalides, I do not know; but I thought that his industry would not be worth much thereafter. I never learned which party was victorious, nor the cause of the war: but I felt for the rest of that day as if I had had my feelings excited and harrowed by witnessing the struggle, the ferocity and carnage, of a human battle before my door.

Kirby and Spence tell us that the battles of ants have long been celebrated and the date of them recorded, though they say that Huber is the only modern author who appears to have witnessed them. "Æneas Sylvius," say they, "after giving a very circumstantial account of one contested with great obstinacy by a great and small species on the trunk of a pear-tree," adds that, "'This action was fought in the pontificate of Eugenius the Fourth, in the presence of Nicholas Pistoriensis, an eminent lawyer, who related the whole history of the battle with the greatest fidelity.' A similar engagement between great and small ants is recorded by Olaus Magnus, in which the small ones, being victorious, are said to have buried the bodies of their own soldiers, but left those of their giant enemies a prey to the birds. This event happened previous to the expulsion of the tyrant Christiern the Second from Sweden." The battle which I witnessed took place in the Presidency of Polk, five years before the passage of Webster's Fugitive-Slave Bill.

Many a village Bose,* fit only to course a mud-turtle in a victualling cellar, sported his heavy quarters in the woods, without the knowledge of his master, and ineffec-

* Bose, a nickname for a dog.

tually smelled at old fox burrows and woodchucks' holes; led perchance by some slight cur which nimbly threaded the wood, and might still inspire a natural terror in its denizens;—now far behind his guide, barking like a canine bull toward some small squirrel which had treed itself for scrutiny, then, cantering off, bending the bushes with his weight, imagining that he is on the track of some stray member of the jerbilla* family.

Once I was surprised to see a cat walking along the stony shore of the pond, for they rarely wander so far from home. The surprise was mutual. Nevertheless the most domestic cat, which has lain on a rug all her days, appears quite at home in the woods, and, by her sly and stealthy behavior, proves herself more native there than the regular inhabitants. Once, when berrying, I met a cat with young kittens in the woods, quite wild, and they all, like their mother, had their backs up and were fiercely spitting at me. A few years before I lived in the woods there was what was called a "winged cat" in one of the farmhouses in Lincoln nearest the pond, Mr. Gilian Baker's. When I called to see her in June, 1842, she was gone a-hunting in the woods, as was her wont (I am not sure whether it was a male or female, and so use the more common pronoun), but her mistress told me that she came into the neighborhood a little more than a year before, in April, and was finally taken into their house; that she was of a dark brownish-gray color, with a white spot on her throat, and white feet, and had a large bushy tail like a fox; that in the winter the fur grew thick and flatted out along her sides, forming stripes ten or twelve inches long by two and a half wide, and under her chin like a muff, the upper side loose, the under matted like felt, and in the spring these appendages dropped off. They

* Jerbilla, or jerboa, a mouse or rat with a pouch; the kangaroo rat is an example.

gave me a pair of her "wings," which I keep still. There is no appearance of a membrane about them. Some thought it was part flying-squirrel or some other wild animal, which is not impossible, for, according to naturalists, prolific hybrids have been produced by the union of the marten and domestic cat. This would have been the right kind of cat for me to keep, if I had kept any; for why should not a poet's cat be winged as well as his horse?

In the fall the loon (*Colymbus glacialis*) came, as usual, to moult and bathe in the pond, making the woods ring with his wild laughter before I had risen. At rumor of his arrival all the Mill-dam sportsmen are on the alert, in gigs and on foot, two by two and three by three, with patent rifles and conical balls and spy-glasses. They come rustling through the woods like autumn leaves, at least ten men to one loon. Some station themselves on this side of the pond, some on that, for the poor bird cannot be omnipresent; if he dive here he must come up there. But now the kind October wind rises, rustling the leaves and rippling the surface of the water, so that no loon can be heard or seen, though his foes sweep the pond with spy-glasses, and make the woods resound with their discharges. The waves generously rise and dash angrily, taking sides with all water-fowl, and our sportsmen must beat a retreat to town, and shop, and unfinished jobs. But they were too often successful. When I went to get a pail of water early in the morning I frequently saw this stately bird sailing out of my cove within a few rods. If I endeavored to overtake him in a boat, in order to see how he would manœuvre, he would dive and be completely lost, so that I did not discover him again, sometimes, till the latter part of the day. But I was more than a match for him on the surface. He commonly went off in a rain.

As I was paddling along the north shore one very calm October afternoon, for such days especially they settle on to the lakes, like the milkweed down, having looked in vain over the pond for a loon, suddenly one, sailing out from the shore toward the middle a few rods in front of me, set up his wild laugh and betrayed himself. I pursued with a paddle and he dived, but when he came up I was nearer than before. He dived again, but I miscalculated the direction he would take, and we were fifty rods apart when he came to the surface this time, for I had helped to widen the interval; and again he laughed loud and long, and with more reason than before. He manœuvred so cunningly that I could not get within half a dozen rods of him. Each time, when he came to the surface, turning his head this way and that, he coolly surveyed the water and the land, and apparently chose his course so that he might come up where there was the widest expanse of water and at the greatest distance from the boat. It was surprising how quickly he made up his mind and put his resolve into execution. He led me at once to the widest part of the pond, and could not be driven from it. While he was thinking one thing in his brain, I was endeavoring to divine his thought in mine. It was a pretty game, played on the smooth surface of the pond, a man against a loon. Suddenly your adversary's checker disappears beneath the board, and the problem is to place yours nearest to where his will appear again. Sometimes he would come up unexpectedly on the opposite side of me, having apparently passed directly under the boat. So long-winded was he and so unweariable, that when he had swum farthest he would immediately plunge again, nevertheless; and then no wit could divine where in the deep pond, beneath the smooth surface, he might be speeding his way like a fish, for he had time and ability to visit the bottom of the pond in its deepest part. It is said that loons have been caught in the New York lakes eighty feet beneath the surface, with hooks set for trout,—though Walden is deeper than that. How surprised must the fishes be to see this ungainly visitor from another sphere speeding his way amid their schools! Yet he appeared to know his course as surely under water as on the surface, and swam much faster there. Once or twice I saw a ripple where he approached the surface, just put his head out to reconnoitre, and instantly dived again. I found that it was as well for me to rest on my oars and wait his reappearing as to endeavor to calculate where he would rise; for again and again, when I was straining my eyes over the surface one way, I would suddenly be startled by his unearthly laugh behind me. But why, after displaying so much cunning, did he invariably betray himself the moment he came up by that loud laugh? Did not his white breast enough betray him? He was indeed a silly loon, I thought. I could commonly hear the plash of the water when he came up, and so also detected him. But after an hour he seemed as fresh as ever, dived as willingly, and swam yet farther than at first. It was surprising to see how serenely he sailed off with unruffled breast when he came to the surface, doing all the work with his webbed feet beneath.

His usual note was this demoniac laughter, yet somewhat like that of a water-fowl; but occasionally, when he had balked me most successfully and come up a long way off, he muttered a long-drawn unearthly howl, probably more like that of a wolf than any bird; as when a beast puts his muzzle to the ground and deliberately howls. This was his looning,—perhaps the wildest sound that is ever heard here, making the woods ring far and wide. I concluded that he laughed in derision of my efforts, confident of his own resources. Though the sky was by this time overcast, the pond was so smooth that I could see where he broke the surface when I did not hear him. His white breast, the stillness of the air, and the smoothness of the water were all against him. At length, having come up fifty rods off, he uttered one of those prolonged howls, as if calling on the god of loons to aid him, and immediately there came a wind from the east and rippled the surface, and filled the whole air with misty rain, and I was impressed as if it were the prayer of the loon answered, and his god was angry with me, and so I left him disappearing far away on the tumultuous surface.

For hours, in fall days, I watched the ducks cunningly tack and veer and hold the middle of the pond, far from the sportsman—tricks which they will have less need to practise in Louisiana bayous. When compelled to rise they would sometimes circle round and round and over the pond at a considerable height, from which they could easily see to other ponds and the river, like black motes in the sky; and, when I thought they had gone off thither long since, they would settle down by a slanting flight of a quarter of a mile on to a distant part which was left free; but what beside safety they got by sailing in the middle of Walden I do not know, unless they love its water for the same reason that I do.

THE CHARACTER SKETCH

OLIVER GOLDSMITH

THE MAN IN BLACK

Oliver Goldsmith (1728–1774) was one of the important men of letters of the eighteenth century, an associate of Addison, Steele, and Johnson. He was born in Ireland, the son of a poor country clergyman. He graduated at Dublin University at the foot of his class. This low rank was not due to any lack of ability, but rather to Goldsmith's happy-go-lucky nature. He wandered about Europe, supposed to be studying medicine, but when he set up practice in London no patients came. Then he became a hack writer, producing books on whatever subjects the publishers desired. For a newspaper he wrote a series of essays called *The Citizen of the World*. He is best remembered as the author of the *Vicar of Wakefield*, a famous novel of rural life in England, and as the author of a comedy which yet holds the stage, *She Stoops to Conquer*, and of two poems, "The Traveller" and "The Deserted Village," which are in almost every collection of English poetry.

The essay here printed is interesting not only in itself but from the fact that the character here sketched is a foreshadowing of the famous Doctor Primrose in the *Vicar of Wakefield*. The impulsive generosity of the Man in Black, his inconsistency, his heart quickly moved by distress,—all these were characteristics of Goldsmith himself.

OLIVER GOLDSMITH

THE MAN IN BLACK

(From *The Citizen of the World*)

Though fond of many acquaintances, I desire an intimacy only with a few. The Man in Black, whom I
have often mentioned, is one whose friendship I could
wish to acquire, because he possesses my esteem. His
manners, it is true, are tinctured with some strange inconsistencies; and he may be justly termed an humorist
in a nation of humorists. Though he is generous even
to profusion, he affects to be thought a prodigy of parsimony and prudence; though his conversation be replete
with the most sordid and selfish maxims, his heart is
dilated with the most unbounded love. I have known
him profess himself a man-hater, while his cheek was
glowing with compassion; and, while his looks were sof-
tened into pity, I have heard him use the language of the
most unbounded ill-nature. Some affect humanity and
tenderness, others boast of having such dispositions from
Nature; but he is the only man I ever knew who seemed
ashamed of his natural benevolence. He takes as much
pains to hide his feelings, as any hypocrite would to conceal his indifference; but on every unguarded moment
the mask drops off, and reveals him to the most super-
ficial observer.

In one of our late excursions into the country, happening to discourse upon the provision that was made for
the poor in England, he seemed amazed how any of his
countrymen could be so foolishly weak as to relieve occasional objects of charity, when the laws had made such

ample provision for their support. "In every parish-house," says he, "the poor are supplied with food, clothes, fire, and a bed to lie on; they want no more, I desire no more myself; yet still they seem discontented.' I'm surprised at the inactivity of our magistrates in not taking up such vagrants, who are only a weight upon the industrious; I'm surprised that the people are found to relieve them, when they must be at the same time sensible that it, in some measure, encourages idleness, extravagance, and imposture. Were I to advise any man for whom I had the least regard, I would caution him by all means not to be imposed upon by their false pretenses: let me assure you, sir, they are impostors, every one of them; and rather merit a prison than relief."

He was proceeding in this strain earnestly, to dissuade me from an imprudence of which I am seldom guilty, when an old man, who still had about him the remnants of tattered finery, implored our compassion. He assured us that he was no common beggar, but forced into the shameful profession to support a dying wife and five hungry children. Being prepossessed against such false-hoods, his story had not the least influence upon me; but it was quite otherwise with the Man in Black; I could see it visibly operate upon his countenance, and effectually interrupt his harangue. I could easily perceive that his heart burned to relieve the five starving children, but he seemed ashamed to discover his weakness to me. While he thus hesitated between compassion and pride, I pretended to look another way, and he seized this opportunity of giving the poor petitioner a piece of silver, bidding him at the same time, in order that I should hear, go work for his bread, and not tease passengers with such impertinent falsehoods for the future.

As he had fancied himself quite unperceived, he continued, as we proceeded, to rail against beggars with as much animosity as before; he threw in some episodes on his own amazing prudence and economy, with his profound skill in discovering impostors; he explained the manner in which he would deal with beggars, were he a magistrate, hinted at enlarging some of the prisons for their reception, and told two stories of ladies that were robbed by beggarmen. He was beginning a third to the same purpose, when a sailor with a wooden leg once more crossed our walks, desiring our pity, and blessing our limbs. I was for going on without taking any notice, but my friend, looking wistfully upon the poor petitioner, bade me stop, and he would show me with how much ease he could at any time detect an impostor.

He now, therefore, assumed a look of importance, and in an angry tone began to examine the sailor, demanding in what engagement he was thus disabled and rendered unfit for service. The sailor replied in a tone as angrily as he, that he had been an officer on board a private ship of war, and that he had lost his leg abroad in defense of those who did nothing at home. At his reply, all my friend's importance vanished in a moment; he had not a single question more to ask; he now only studied what method he should take to relieve him unobserved. He had, however, no easy part to act, as he was obliged to preserve the appearance of ill-nature before me, and yet relieve himself by relieving the sailor. Casting, therefore, a furious look upon some bundles of chips which the fellow carried in a string at his back, my friend demanded how he sold his matches; but not waiting for a reply, desired in a surly tone to have a shilling's worth. The sailor seemed at first surprised at his demand, but soon recollecting himself, and presenting his whole bundle—"Here, master," says he, "take all my cargo, and a blessing into the bargain."

It is impossible to describe with what an air of triumph

my friend marched off with his new purchase; he assured me that he was firmly of opinion that those fellows must have stolen their goods who could thus afford to sell them for half value. He informed me of several different uses to which those chips might be applied; he expatiated largely upon the savings that would result from lighting candles with a match instead of thrusting them into the fire. He averred that he would as soon have parted with a tooth as his money to those vagabonds, unless for some valuable consideration. I cannot tell how long this panegyric upon frugality and matches might have continued, had not his attention been called off by another object more distressful than either of the former. A woman in rags, with one child in her arms, and another on her back, was attempting to sing ballads, but with such a mournful voice that it was difficult to determine whether she was singing or crying. A wretch who in the deepest distress still aimed at good-humor, was an object my friend was by no means capable of withstanding; his vivacity and his discourse were instantly interrupted; upon this occasion his very dissimulation had forsaken him. Even in my presence, he immediately applied his hands to his pockets, in order to relieve her; but guess his confusion, when he found he had already given away all the money he carried about him to former objects. The misery painted in the woman's visage was not half so strongly expressed as the agony in his. He continued to search for some time, but to no purpose, till, at length, recollecting himself, with a face of ineffable good-nature, as he had no money, he put into her hands his shilling's worth of matches.

ROBERT LOUIS STEVENSON

THE HUNTER'S FAMILY

The following essay, like the one on The Sea Fogs, is taken from *The Silverado Squatters*, the book which records the life of the Stevensons in the mountains of California. His frail health made it necessary to have some assistance in their cabin, and to this fact we owe the minute portrayal of the two men, Irvine and Rufe. As Irvine loafed about, talking boastfully of his own achievements, he little imagined that every attitude, every word, was being recorded upon a mind more sensitive than any photographic film, so that not only his image, but his very self would be set forth on paper, and he would be known to men in distant lands and other times. Such is the miracle wrought by literature.

ROBERT LOUIS STEVENSON

THE HUNTER'S FAMILY

(From *The Silverado Squatters*)

There is quite a large race or class of people in America, for whom we scarcely seem to have a parallel in England. Of pure white blood, they are unknown or unrecognizable in towns; inhabit the fringe of settlements and the deep, quiet places of the country; rebellious to all labor, and pettily thievish, like the English gypsies; rustically ignorant, but with a touch of wood lore and the dexterity of the savage. Whence they came is a moot point. At the time of the war,* they poured north in crowds to escape the conscription; lived during summer on fruits, wild animals, and petty theft; and at the approach of winter, when these supplies failed, built great fires in the forest, and there died stoically by starvation. They are widely scattered, however, and easily recognized. Loutish, but not ill-looking, they will sit all day, swinging their legs on a field fence, the mind seemingly as devoid of all reflection as a Suffolk peasant's, careless of politics, for the most part incapable of reading, but with a rebellious vanity and a strong sense of independence. Hunting is their most congenial business, or, if the occasion offers, a little amateur detection. In tracking a criminal, following a particular horse along a beaten highway, and drawing inductions from a hair or a footprint, one of those somnolent, grinning Hodges will suddenly display activity of body and finesse of mind. By their names ye may know them, the women figuring as Loveina, Larsenia, Serena, Leanna, Orreana; the men answering to Alvin,

* The reference is to the Civil War.

153

Alva, or Orion, pronounced Orrion, with the accent on the first. Whether they are indeed a race, or whether this is the form of degeneracy common to all backwoodsmen, they are at least known by a generic byword, as Poor Whites or Lowdowners.

I will not say that the Hanson family was Poor White, because the name savors of offense; but I may go as far as this—they were, in many points, not unsimilar to the people usually so called. Rufe himself combined two of the qualifications, for he was both a hunter and an amateur detective. It was he who pursued Russel and Dollar, the robbers of the Lakeport stage, and captured them the very morning after the exploit, while they were still sleeping in a hay-field. Russel, a drunken Scotch carpenter, was even an acquaintance of his own, and he expressed much grave commiseration for his fate. In all that he said and did, Rufe was grave. I never saw him hurried. When he spoke, he took out his pipe with ceremonial deliberation, looked east and west, and then, in quiet tones and few words, stated his business or told his story. His gait was to match; it would never have surprised you if, at any step, he had turned round and walked away again, so warily and slowly, and with so much seeming hesitation did he go about. He lay long in bed in the morning—rarely, indeed, rose before noon; he loved all games, from poker to clerical croquet, and in the Toll House croquet ground I have seen him toiling at the latter with the devotion of a curate. He took an interest in education, was an active member of the local school board, and when I was there, he had recently lost the schoolhouse key. His wagon was broken, but it never seemed to occur to him to mend it. Like all truly idle people, he had an artistic eye. He chose the print stuff for his wife's dresses, and counselled her in the making of a patchwork quilt, always, as she thought, wrongly, but to the more educated eye, always with bizarre and admirable taste—the taste of an Indian. With all this, he was a perfect, unoffending gentleman in word and act. Take his clay pipe from him, and he was fit for any society but that of fools. Quiet as he was, there burned a deep, permanent excitement in his dark blue eyes; and when this grave man smiled, it was like sunshine in a shady place.

Mrs. Hanson (*née*, if you please, Lovelands) was more commonplace than her lord. She was a comely woman, too, plump, fair-colored, with wonderful white teeth; and in her print dresses (chosen by Rufe) and with a large sunbonnet shading her valued complexion, made, I assure you, a very agreeable figure. But she was on the surface, what there was of her, outspoken and loud-spoken. Her noisy laughter had none of the charm of one of Hanson's rare, slow-spreading smiles; there was no reticence, no mystery, no manner about the woman; she was a first-class dairymaid, but her husband was an unknown quantity between the savage and the nobleman. She was often in and out with us, merry, and healthy, and fair; he came far seldomer—only, indeed, when there was business, or now and again, to pay a visit of ceremony, brushed up for the occasion, with his wife on his arm, and a clean clay pipe in his teeth. These visits, in our forest state, had quite the air of an event, and turned our red canyon into a salon.

Such was the pair who ruled in the old Silverado Hotel, among the windy trees, on the mountain shoulder overlooking the whole length of Napa Valley, as the man aloft looks down on the ship's deck. There they kept house, with sundry horses and fowls, and a family of sons, Daniel Webster, and I think George Washington, among the number. Nor did they want visitors. An old gentleman, of singular stolidity, and called Breedlove—I think

he had crossed the plains in the same caravan with Rufe
—housed with them for a while during our stay; and they
had besides a permanent lodger, in the form of Mrs.
Hanson's brother, Irvine Lovelands. I spell Irvine by
guess; for I could get no information on the subject, just
as I could never find out, in spite of many inquiries,
whether or not Rufe was a contraction for Rufus. They
were all cheerfully at sea about their names in that generation. And this is surely the more notable where the
names are all so strange, and even the family names
appear to have been coined. At one time, at least, the
ancestors of all these Alvins and Alvas, Loveinas, Lovelands, and Breedloves, must have taken serious counsel
and found a certain poetry in these denominations; that
must have been, then, their form of literature. But
still times change; and their next descendants, the George
Washingtons and Daniel Websters, will at least be clear
upon the point. And anyway, and however his name
should be spelled, this Irvine Lovelands was the most un-
mitigated Caliban I ever knew.

Our very first morning at Silverado, when we were full
of business, patching up doors and windows, making beds
and seats, and getting our rough lodging into shape,
Irvine and his sister made their appearance together, she
for neighborliness and general curiosity; he, because he
was working for me, to my sorrow, cutting firewood at I
forget how much a day. The way that he set about
cutting wood was characteristic. We were at that moment patching up and unpacking in the kitchen. Down
he sat on one side, and down sat his sister on the other.
Both were chewing pine-tree gum, and he, to my annoyance, accompanied that simple pleasure with profuse ex-
pectoration. She rattled away, talking up hill and down
dale, laughing, tossing her head, showing her brilliant
teeth. He looked on in silence, now spitting heavily on

the floor, now putting his head back and uttering a loud, discordant, joyless laugh. He had a tangle of shock hair, the color of wool; his mouth was a grin; although as strong as a horse, he looked neither heavy nor yet adroit, only leggy, coltish, and in the road. But it was plain he was in high spirits, thoroughly enjoying his visit; and he laughed frankly whenever we failed to accomplish what we were about. This was scarcely helpful: it was even, to amateur carpenters, embarrassing; but it lasted until we knocked off work and began to get dinner. Then Mrs. Hanson remembered she should have been gone an hour ago; and the pair retired, and the lady's laughter died away among the nutmegs down the path. That was Irvine's first day's work in my employment—the devil take him!

The next morning he returned and, as he was this time alone, he bestowed his conversation upon us with great liberality. He prided himself on his intelligence; asked us if we knew the schoolma'am. *He* didn't think much of her, anyway. He had tried her, he had. He had put a question to her. If a tree a hundred feet high were to fall a foot a day, how long would it take to fall right down? She had not been able to solve the problem. "She don't know nothing," he opined. He told us how a friend of his kept a school with a revolver, and chuckled mightily over that; his friend could teach school, he could. All the time he kept chewing gum and spitting. He would stand a while looking down; and then he would toss back his shock of hair, and laugh hoarsely, and spit, and bring forward a new subject. A man, he told us, who bore a grudge against him, had poisoned his dog. "That was a low thing for a man to do now, wasn't it? It wasn't like a man, that, nohow. But I got even with him: I pisoned *his* dog." His clumsy utterance, his rude embarrassed manner, set a fresh value on the stupidity of his remarks. I do not think I ever appreciated the meaning of two words until I knew Irvine—the verb, loaf, and the noun, oaf; between them, they complete his portrait. He could lounge, and wriggle, and rub himself against the wall, and grin, and be more in everybody's way than any other two people that I ever set my eyes on. Nothing that he did became him; and yet you were conscious that he was one of your own race, that his mind was cumbrously at work, revolving the problem of existence like the quid of gum, and in his own cloudy manner enjoying life, and passing judgment on his fellows. Above all things, he was delighted with himself. You would not have thought it, from his uneasy manners and troubled, struggling utterance; but he loved himself to the marrow, and was happy and proud like a peacock on a rail.

His self-esteem was, indeed, the one joint in his harness. He could be got to work, and even kept at work, by flattery. As long as my wife stood over him, crying out how strong he was, so long exactly he would stick to the matter in hand; and the moment she turned her back, or ceased to praise him, he would stop. His physical strength was wonderful; and to have a woman stand by and admire his achievements, warmed his heart like sunshine. Yet he was as cowardly as he was powerful, and felt no shame in owning to the weakness. Something was once wanted from the crazy platform over the shaft, and he at once refused to venture there—"did not like," as he said, "foolen' round them kind o' places," and let my wife go instead of him, looking on with a grin. Vanity, where it rules, is usually more heroic: but Irvine steadily approved himself, and expected others to approve him; rather looked down upon my wife, and decidedly expected her to look up to him, on the strength of his superior prudence.

Yet the strangest part of the whole matter was perhaps this, that Irvine was as beautiful as a statue. His features were, in themselves, perfect; it was only his cloudy, uncouth, and coarse expression that disfigured them. So much strength residing in so spare a frame was proof sufficient of the accuracy of his shape. He must have been built somewhat after the pattern of Jack Sheppard; but the famous housebreaker, we may be certain, was no lout. It was by the extraordinary powers of his mind no less than by the vigor of his body, that he broke his strong prison with such imperfect implements, turning the very obstacles to service. Irvine, in the same case, would have sat down and spat, and grumbled curses. He had the soul of a fat sheep, but, regarded as an artist's model, the exterior of a Greek god. It was a cruel thought to persons less favored in their birth, that this creature, endowed—to use the language of theatres—with extraordinary "means," should so manage to misemploy them that he looked ugly and almost deformed. It was only by an effort of abstraction, and after many days, that you discovered what he was.

By playing on the oaf's conceit, and standing closely over him, we got a path made round the corner of the dump to our door, so that we could come and go with decent ease; and he even enjoyed the work, for in that there were boulders to be plucked up bodily, bushes to be uprooted, and other occasions for athletic display: but cutting wood was a different matter. Anybody could cut wood; and, besides, my wife was tired of supervising him, and had other things to attend to. And, in short, days went by, and Irvine came daily, and talked and lounged and spat; but the firewood remained intact as sleepers on the platform or growing trees upon the mountainside. Irvine as a wood-cutter, we could tolerate; but Irvine as a friend of the family, at so much a day, was too bald an imposition, and at length, on the afternoon of the fourth or fifth day of our connection, I explained to him, as clearly as I could, the light in which I had grown to regard his presence. I pointed out to him that I could not continue to give him a salary for spitting on the floor; and this expression, which came after a good many others, at last penetrated his obdurate wits. He rose at once, and said if that was the way he was going to be spoke to, he reckoned he would quit. And, no one interposing, he departed.

So far, so good. But we had no firewood. The next afternoon, I strolled down to Rufe's and consulted him on the subject. It was a very droll interview, in the large, bare north room of the Silverado Hotel, Mrs. Hanson's patchwork on a frame, and Rufe, and his wife, and I, and the oaf himself, all more or less embarrassed. Rufe announced there was nobody in the neighborhood but Irvine who could do a day's work for anybody. Irvine, thereupon, refused to have any more to do with my service; he "wouldn't work no more for a man as had spoke to him 's I had done." I found myself on the point of the last humiliation—driven to beseech the creature whom I had just dismissed with insult: but I took the high hand in despair, said there must be no talk of Irvine coming back unless matters were to be differently managed; that I would rather chop firewood for myself than be fooled; and, in short, the Hansons being eager for the lad's hire, I so imposed upon them with merely affected resolution, that they ended by begging me to re-employ him again on a solemn promise that he should be more industrious. The promise, I am bound to say, was kept. We soon had a fine pile of firewood at our door; and if Caliban gave me the cold shoulder and spared me his conversation, I thought none the worse of him for that, nor did I find my days much longer for the deprivation.

The leading spirit of the family was, I am inclined to fancy, Mrs. Hanson. Her social brilliancy somewhat dazzled the others, and she had more of the small change of sense. It was she who faced Kelmar, for instance; and perhaps, if she had been alone, Kelmar would have had no rule within her doors. Rufe, to be sure, had a fine, sober, open-air attitude of mind, seeing the world without exaggeration—perhaps, we may even say, without enough; for he lacked, along with the others, that commercial idealism which puts so high a value on time and money. Sanity itself is a kind of convention. Perhaps Rufe was wrong; but, looking on life plainly, he was unable to perceive that croquet or poker were in any way less important than, for instance, mending his wagon. Even his own profession, hunting, was dear to him mainly as a sort of play; even that he would have neglected, had it not appealed to his imagination. His hunting-suit, for instance, had cost I should be afraid to say how many bucks—the currency in which he paid his way: it was all befringed, after the Indian fashion, and it was dear to his heart. The pictorial side of his daily business was never forgotten. He was even anxious to stand for his picture in those buckskin hunting clothes; and I remember how he once warmed almost into enthusiasm, his dark blue eyes growing perceptibly larger, as he planned the composition in which he should appear, "with the horns of some real big bucks, and dogs, and a camp on a crick" (creek, stream).

There was no trace in Irvine of this woodland poetry. He did not care for hunting, nor yet for buckskin suits. He had never observed scenery. The world, as it appeared to him, was almost obliterated by his own great grinning figure in the foreground: Caliban Malvolio. And it seems to me as if, in the persons of these brothers-in-law, we had the two sides of rusticity fairly well rep-

resented: the hunter living really in nature; the clod-
hopper living merely out of society: the one bent up in
every corporal agent to capacity in one pursuit, doing at
least one thing keenly and thoughtfully, and thoroughly
alive to all that touches it; the other in the inert and
bestial state, walking in a faint dream, and taking so
dim an impression of the myriad sides of life that he is
truly conscious of nothing but himself. It is only in
the fastnesses of nature, forests, mountains, and the
back of man's beyond, that a creature endowed with five
senses can grow up into the perfection of this crass and
earthy vanity. In towns or the busier country sides,
he is roughly reminded of other men's existence; and if
he learns no more, he learns at least to fear contempt.
But Irvine had come scathless through life, conscious
only of himself, of his great strength and intelligence;
and in the silence of the universe, to which he did not
listen, dwelling with delight on the sound of his own
thoughts.

JULIAN STREET

THE SPIRIT OF THEODORE ROOSEVELT

Julian Street (1879———) an American journalist of to-day, was born in Chicago, and received his education in the public schools of that city and at Ridley College. He entered journalism, becoming a reporter on the New York *Mail* (then the *Mail and Express*), in 1899, and was for a time dramatic editor. He has been a frequent contributor to magazines, and has published a number of books, of which the best known are a humorous story, *The Need of Change*, some sketches of travel called *Abroad at Home* and *American Adventures*, also a recent book on *Mysterious Japan*.

His work as a writer of magazine articles brought him into relations with Theodore Roosevelt, and, like many other journalists, he became a warm admirer of the Colonel. In 1915 he published a sketch of Roosevelt with the title *The Most Interesting American*. In this he pointed out the fact that Theodore Roosevelt combined within himself men of many types: he was a physical-culture expert, a historian, a biographer, an essayist, a natural scientist, a big-game hunter, an explorer and discoverer, a critic, a former cowboy, the holder of a dozen LL.D.'s, an editor, a former member of the State legislature, a practical reformer, a veteran colonel of cavalry, a former Assistant Secretary of the Navy, a former governor, a Nobel prize winner, a former Vice-president and former President—the youngest who ever held that position. On the death of Theodore Roosevelt, Mr. Street wrote the fine tribute here printed; it appeared first in *Collier's*, and is now published as part of the volume, *The Most Interesting American*.

JULIAN STREET

THE SPIRIT OF THEODORE ROOSEVELT *

(From *The Most Interesting American*)

We, whom Theodore Roosevelt used proudly and affectionately to call his "fellow Americans," have always listened with great relish to characteristic stories of him. His qualities, physical and spiritual, were so utterly his own, his individuality so intense and overmastering, that he seemed somehow to be projected among us, to be intimately known even to those of us who had never touched his hand or even seen him. It was this curious feeling as of personal acquaintance with him that caused us so to delight in the flavor of a typical Roosevelt story.

"Isn't that just like him!" we would say, as we might of a story hitting off familiar traits of our own father.

But whereas, on the night of January 5, 1919, a Roosevelt story might by many of us have been regarded merely as something entertaining, the next morning witnessed a great change. The wand of Death touching him as he slept, releasing him to further high adventure, to great, final explorations, transformed not him alone, but the environment and the legend of him. To every possession of his, from the wife and children he loved to such small objects as that inkstand, made from an elephant's foot, which stood upon his desk at Sagamore Hill, or the very pens and pencils there, thenceforth attached a quite new sacredness. And so, for us, his fellow Americans,

* Copyright, *Collier's*, February 1, 1919; also Century Co., 1920. Reprinted by permission of the author and of the publishers.

new sacredness attaches now to the rich legacy of wisdom he has left us, to every thought of his that we can learn, to every belief he held, and consequently to every authentic story that can in any way contribute to our knowledge of him.

In the vast amount of matter that has been printed of the Colonel I do not recall having seen any reference to a certain theory that he had (and, having it, of course he put it into practice) in connection with the bringing up of children. It was a characteristic theory, and now it, like all else, takes on a new significance.

As long since as when he was Governor of New York it was his practice to go every Saturday afternoon for a tramp in the country with Mrs. Roosevelt and the children. And it was understood between them that in the course of all such tramps he would lead them to some physical obstacle which must be overcome. Sometimes it would be merely the obstacle of long distance over a difficult terrain, calling for sustained effort in face of great fatigue; sometimes it would be a wide brook to be crossed at a difficult place; sometimes a deep ravine full of tangled underbrush to be traversed; and on one memorable occasion, less than a fortnight before the Colonel was nominated for Vice-President—that nomination designed by political enemies within his own party to terminate his political career—there was a steep cliff of crumbling slate to be ascended and descended.

The idea that Colonel and Mrs. Roosevelt attempted to fasten in the children's minds was that life frequently presents obstacles comparable with those encountered on these walks, and that it is the part of good manhood and good womanhood squarely to meet and surmount them, going through or over, but never around. Thus early the Roosevelt children, whose later record has been so worthy of their father and their mother, had begun to learn pri-

mary lessons in resourcefulness, perseverance, courage,
stoicism, and disregard for danger—for sometimes, as in
the Adventure of the Slate Cliff, there was danger.

The bank, soft and almost perpendicular, at first appeared insurmountable, but after an hour and a half all
but one of that day's walking party had managed to
climb up and down again. The exception was Alice
Roosevelt, then a girl of sixteen, who, having reached
the top, found herself unable to descend.

On this day Elon Hooker, an old friend of the Roose-
velts, was with them. Walking along the base of the
cliff, this young man found a stout tree growing up beside it. Climbing the tree, he leaned out and, seizing
with one hand a hummock of slate at the crest of the
little precipice, offered his arm as a bridge over which
Alice could step into the tree, whence it would be no
very difficult matter to climb down to earth.

The hummock was less secure than it appeared. As
she stepped upon his arm the slate to which he was holding broke away and his arm fell beneath her. She had,
however, managed to grasp with one hand a branch, and
to this she clung until he succeeded in catching her and
drawing her safely into the tree.

On reaching the ground they discovered that the fallen
mass of slate had struck the Colonel fairly on the head,
laying open his scalp from the forehead to a corresponding
point at the back of the skull. Though the wound bled
freely, they were immediately reassured by his smile.
Finding a brook, they washed the gash as best they
could; later a surgeon took a dozen stitches in the
Colonel's scalp; and when, some ten days after, he attended the Republican National Convention he was none
the worse for the accident. Few persons, indeed, knew
of it at all, for it was characteristic of him to avoid any
mention of his injuries or ailments, and if forced to men-

tion them he would invariably pass them off as being of no consequence.

Thus, for example, when it became known a twelve-month or so ago that he had been for many years stone blind in the left eye, as the result of a blow received in boxing, the news came as a surprise to numerous friends who knew him well. Yet he had been blind in that eye when he shot lions in Africa. He was not in the least sensitive about his blindness, nor do I think he tried particularly to conceal it. It was simply that he had an aversion, resembling that of the aboriginal American, for the discussion of bodily ills; a contempt for the inconvenience or suffering resulting from them. And still, when others suffered physically or spiritually, he was the most solicitous, the gentlest, the tenderest of men.

It was like him, too, that throughout the afternoon on which he went to the hospital for a grave operation, a year before his death, he continued to dictate letters to his secretary, and that while dictating he had a hemorrhage and fainted three times, only to revive and resume his dictation. And until the doctor forbade it, he even contemplated going that night to a dinner at which he had agreed to speak.

On his hunting trips, when travelling, and more lately when confined to his bed in the hospital, he utilized every moment of his time for work, study, and reflection; he would concentrate upon a book or a conversation while enduring pain to a degree that would have rendered it impossible for most men to think consecutively, let alone converse upon important topics with a succession of visitors.

He was afraid neither to live nor to die. And in the purely orthodox sense he had no cause to fear death, for his soul was as clean as that of a little child. The ultimate biographer of Roosevelt will not have so much as one single item to gloss over or conceal. And I am not sure that that is not the finest thing that may be said of any man.

Until a year ago I never heard him speak of death, but since then I have known him to speak of it more than once. I am wondering now if it merely happened so, or whether, as he lay there in the hospital a year ago, and again in the last months of the year just past, he may not have had a premonition that the end was perhaps nearer than those about him supposed. Certainly he knew a year ago, at the time of the operation for an abscess in the middle ear, which rapidly extended to the inner ear, that he was at death's door. Dr. Arthur B. Duel, his surgeon, told him so, and the Colonel promptly expressed a brave resignation.

I saw him in the hospital a few days after the operation. He was reading a book. After we had spoken a few words he said:

"Lying here, I have often thought how glad I would be to go now if by doing so I could only bring the boys back safe to Mrs. Roosevelt."

One day at luncheon last April, when we all thought him as vigorous as ever, he spoke again of his boys, and there was in what he said as much apprehension for them as he ever allowed himself to show—or perhaps I should say as much apprehension of the blow that the loss of any one of them would be to the remainder of the family.

"Mrs. Roosevelt has been perfectly wonderful," he said, "about their going to fight. We both realize that we have a very full, interesting, satisfying life to look back upon. Whatever may come now, we have had more than thirty years of happiness together, with all our children spared to us."

And again, less than a month ago, as I write, when I called at the hospital, Mrs. Roosevelt—who always stayed there with him—spoke in the same terms, though in the interim the blow had fallen. It was of Quentin, the eagle, that she spoke.

"We have been until now a singularly united family," she said. "This is the first loss from our immediate circle. Life has been kind to us. We have much to be thankful for."

The story I have told of his walks with the children and the obstacles over which he led them was, until the morning of January 6, only a typical Roosevelt story. Since then it has become an allegory. For his feeling for us all was in a very fine sense paternal. He was the father; we the children. "Face the obstacles," he always urged us. "Go through or over; never around."

Or to quote his own words, uttered in that great speech twenty years ago:

"*I preach to you, then, my countrymen, that our country calls not for the life of ease, but for the life of strenuous endeavor. The twentieth century looms before us big with the fate of many nations. If we stand idly by, if we seek merely swollen, slothful ease and ignoble peace, if we shrink from the hard contests where men must win at hazard of their lives and at the risk of all they hold dear, then the bolder and stronger people will pass by us and will win for themselves the domination of the world.*

"*Let us therefore boldly face the life of strife, resolute to do our duty well and manfully; resolute to uphold righteousness by deed and by word; resolute to be both honest and brave, to serve high ideals, yet to use practical methods. Above all, let us not shrink from strife, moral or physical, within or without the Nation, provided we are certain the strife is justified; for it is only through strife, through hard and dangerous endeavor, that we shall ultimately win the goal of true national greatness.*"

That, I believe, was the essence of Roosevelt's personal and national philosophy. Simply he thought and spoke and lived and died. And that, without exception, has been true of all our greatest men. Like Lincoln and Franklin, he was one of us. When he spoke we understood him. He never juggled thoughts or words to baffle us, confuse us, stupefy us with the brilliancy of his performance. Nor did he ever speak or write to mask a purpose, or a lack of purpose. He never thought, as he tried to set down his ideas: "Now I am writing something that will live. Now I am making history." He was impatient of such notions, just as he was impatient of the applause that interrupted him when he was making public speeches. Time and again I have seen him hold up his hand to stop applause. He wanted to go on. It was the thing to be accomplished that obsessed him.

Thinking of the ingratitude that we have sometimes shown him, and of the follies we have committed, on occasion, in face of his exhortation to be brave and prompt and ready, I once asked him how he had kept from becoming cynical about mankind.

"I am not cynical," he said, "because I have observed that just when our people seem to be becoming altogether hopeless they have a way of suddenly turning around and doing something perfectly magnificent."

What a prophecy that was!—for he said it in the hour of our national shame, when we were crying gratefully: "He kept us out of war!"

Well may we be thankful that Roosevelt lived to see his profound faith in us justified; to see us at last take up arms in answer to his repeated call; to see us quit "the life of ease" for that of "strenuous endeavor"; to see us spurn "ignoble peace" and enter the "hard contest where men must win at hazard of their lives." That the poison of pacifism did not ruin the nation is due to the fact that we had Roosevelt as an antitoxin.

Thus his greatest single service to his country was performed, not while he was President, but in the last years of his life; not while he held the reins of government, but as a private citizen whose unofficial power lay solely in the nation's admiration for him; its faith in him and in his vision; its heed to what he said.

There will, of course, be a memorial to Roosevelt. It will be a noble thing of marble. But such a thing, however glorious, will mean much more to us than it could mean to him. We shall erect it to give ourselves the mournful satisfaction of doing our dead hero honor. But let us not forget, meanwhile, that the one memorial he would have wished cannot be built of tangible materials, but must be made of thoughts and deeds.

He has taken his last tramp with his own children, and with us. He has guided them, and us, up to the last obstacle we were destined to meet and overcome under his leadership. And the one thing he would ask of us is this: That we go on without him. That we learn the simple lessons he has taught by precept and example. That we be foresighted, prompt, practical, honest, resolute, courageous.

So, in ourselves, we will make his spirit live.

THE CRITICAL ESSAY

JOHN RUSKIN

WHAT AND HOW TO READ

A sketch of Ruskin's life is given on page 104. On one side he was an artist, on the other side a reformer. Even when he writes about books, he does not aim to lead us upon pleasant literary rambles, but tells us plainly that we are reading the wrong books, and reading them the wrong way. This is not very complimentary, it is true; if you are looking for compliments, if you are afraid of criticism, do not read Ruskin. But if you are willing to face honest criticism, if you have the mental vigor to follow a great thinker, then Ruskin has a message for you. In another essay, Ruskin says: "No book is worth anything which is not worth much; nor is it serviceable until it has been read and re-read and loved and loved again, and every passage marked, so that you can refer to the passages you want in it, as a soldier can seize the weapon he needs in an armory, or a housewife bring the spice she needs from her store." As you read the following essay, decide what passages you would mark in this way.

JOHN RUSKIN

WHAT AND HOW TO READ

(From *Sesame and Lilies*, Lecture I)

I want to speak to you about books; and about the way we read them, and could, or should read them. A grave subject, you will say; and a wide one! Yes; so wide that I shall make no effort to touch the compass of it. I will try only to bring before you a few simple thoughts about reading, which press themselves upon me every day more deeply, as I watch the course of the public mind with respect to our daily enlarging means of education, and the answeringly wider-spreading, on the levels, of the irrigation of literature. It happens that I have practically some connection with schools for different classes of youth; and I receive many letters from parents respecting the education of their children. In the mass of these letters, I am always struck by the precedence which the idea of a "position in life" takes above all other thoughts in the parents'—more especially in the mothers'—minds. . . .

Indeed, among the ideas most prevalent and effective in the mind of this busiest of countries, I suppose the first—at least that which is confessed with the greatest frankness, and put forward as the fittest stimulus to youthful exertion—is this of "advancement in life." My main purpose this evening is to determine, with you, what this idea practically includes, and what it should include.

You will grant that moderately honest men desire place and office, at least in some measure, for the sake of their beneficent power; and would wish to associate rather with sensible and well-informed persons than with fools and ignorant persons, whether they are seen in the company of the sensible ones or not. And finally, without being troubled by repetition of any common truisms about the preciousness of friends, and the influence of companions, you will admit, doubtless, that according to the sincerity of our desire that our friends may be true, and our companions wise,—and in proportion to the earnestness and discretion with which we choose both, will be the general chances of our happiness and usefulness.

But, granting that we had both the will and the sense to choose our friends well, how few of us have the power! or, at least, how limited, for most, is the sphere of choice! Nearly all our associations are determined by chance or necessity; and restricted within a narrow circle. We cannot know whom we would; and those whom we know, we cannot have at our side when we most need them. All the higher circles of human intelligence are, to those beneath, only momentarily and partially open. We may, by good fortune, obtain a glimpse of a great poet, and hear the sound of his voice; or put a question to a man of science, and be answered good-humoredly. We may intrude ten minutes' talk on a cabinet minister, answered probably with words worse than silence, being deceptive; or snatch, once or twice in our lives, the privilege of throwing a bouquet in the path of a Princess, or arresting the kind glance of a Queen. And yet these momentary chances we covet; and spend our years, and passions, and powers in pursuit of little more than these; while, meantime, there is a society continually open to us, of people who will talk to us as long as we like, whatever our rank or occupation;—talk to us in the best words they can choose, and with thanks if we listen to them. And this society, because it is so numerous and so gentle,

—and can be kept waiting round us all day long, not to grant audience, but to gain it;—kings and statesmen lingering patiently in those plainly furnished and narrow anterooms, our bookcase shelves,—we make no account of that company,—perhaps never listen to a word they would say, all day long!

You may tell me, perhaps, or think within yourselves, that the apathy with which we regard this company of the noble, who are praying us to listen to them, and the passion with which we pursue the company, probably of the ignoble, who despise us, or who have nothing to teach us, are grounded in this,—that we can see the faces of the living men, and it is themselves, and not their sayings, with which we desire to become familiar. But it is not so. Suppose you never were to see their faces;—suppose you could be put behind a screen in the statesman's cabinet, or the prince's chamber, would you not be glad to listen to their words, though you were forbidden to advance beyond the screen? And when the screen is only a little less, folded in two, instead of four, and you can be hidden behind the cover of the two boards that bind a book, and listen, all day long, not to the casual talk, but to the studied, determined, chosen addresses of the wisest of men;—this station of audience, and honorable privy council, you despise!

But perhaps you will say that it is because the living people talk of things that are passing, and are of immediate interest to you, that you desire to hear them. Nay; that cannot be so, for the living people will themselves tell you about passing matters, much better in their writings than in their careless talk. But I admit that this motive does influence you, so far as you prefer those rapid and ephemeral writings to slow and enduring writings—books, properly so called. For all books are divisible into two classes, the books of the hour, and the books of all time. Mark this distinction—it is not one of quality only. It is not merely the bad book that does not last, and the good one that does. It is a distinction of species. There are good books for the hour, and good ones for all time; bad books for the hour, and bad ones for all time. I must define the two kinds before I go farther.

The good book of the hour, then,—I do not speak of the bad ones—is simply the useful or pleasant talk of some person whom you cannot otherwise converse with, printed for you. Very useful often, telling you what you need to know; very pleasant often, as a sensible friend's present talk would be. These bright accounts of travels; good-humored and witty discussions of questions; lively or pathetic story-telling in the form of novel; firm fact-telling, by the real agents concerned in the events of passing history;—all these books of the hour, multiplying among us as education becomes more general, are a peculiar characteristic and possession of the present age; we ought to be entirely thankful for them, and entirely ashamed of ourselves if we make no good use of them. But we make the worst possible use, if we allow them to usurp the place of true books: for, strictly speaking, they are not books at all, but merely letters or newspapers in good print. Our friend's letter may be delightful, or necessary, to-day; whether worth keeping or not, is to be considered. The newspaper may be entirely proper at breakfast time, but assuredly it is not reading for all day. So, though bound up in a volume, the long letter which gives you so pleasant an account of the inns, and roads, and weather last year at such a place, or which tells you that amusing story, or gives you the real circumstances of such and such events, however valuable for occasional reference, may not be, in the real sense of the word, a "book" at all, nor, in the real sense, to be "read."

A book is essentially not a talked thing, but a written

thing; and written, not with the view of mere communication, but of permanence. The book of talk is printed
only because its author cannot speak to thousands of
people at once; if he could, he would—the volume is
mere *multiplication* of his voice. You cannot talk to your
friend in India; if you could, you would; you write instead: that is mere *conveyance* of voice. But a book is
written, not to multiply the voice merely, not to carry it
merely, but to preserve it. The author has something
to say which he perceives to be true and useful, or help-
fully beautiful. So far as he knows, no one has yet said
it; so far as he knows, no one else can say it. He is bound
to say it, clearly and melodiously if he may; clearly, at
all events. In the sum of his life he finds this to be the
thing, or group of things, manifest to him;—this the
piece of true knowledge, or sight, which his share of sunshine and earth has permitted him to seize. He would
fain set it down forever; engrave it on rock, if he could;
saying, "This is the best of me; for the rest, I ate, and
drank, and slept, loved, and hated, like another; my life
was as the vapor, and is not; but this I saw and knew;
this, if anything of mine, is worth your memory." That
is his "writing"; it is, in his small human way, and with
whatever degree of true inspiration is in him, his inscription, or scripture. That is a "Book."

Perhaps you think no books were ever so written?

But, again, I ask you, do you at all believe in honesty,
or at all in kindness? or do you think there is never any
honesty or benevolence in wise people? None of us, I
hope, are so unhappy as to think that. Well, whatever
bit of a wise man's work is honestly and benevolently
done, that bit is his book, or his piece of art. It is mixed
always with evil fragments—ill-done, redundant, affected
work. But if you read rightly, you will easily discover
the true bits, and those *are* the book.

Now books of this kind have been written in all ages

by their greatest men;—by great leaders, great statesmen, and great thinkers. These are all at your choice;
and life is short. You have heard as much before;—yet
have you measured and mapped out this short life and
its possibilities? Do you know, if you read this, that
you cannot read that—that what you lose to-day you
cannot gain to-morrow? Will you go and gossip with
your housemaid, or your stable-boy, when you may talk
with queens and kings; or flatter yourselves that it is
with any worthy consciousness of your own claims to
respect that you jostle with the common crowd for *entrée*
here, and audience there, when all the while this eternal
court is open to you, with its society wide as the world,
multitudinous as its days, the chosen, and the mighty, of
every place and time? Into that you may enter always;
in that you may take fellowship and rank according to
your wish; from that, once entered into it, you can never
be outcast but by your own fault; by your aristocracy of
companionship there, your own inherent aristocracy will
be assuredly tested, and the motives with which you strive
to take high place in the society of the living, measured,
as to all the truth and sincerity that are in them, by the
place you desire to take in this company of the dead.

"The place you desire," and the place you *fit yourself
for*, I must also say; because, observe, this court of the
past differs from all living aristocracy in this:—it is open
to labor and to merit, but to nothing else. No wealth
will bribe, no name overawe, no artifice deceive, the
guardian of those Elysian gates. In the deep sense, no
vile or vulgar person ever enters there. At the portières
of that silent Faubourg St. Germain, there is but brief
question, "Do you deserve to enter? Pass. Do you
ask to be the companion of nobles? Make yourself noble,
and you shall be. Do you long for the conversation of the
wise? Learn to understand it, and you shall hear it.

But on other terms?—No. If you will not rise to us, we cannot stoop to you. The living lord may assume courtesy, the living philosopher explain his thought to you with considerable pain; but here we neither feign nor interpret; you must rise to the level of our thoughts if you would be gladdened by them, and share our feelings, if you would recognize our presence."

This, then, is what you have to do, and I admit that it is much. You must, in a word, love these people, if you are to be among them. No ambition is of any use. They scorn your ambition. You must love them, and show your love in these two following ways.

I. First, by a true desire to be taught by them, and to enter into their thoughts. To enter into theirs, observe; not to find your own expressed by them. If the person who wrote the book is not wiser than you, you need not read it; if he be, he will think differently from you in many respects.

Very ready we are to say of a book, "How good this is —that's exactly what I think!" But the right feeling is, "How strange that is! I never thought of that before, and yet I see it is true; or if I do not now, I hope I shall, some day." But whether thus submissively or not, at least be sure that you go to the author to get at *his* meaning, not to find yours. Judge it afterward, if you think yourself qualified to do so; but ascertain it first. And be sure also, if the author is worth anything, that you will not get at his meaning all at once;—nay, that at his whole meaning you will not for a long time arrive in any wise. Not that he does not say what he means, and in strong words too; but he cannot say it all; and what is more strange, will not, but in a hidden way and in parables, in order that he may be sure you want it. I cannot quite see the reason of this, nor analyze that cruel reticence in the breasts of wise men which makes them always hide their deeper thought. They do not give it to you by way of help, but of reward, and will make themselves sure that you deserve it before they allow you to reach it. But it is the same with the physical type of wisdom, gold. There seems, to you and me, no reason why the electric forces of the earth should not carry whatever there is of gold within it at once to the mountain tops, so that kings and people might know that all the gold they could get was there; and without any trouble of digging, or anxiety, or chance, or waste of time, cut it away, and coin as much as they needed. But Nature does not manage it so. She puts it in little fissures in the earth, nobody knows where: you may dig long and find none; you must dig painfully to find any.

And it is just the same with men's best wisdom. When you come to a good book, you must ask yourself, "Am I inclined to work as an Australian miner would? Are my pickaxes and shovels in good order, and am I in good trim myself, my sleeves well up to the elbow, and my breath good, and my temper?" And, keeping the figure a little longer, even at cost of tiresomeness, for it is a thoroughly useful one, the metal you are in search of being the author's mind or meaning, his words are as the rock which you have to crush and smelt in order to get at it. And your pickaxes are your own care, wit, and learning; your smelting-furnace is your own thoughtful soul. Do not hope to get at any good author's meaning without those tools and that fire; often you will need sharpest, finest chiselling, and patientest fusing, before you can gather one grain of the metal.

And, therefore, first of all, I tell you, earnestly and authoritatively, (I *know* I am right in this,) you must get into the habit of looking intensely at words, and assuring yourself of their meaning, syllable by syllable—nay letter by letter. For though it is only by reason of the opposition of letters in the function of signs, to sounds in functions of signs, that the study of books is called "literature," and that a man versed in it is called, by the consent of nations, a man of letters instead of a man of books, or of words, you may yet connect with that accidental nomenclature this real principle;—that you might read all the books in the British Museum (if you could live long enough), and remain an utterly "illiterate," uneducated person; but that if you read ten pages of a good book, letter by letter,—that is to say, with real accuracy, —you are for evermore in some measure an educated person. The entire difference between education and non-education (as regards the merely intellectual part of it), consists in this accuracy. A well-educated gentleman may not know many languages,—may not be able to speak any but his own,—may have read very few books. But whatever language he knows, he knows precisely; whatever word he pronounces he pronounces rightly; above all, he is learned in the *peerage* of words; knows the words of true descent and ancient blood at a glance, from words of modern canaille; remembers all their ancestry —their intermarriages, distantest relationships, and the extent to which they were admitted, and offices they held, among the national noblesse of words at any time, and in any country. . . .

Now, in order to deal with words rightly, this is the habit you must form. Nearly every word in your language has been first a word of some other language—of Saxon, German, French, Latin, or Greek (not to speak of eastern and primitive dialects). And many words have been all these;—that is to say, have been Greek first, Latin next, French or German next, and English last; undergoing a certain change of sense and use on the lips of each nation; but retaining a deep vital meaning which all good scholars feel in employing them, even at this day.

If you do not know the Greek alphabet, learn it; young or old—girl or boy—whoever you may be, if you think of reading seriously (which, of course, implies that you have some leisure at command), learn your Greek alphabet; then get good dictionaries of all these languages, and whenever you are in doubt about a word, hunt it down patiently. Read Max Müller's lectures thoroughly, to begin with; and, after that, never let a word escape you that looks suspicious. It is severe work; but you will find it, even at first, interesting, and at last, endlessly amusing. And the general gain to your character, in power and precision, will be quite incalculable.

Mind, this does not imply knowing, or trying to know, Greek, or Latin, or French. It takes a whole life to learn any language perfectly. But you can easily ascertain the meanings through which the English word has passed; and those which in a good writer's work it must still bear.

And now, merely for example's sake, I will, with your permission, read a few lines of a true book with you, carefully; and see what will come out of them. I will take a book perfectly known to you all; no English words are more familiar to us, yet nothing perhaps has been less read with sincerity. I will take these few following lines of "Lycidas":

"Last came, and last did go,
   The pilot of the Galilean lake;
   Two massy keys he bore of metals twain,
   (The golden opes, the iron shuts amain),
   He shook his mitred locks, and stern bespake,
   How well could I have spared for thee, young swain,
   Enow of such as for their bellies' sake
   Creep, and intrude, and climb into the fold!
   Of other care they little reckoning make,
   Than how to scramble at the shearers' feast,
   And shove away the worthy bidden guest;

Blind mouths! that scarce themselves know how to hold
A sheep-hook, or have learn'd aught else, the least
That to the faithful herdsman's art belongs!
What recks it them? What need they? They are sped;
And when they list, their lean and flashy songs
Grate on their scrannel pipes of wretched straw;
The hungry sheep look up, and are not fed,
But, swoln with wind, and the rank mist they draw,
Rot inwardly, and foul contagion spread;
Besides what the grim wolf with privy paw
Daily devours apace, and nothing said."

Let us think over this passage, and examine its words.
First, is it not singular to find Milton assigning to St.
Peter, not only his full episcopal function, but the very
types of it which Protestants usually refuse most pas-
sionately? His "mitred" locks! Milton was no Bishop-
lover; how comes St. Peter to be "mitred"? "Two
massy keys he bore." Is this, then, the power of the
keys claimed by the Bishops of Rome, and is it acknowledged here by Milton only in a poetical license for the
sake of its picturesqueness, that he may get the gleam
of the golden keys to help his effect? Do not think it.
Great men do not play stage tricks with doctrines of life
and death: only little men do that. Milton means what
he says; and means it with his might too—is going to
put the whole strength of his spirit presently into the
saying of it. For though not a lover of false bishops, he
was a lover of true ones; and the Lake-pilot is here, in
his thoughts, the type and head of true episcopal power.
For Milton reads that text, "I will give unto thee the
keys of the kingdom of Heaven" quite honestly. Puritan
though he be, he would not blot it out of the book because there have been bad bishops; nay, in order to
understand him, we must understand that verse first; it
will not do to eye it askance, or whisper it under our
breath, as if it were a weapon of an adverse sect. It is

a solemn, universal assertion, deeply to be kept in mind by all sects. But perhaps we shall be better able to reason on it if we go on a little farther, and come back to it. For clearly, this marked insistence on the power of the true episcopate is to make us feel more weightily what is to be charged against the false claimants of episcopate; or generally, against false claimants of power and rank in the body of the clergy; they who, "for their bellies' sake, creep, and intrude, and climb into the fold."

Do not think Milton uses those three words to fill up his verse, as a loose writer would. He needs all the three; specially those three, and no more than those— "creep," and "intrude," and "climb"; no other words would or could serve the turn, and no more could be added. For they exhaustively comprehend the three classes, correspondent to the three characters, of men who dishonestly seek ecclesiastical power. First, those who "*creep*" into the fold; who do not care for office, nor name, but for secret influence, and do all things occultly and cunningly, consenting to any servility of office or conduct, so only that they may intimately discern, and unawares direct, the minds of men. Then those who "intrude" (thrust, that is) themselves into the fold, who by natural insolence of heart, and stout eloquence of tongue, and fearlessly perseverant self-assertion, obtain hearing and authority with the common crowd. Lastly, those who "climb," who by labor and learning, both stout and sound, but selfishly exerted in the cause of their own ambition, gain high dignities and authorities, and become "lords over the heritage," though not "ensamples to the flock."

Now go on:—

> "Of other care they little reckoning make,
> Than how to scramble at the shearers' feast;
> *Blind mouths*—"

I pause again, for this is a strange expression; a broken metaphor, one might think, careless and unscholarly.

Not so: its very audacity and pithiness are intended to make us look close at the phrase and remember it. Those two monosyllables express the precisely accurate contraries of right character, in the two great offices of the Church—those of bishop and pastor.

A Bishop means a person who sees.

A Pastor means one who feeds.

The most unbishoply character a man can have is therefore to be Blind.

The most unpastoral is, instead of feeding, to want to be fed,—to be a Mouth.

Take the two reverses together, and you have "blind mouths." We may advisably follow out this idea a little. Nearly all the evils in the Church have arisen from bishops desiring *power* more than *light*. They want authority, not outlook. Whereas their real office is not to rule; though it may be vigorously to exhort and rebuke; it is the king's office to rule; the bishop's office is to *oversee* the flock; to number it, sheep by sheep; to be ready always to give full account of it. Now it is clear he cannot give account of the souls, if he has not so much as numbered the bodies of his flock. The first thing, therefore, that a bishop has to do is at least to put himself in a position in which, at any moment, he can obtain the history from childhood of every living soul in his diocese, and of its present state. Down in that back street, Bill and Nancy, knocking each other's teeth out! —Does the bishop know all about it? Has he his eye upon them? Has he *had* his eye upon them? Can he circumstantially explain to us how Bill got into the habit of beating Nancy about the head? If he cannot, he is no bishop, though he had a mitre as high as Salisbury steeple; he is no bishop—he has sought to be at the helm instead of the masthead; he has no sight of things. "Nay," you say, it is not his duty to look after Bill in the back street. What! the fat sheep that have full fleeces—you think it is only those he should look after, while (go back to your Milton) "the hungry sheep look up, and are not fed, besides what the grim wolf, with privy paw" (bishops knowing nothing about it) "daily devours apace, and nothing said"?

"But that's not our idea of a bishop." Perhaps not; but it was St. Paul's; and it was Milton's. They may be right, or we may be; but we must not think we are reading either one or the other by putting our meaning into their words.

I go on.

"But, swollen with wind, and the rank mist they draw."

This is to meet the vulgar answer that "if the poor are not looked after in their bodies, they are in their souls; they have spiritual food."

And Milton says, "They have no such thing as spiritual food; they are only swollen with wind." At first you may think that is a coarse type, and an obscure one. But again, it is a quite literally accurate one. Take up your Latin and Greek dictionaries, and find out the meaning of "Spirit." It is only a contraction of the Latin word "breath," and an indistinct translation of the Greek word for "wind." The same word is used in writing, "The wind bloweth where it listeth"; and in writing, "So is every one that is born of the Spirit"; born of the *breath*, that is; for it means the breath of God, in soul and body. We have the true sense of it in our words "inspiration" and "expire." Now, there are two kinds of breath with which the flock may be filled; God's breath, and man's. The breath of God is health, and life, and peace to them, as the air of heaven is to the flocks on the hills; but man's breath—the word which *he* calls spiritual, —is disease and contagion to them, as the fog of the fen. They rot inwardly with it; they are puffed up by it, as a dead body by the vapors of its own decomposition. This is literally true of all false religious teaching; the first and last, and fatalest sign of it is that "puffing up." Your converted children, who teach their parents; your converted convicts, who teach honest men; your converted dunces, who, having lived in cretinous stupefaction half their lives, suddenly awakening to the fact of there being a God, fancy themselves therefore His peculiar people and messengers; your sectarians of every species, small and great, Catholic or Protestant, of high church or low, in so far as they think themselves exclusively in the right and others wrong; and pre-eminently, in every sect, those who hold that men can be saved by thinking rightly instead of doing rightly, by word instead of act, and wish instead of work:—these are the true fog-children—clouds, these, without water; bodies, these, of putrescent vapor and skin, without blood or flesh: blown bagpipes for the fiends to pipe with—corrupt, and corrupting,—"Swollen with wind, and the rank mist they draw."

Lastly, let us return to the lines respecting the power of the keys, for now we can understand them. Note the difference between Milton and Dante in their interpretation of this power: for once, the latter is weaker in thought; he supposes *both* the keys to be of the gate of heaven; one is of gold, the other of silver: they are given by St. Peter to the sentinel angel; and it is not easy to determine the meaning either of the substances of the three steps of the gate, or of the two keys. But Milton makes one, of gold, the key of heaven; the other, of iron, the key of the prison, in which the wicked teachers are to be bound who "have taken away the key of knowledge, yet entered not in themselves."

We have seen that the duties of bishop and pastor are to see, and feed; and, of all who do so, it is said, "He that watereth, shall be watered also himself." But the reverse is truth also. He that watereth not, shall be *withered* himself, and he that seeth not, shall himself be shut out of sight,—shut into the perpetual prison-house. And that prison opens here, as well as hereafter: he who is to be bound in heaven must first be bound on earth. That command to the strong angels, of which the rock-apostle is the image, "Take him, and bind him hand and foot, and cast him out," issues, in its measure, against the teacher, for every help withheld, and for every truth refused, and for every falsehood enforced; so that he is more strictly fettered the more he fetters, and farther outcast, as he more and more misleads, till at last the bars of the iron cage close upon him, and as "the golden opes, the iron shuts amain."

We have got something out of the lines, I think, and much more is yet to be found in them; but we have done enough by way of example of the kind of word-by-word examination of your author which is rightly called "reading"; watching every accent and expression, and putting ourselves always in the author's place, annihilating our own personality, and seeking to enter into his, so as to be able assuredly to say, "Thus Milton thought," not "Thus I thought, in mis-reading Milton."

THOMAS B. MACAULAY

BUNYAN'S "PILGRIM'S PROGRESS"

Thomas Babington Macaulay (1800–1859) was one of the eminent writers of the Victorian age. He was educated at Cambridge University, where he was distinguished as a debater, and famous for his ability to remember everything that he read, often in the exact words of the book. To the *Edinburgh Review* he contributed a number of essays on historical and literary topics. He served several terms in Parliament, had a seat in the Cabinet, and went to India as a member of the Supreme Council. He wrote a *History of England* that was so popular that its sales exceeded those of the novels of the time. He also wrote some stirring ballads called the *Lays of Ancient Rome*, and contributed to the *Encyclopædia Britannica* articles upon Samuel Johnson, Bunyan, and Goldsmith.

Macaulay had the power to make his readers see the persons and scenes he described. His marvellous memory enabled him, as in this essay, to bring in a mass of details. Yet he never lets the detail become confusing; he carries us along as over a well-marked road, we know where we are, and he knows exactly where he is taking us. His style is always clear; he is fond of using balanced sentences and sharp antitheses; his statements are always positive; when he makes a general statement he usually follows it by a concrete example. All these characteristics are seen in the essay on Bunyan's *Pilgrim's Progress*. It was first published in the *Edinburgh Review* for December, 1832.

THOMAS B. MACAULAY

BUNYAN'S "PILGRIM'S PROGRESS" *

(From Macaulay's *Literary Essays*)

This is an eminently beautiful and splendid edition of
a book which well deserves all that the printer and the
engraver can do for it. The *Life of Bunyan* is, of course,
not a performance which can add much to the literary
reputation of such a writer as Mr. Southey. But it is
written in excellent English, and, for the most part, in
an excellent spirit. Mr. Southey propounds, we need
not say, many opinions from which we altogether dissent;
and his attempts to excuse the odious persecution to
which Bunyan was subjected have sometimes moved our
indignation. But we will avoid this topic. We are at
present much more inclined to join in paying homage to
the genius of a great man than to engage in a controversy
concerning Church government and toleration.

We must not pass without notice the engravings with
which this volume is decorated. Some of Mr. Heath's
woodcuts are admirably designed and executed. Mr.
Martin's illustrations do not please us quite so well. His
Valley of the Shadow of Death is not that Valley of the
Shadow of Death which Bunyan imagined. At all
events, it is not that dark and horrible glen which has
from childhood been in our mind's eye. The valley is a
cavern: the quagmire is a lake: the straight path runs
zigzag: and Christian appears like a speck in the darkness of the immense vault. We miss, too, those hideous

* *The Pilgrim's Progress, with a Life of John Bunyan.* By Robert
Southey, Esq., LL.D., Poet-Laureate. Illustrated with Engravings. 8vo. London: 1830.

forms which make so striking a part of the description of Bunyan, and which Salvator Rosa would have loved to draw.

The characteristic peculiarity of the *Pilgrim's Progress* is that it is the only work of its kind which possesses a strong human interest. Other allegories only amuse the fancy. The allegory of Bunyan has been read by many thousands with tears. There are some good allegories in Johnson's works, and some of still higher merit by Addison. In these performances there is, perhaps, as much wit and ingenuity as in the *Pilgrim's Progress*. But the pleasure which is produced by the Vision of Mirza,* the Vision of Theodore, the Genealogy of Wit, or the Contest between Rest and Labor, is exactly similar to the pleasure which we derive from one of Cowley's odes or from a canto of Hudibras. It is a pleasure which belongs wholly to the understanding, and in which the feelings have no part whatever. Nay, even Spenser himself, though assuredly one of the greatest poets that ever lived, could not succeed in the attempt to make allegory interesting. It was in vain that he lavished the riches of his mind on the House of Pride and the House of Temperance. One unpardonable fault, the fault of tediousness, pervades the whole of the *Fairy Queen*. We become sick of Cardinal Virtues and Deadly Sins, and long for the society of plain men and women. Of the persons who read the first canto, not one in ten reaches the end of the first book, and not one in a hundred perseveres to the end of the poem. Very few and very weary are those who are in at the death of the Blatant Beast. If the last six books, which are said to have been destroyed in Ireland, had been preserved, we doubt whether any heart less stout than that of a commentator would have held out to the end.

* This and the following are titles of Addison's *Spectator* papers.

It is not so with the *Pilgrim's Progress*. That wonderful book, while it obtains admiration from the most fastidious critics, is loved by those who are too simple to admire it. Dr. Johnson, all whose studies were desultory, and who hated, as he said, to read books through, made an exception in favor of the *Pilgrim's Progress*. That work, he said, was one of the two or three works which he wished longer. It was by no common merit that the illiterate sectary extracted praise like this from the most pedantic of critics and the most bigoted of Tories. In the wildest parts of Scotland the *Pilgrim's Progress* is the delight of the peasantry. In every nursery the *Pilgrim's Progress* is a greater favorite than *Jack the Giant-killer*. Every reader knows the straight and narrow path as well as he knows a road in which he has gone backwar l and forward a hundred times. This is the highest miracle of genius,—that things which are not should be as though they were,—that the imaginations of one mind should become the personal recollections of another. And this miracle the tinker has wrought. There is no ascent, no declivity, no resting place, no turnstile, with which we are not perfectly acquainted. The wicket gate, and the desolate swamp which separates it from the City of Destruction, the long line of road, as straight as a rule can make it, the Interpreter's house and all its fair shows, the prisoner in the iron cage, the palace, at the doors of which armed men kept guard, and on the battlements of which walked persons clothed all in gold, the cross and the sepulchre, the steep hill and the pleasant arbor, the stately front of the House Beautiful by the wayside, the low green valley of Humiliation, rich with grass and covered with flocks, all are as well known to us as the sights of our own street. Then we come to the narrow place where Apollyon strode right across the whole breadth of the way, to stop the journey of Christian, and where afterward the pillar was set up to testify how bravely the pilgrim had fought the good fight. As we advance, the valley becomes deeper and deeper. The shade of the precipices on both sides falls blacker and blacker. The clouds gather overhead. Doleful voices, the clanking of chains, and the rushing of many feet to and fro, are heard through the darkness. The way, hardly discernible in gloom, runs close by the mouth of the burning pit, which sends forth its flames, its noisome smoke, and its hideous shapes, to terrify the adventurer. Thence he goes on, amidst the snares and pitfalls, with the mangled bodies of those who have perished lying in the ditch by his side. At the end of the long dark valley he passes the dens in which the old giants dwelt, amidst the bones of those whom they had slain.

Then the road passes straight on through a waste moor, till at length the towers of a distant city appear before the traveller; and soon he is in the midst of the innumerable multitudes of Vanity Fair. There are the jugglers and the apes, the shops and the puppet-shows. There are Italian Row, and French Row, and Spanish Row, and British Row, with their crowds of buyers, sellers, and loungers, jabbering all the languages of the earth.

Thence we go on by the little hill of the silver-mine, and through the meadow of lilies, along the bank of that pleasant river which is bordered on both sides by fruit-trees. On the left branches off the path leading to the horrible castle, the courtyard of which is paved with the skulls of pilgrims; and right onward are the sheepfolds and orchards of the Delectable Mountains.

From the Delectable Mountains, the way lies through the fogs and briers of the Enchanted Ground, with here and there a bed of soft cushions spread under a green arbor. And beyond is the land of Beulah, where the flowers, the grapes, and the songs of birds never cease, and where the sun shines night and day. Thence are plainly seen the golden pavements and streets of pearl, on the other side of that black and cold river over which there is no bridge.

All the stages of the journey, all the forms which cross or overtake the pilgrims, giants and hobgoblins, ill-favored ones and shining ones, the tall, comely, swarthy Madam Bubble, with her great purse by her side, and her fingers playing with the money, the black man in the bright vesture, Mr. Worldly Wiseman and my Lord Hategood, Mr. Talkative, and Mrs. Timorous, all are actually existing beings to us. We follow the travellers through their allegorical progress with interest not inferior to that with which we follow Elizabeth from Siberia to Moscow, or Jeanie Deans from Edinburgh to London. Bunyan is almost the only writer who ever gave to the abstract the interest of the concrete. In the works of many celebrated authors, men are mere personifications. We have not an Othello, but jealousy, not an Iago, but perfidy, not a Brutus, but patriotism. The mind of Bunyan, on the contrary, was so imaginative that personifications, when he dealt with them, became men. A dialogue between two qualities, in his dream, has more dramatic effect than a dialogue between two human beings in most plays.

The *Pilgrim's Progress* undoubtedly is not a perfect allegory. The types are often inconsistent with each other; and sometimes the allegorical disguise is altogether thrown off. The river, for example, is emblematic of death; and we are told that every human being must pass through the river. But Faithful does not pass through it. He is martyred, not in shadow, but in reality, at Vanity Fair. Hopeful talks to Christian about Esau's birthright and about his own convictions of sin as Bunyan might have talked with one of his own congregation.

The damsels at the House Beautiful catechise Christiana's boys, as any good ladies might catechise any boys at a Sunday-school. But we do not believe that any man, whatever might be his genius, and whatever his good luck, could long continue a figurative history without falling into many inconsistencies. We are sure that inconsistencies, scarcely less gross than the worst into which Bunyan has fallen, may be found in the shortest and most elaborate allegories of the *Spectator* and the *Rambler*. The *Tale of a Tub* * and the *History of John Bull* swarm with similar errors, if the name of error can be properly applied to that which is unavoidable. It is not easy to make a simile go on all fours. But we believe that no human ingenuity could produce such a centipede as a long allegory in which the correspondence between the outward sign and the thing signified should be exactly preserved. Certainly no writer, ancient or modern, has yet achieved the adventure. The best thing, on the whole, that an allegorist can do, is to present to his readers a succession of analogies, each of which may separately be striking and happy, without looking very nicely to see whether they harmonize with each other. This Bunyan has done; and, though a minute scrutiny may detect inconsistencies in every page of his tale, the general effect which the tale produces on all persons, learned and unlearned, proves that he has done well. The passages which it is most difficult to defend are those in which he altogether drops the allegory, and puts into the mouth of his pilgrims religious ejaculations and disquisitions better suited to his own pulpit at Bedford or Reading than to the Enchanted Ground or the Interpreter's Garden. Yet even these passages, though we will not undertake to defend them against the objections

* The *Tale of a Tub* is by Jonathan Swift; the *History of John Bull* by John Arbuthnot. Both are prose allegories.

of critics, we feel that we could ill spare. We feel that the story owes much of its charm to these occasional glimpses of solemn and affecting subjects, which will not be hidden, which force themselves through the veil, and appear before us in their native aspect. The effect is not unlike that which is said to have been produced on the ancient stage, when the eyes of the actor were seen flaming through his mask, and giving life and expression to what would else have been an inanimate and uninteresting disguise.

It is very amusing and very instructive to compare the *Pilgrim's Progress* with the *Grace Abounding*. The latter work is indeed one of the most remarkable pieces of autobiography in the world. It is a full and open confession of the fancies which passed through the mind of an illiterate man, whose affections were warm, whose nerves were irritable, whose imagination was ungovernable, and who was under the influence of the strongest religious excitement. In whatever age Bunyan had lived, the history of his feelings would, in all probability, have been very curious. But the time in which his lot was cast was the time of a great stirring of the human mind. A tremendous burst of public feeling, produced by the tyranny of the hierarchy, menaced the old ecclesiastical institutions with destruction. To the gloomy regularity of one intolerant Church had succeeded the license of innumerable sects, drunk with the sweet and heady must of their new liberty. Fanaticism, engendered by persecution and destined to engender persecution in turn, spread rapidly through society. Even the strongest and most commanding minds were not proof against this strange taint. Any time might have produced George Fox and James Naylor. But to one time alone belong the frantic delusions of such a statesman as Vane, and the hysterical tears of such a soldier as Cromwell.

The history of Bunyan is the history of a most excitable mind in an age of excitement. By most of his biographers he has been treated with gross injustice. They have understood in a popular sense all those strong terms of self-condemnation which he employed in a theological sense. They have, therefore, represented him as an abandoned wretch, reclaimed by means almost miraculous; or, to use their favorite metaphor, "as a brand plucked from the burning." Mr. Ivimey calls him the depraved Bunyan, and the wicked tinker of Elstow. Surely Mr. Ivimey ought to have been too familiar with the bitter accusations which the most pious people are in the habit of bringing against themselves, to understand literally all the strong expressions which are to be found in the *Grace Abounding*. It is quite clear, as Mr. Southey most justly remarks, that Bunyan never was a vicious man. He married very early; and he solemnly declares that he was strictly faithful to his wife. He does not appear to have been a drunkard. He owns, indeed, that when a boy he never spoke without an oath. But a single admonition cured him of this bad habit for life; and the cure must have been wrought early; for at eighteen he was in the army of the Parliament; and, if he had carried the vice of profaneness into that service, he would doubtless have received something more than an admonition from Sergeant Bind-their-kings-in-chains, or Captain Hew-Agag-in-pieces-before-the-Lord. Bell-ringing, and playing at hockey on Sundays, seem to have been the worst vices of this depraved tinker. They would have passed for virtues with Archbishop Laud. It is quite clear that, from a very early age, Bunyan was a man of a strict life and of a tender conscience. "He had been," says Mr. Southey, "a blackguard." Even this we think too hard a censure. Bunyan was not, we admit, so fine a gentleman as Lord Digby; but he was a blackguard no otherwise than as every tinker that ever lived has been a blackguard. Indeed, Mr. Southey acknowledges this. "Such he might have been expected to be by his birth, breeding, and vocation. Scarcely, indeed, by possibility, could he have been otherwise." A man whose manners and sentiments are decidedly below those of his class deserves to be called a blackguard. But it is surely unfair to apply so strong a word of reproach to one who is only what the great mass of every community must inevitably be.

Those horrible internal conflicts which Bunyan has described with so much power of language prove, not that he was a worse man than his neighbors, but that his mind was constantly occupied by religious considerations, that his fervor exceeded his knowledge, and that his imagination exercised despotic power over his body and mind. He heard voices from heaven. He saw strange visions of distant hills, pleasant and sunny as his own Delectable Mountains. From those abodes he was shut out, and placed in a dark and horrible wilderness, where he wandered through ice and snow, striving to make his way into the happy region of light. At one time he was seized with an inclination to work miracles. At another time he thought himself actually possessed by the devil. He could distinguish the blasphemous whispers. He felt his infernal enemy pulling at his clothes behind him. He spurned with his feet and struck with his hands at the destroyer. Sometimes he was tempted to sell his part in the salvation of mankind. Sometimes a violent impulse urged him to start up from his food, to fall on his knees, and to break forth into prayer. At length he fancied that he had committed the unpardonable sin. His agony convulsed his robust frame. It was, he says, as if his breast-bone would split; and this he took for a sign that he was destined to burst asunder like Judas.

The agitation of his nerves made all his movements tremulous; and this trembling, he supposed, was a visible mark of his reprobation, like that which had been set on Cain. At one time, indeed, an encouraging voice seemed to rush in at the window, like the noise of wind, but very pleasant, and commanded, as he says, a great calm in his soul. At another time a word of comfort "was spoke loud unto him; it showed a great word; it seemed to be writ in great letters." But these intervals of ease were short. His state, during two years and a half, was generally the most horrible that the human mind can imagine. "I walked," says he, with his own peculiar eloquence, "to a neighboring town; and sat down upon a settle in the street, and fell into a very deep pause about the most fearful state my sin had brought me to; and, after long musing, I lifted up my head; but methought I saw as if the sun that shineth in the heavens did grudge to give me light; and as if the very stones in the street, and the tiles upon the houses, did band themselves against me. Methought that they all combined together to banish me out of the world. I was abhorred of them, and unfit to dwell among them, because I had sinned against the Saviour. Oh, how happy now was every creature over I! for they stood fast, and kept their station. But I was gone and lost." Scarcely any madhouse could produce an instance of delusion so strong, or of misery so acute.

It was through this valley of the Shadow of Death, overhung by darkness, peopled with devils, resounding with blasphemy and lamentation, and passing amidst quagmires, snares, and pitfalls, close by the very mouth of hell, that Bunyan journeyed to that bright and fruitful land of Beulah, in which he sojourned during the latter period of his pilgrimage. The only trace which his cruel sufferings and temptations seem to have left behind them was an affectionate compassion for those who were still in the state in which he had once been. Religion has scarcely ever worn a form so calm and soothing as in his allegory. The feeling which predominates through the whole book is a feeling of tenderness for weak, timid, and harassed minds. The character of Mr. Fearing, of Mr. Feeblemind, of Mr. Despondency and his daughter Miss Muchafraid, the account of poor Littlefaith who was robbed by the three thieves of his spending money, the description of Christian's terror in the dungeons of Giant Despair and in his passage through the river, all clearly show how strong a sympathy Bunyan felt, after his own mind had become clear and cheerful, for persons afflicted with religious melancholy.

Mr. Southey, who has no love for the Calvinists, admits that, if Calvinism had never worn a blacker appearance than in Bunyan's works, it would never have become a term of reproach. In fact, those works of Bunyan with which we are acquainted are by no means more Calvinistic than the articles and homilies of the Church of England. The moderation of his opinions on the subject of predestination gave offense to some zealous persons. We have seen an absurd allegory, the heroine of which is named Hephzibah, written by some raving supralapsarian* preacher who was dissatisfied with the mild theology of the *Pilgrim's Progress.* In this foolish book, if we recollect rightly, the Interpreter is called the Enlightener, and the House Beautiful is Castle Strength. Mr. Southey tells us that the Catholics had also their *Pilgrim's Progress,* without a Giant Pope, in which the Interpreter is the Director, and the House Beautiful Grace's Hall. It is surely a remarkable proof of the

* Supralapsarian, a theological term signifying one who believes that before men were created, God had determined which ones were to be saved and which were to be damned.

power of Bunyan's genius, that two religious parties, both of which regarded his opinions as heterodox, should have had recourse to him for assistance.

There are, we think, some characters and scenes in the *Pilgrim's Progress*, which can be fully comprehended and enjoyed only by persons familiar with the history of the times through which Bunyan lived. The character of Mr. Greatheart, the guide, is an example. His fighting is, of course, allegorical; but the allegory is not strictly preserved. He delivers a sermon on imputed righteousness to his companions; and, soon after, he gives battle to Giant Grim, who had taken upon him to back the lions. He expounds the fifty-third chapter of Isaiah to the household and guests of Gaius; and then he sallies out to attack Slaygood, who was of the nature of flesh-eaters, in his den. These are inconsistencies; but they are inconsistencies which add, we think, to the interest of the narrative. We have not the least doubt that Bunyan had in view some stout old Greatheart of Naseby and Worcester, who prayed with his men before he drilled them, who knew the spiritual state of every dragoon in his troop, and who, with the praises of God in his mouth, and a two-edged sword in his hand, had turned to flight, on many fields of battle, the swearing, drunken bravoes of Rupert and Lunsford.

Every age produces such men as By-ends. But the middle of the seventeenth century was eminently prolific of such men. Mr. Southey thinks that the satire was aimed at some particular individual; and this seems by no means improbable. At all events, Bunyan must have known many of those hypocrites who followed religion only when religion walked in silver slippers, when the sun shone, and when the people applauded. Indeed, he might have easily found all the kindred of By-ends among the public men of his time. He might have found among the peers my Lord Turn-about, my Lord Time-server, and my Lord Fair-speech; in the House of Commons, Mr. Smooth-man, Mr. Any-thing, and Mr. Facing-both-ways; nor would "the parson of the parish, Mr. Two-tongues," have been wanting. The town of Bedford probably contained more than one politician who, after contriving to raise an estate by seeking the Lord during the reign of the saints, contrived to keep what he had got by persecuting the saints during the reign of the strumpets, and more than one priest who, during repeated changes in the discipline and doctrines of the church, had remained constant to nothing but his benefice.

One of the most remarkable passages in the *Pilgrim's Progress* is that in which the proceedings against Faith-ful are described. It is impossible to doubt that Bunyan intended to satirize the mode in which state trials were conducted under Charles the Second. The license given to the witnesses for the prosecution, the shameless par-tiality and ferocious insolence of the judge, the precipi-tancy and the blind rancor of the jury, remind us of those odious mummeries which, from the Restoration to the Revolution, were merely forms preliminary to hanging, drawing, and quartering. Lord Hategood performs the office of counsel for the prisoners as well as Scroggs him-self could have performed it.

"JUDGE. Thou runagate, heretic, and traitor, hast thou heard what these honest gentlemen have witnessed against thee?

"FAITHFUL. May I speak a few words in my own defense?

"JUDGE. Sirrah, sirrah! thou deservest to live no longer, but to be slain immediately upon the place; yet, that all men may see our gentleness to thee, let us hear what thou, vile runagate, hast to say."

No person who knows the state trials can be at a loss for parallel cases. Indeed, write what Bunyan would, the baseness and cruelty of the lawyers of those times "sinned up to it still," and even went beyond it. The imaginary trial of Faithful, before a jury composed of personified vices, was just and merciful, when compared with the real trial of Alice Lisle before that tribunal where all the vices sat in the person of Jefferies.

The style of Bunyan is delightful to every reader, and invaluable as a study to every person who wishes to obtain a wide command over the English language. The vocabulary is the vocabulary of the common people. There is not an expression, if we except a few technical terms of theology, which would puzzle the rudest peasant. We have observed several pages which do not contain a single word of more than two syllables. Yet no writer has said more exactly what he meant to say. For magnificence, for pathos, for vehement exhortation, for subtle disquisition, for every purpose of the poet, the orator, and the divine, this homely dialect, the dialect of plain working men, was perfectly sufficient. There is no book in our literature on which we would so readily stake the fame of the old unpolluted English language, no book which shows so well how rich that language is in its own proper wealth, and how little it has been improved by all that it has borrowed.

Cowper said, forty or fifty years ago, that he dared not name John Bunyan in his verse, for fear of moving a sneer. To our refined forefathers, we suppose, Lord Roscommon's *Essay on Translated Verse*, and the Duke of Buckinghamshire's *Essay on Poetry*, appeared to be compositions infinitely superior to the allegory of the preaching tinker. We live in better times; and we are not afraid to say, that, though there were many clever men in England during the latter half of the seventeenth century, there were only two great creative minds. One of those minds produced the *Paradise Lost*, the other the *Pilgrim's Progress*.

J. SALWYN SCHAPIRO

WELLS'S "OUTLINE OF HISTORY"

J. Salwyn Schapiro (1879———) is assistant professor of History in the College of the City of New York. He received his early education in the public schools of Hudson, New York, and his collegiate training at the College of the City of New York and at Columbia University, receiving the degree of Doctor of Philosophy from Columbia in 1909. He is the author of *Social Reform and the Reformation* and *Modern and Contemporary European History*.

The review here given appeared originally in the New York *Nation*. It is longer than most reviews, partly because of the importance of the book to be discussed, partly because of the method of treatment adopted by the reviewer. The article has three main divisions: (a) a general discussion of the subject of history, with reference to Mr. Wells; (b) a summary of the *Outline of History*, with comment; (c) an estimate of Mr. Wells's whole literary product, for the purpose of pointing out features which are common to all his writings.

J. SALWYN SCHAPIRO

H. G. WELLS'S "OUTLINE OF HISTORY"

(This article appeared in *The Nation* for February 3, 1921. It is reprinted by permission of the author and of the editor of *The Nation*.)

I

In *The Outline of History* Mr. Wells has performed at least one remarkable feat: he has interested the average intelligent reader in history. No professional historian now living has ever done it or could do it. The average intelligent person will read fiction, essays, philosophy, science, and sometimes even poetry; but he will not read history. And the reason for this is obvious. History has recently been written for one of two audiences. One of these audiences consists of students in school and college to whom history is presented as an endless and tiresome succession of dates, battles, political parties, the "heroic dead," politicians, kings, and generals. Examinations once over, these students promptly proceed to forget all about it. But the memory of horrors associated with studying history lingers, and in after-life nothing will induce them to open a book on this subject. Or history has been written by the Ph. Deified for the Ph. Deified, generally in a language unknown to living men. When an ordinary person happens across a volume of this type and begins reading it, he is at first mystified, then dismayed, and ends·by giving the book as a gift to a deserving nephew. Now and then a Macaulay, a Green, a Michelet, a Treitschke, a Mommsen, a Bancroft comes along and writes a history so vivid, so full of the life and color that characterize man even at his lowest and stupidest that the reader overcomes his antipathy for the subject and pursues it with avidity.

Mr. Wells, by profession a novelist and by temperament a reformer, has now essayed the task. In spite of the fact that he is not a member of the guild of historians and has therefore received no training in what is termed scientific history, he is nevertheless in many ways remarkably well qualified for it. In the first place, he has a strong, subtle, and profound sense of human relationships. Few men of our day have so keen a realization of the forces in life that make or mar individuals and societies. In the second place, Mr. Wells possesses unusual powers of imagination, an essential gift in one who essays to write history, for it takes imagination to see reality. The unimaginative see only forms, appearances, and semblances, never reality. Finally, Mr. Wells can write superlatively well. A reader can rest assured as he takes up these two rather large volumes that they will hold his attention throughout.

To Mr. Wells, as to many other thoughtful men, the World War and the class wars that followed in its wake revealed a civilization sick unto death. A true lover of mankind, he was moved to inquire into the origin of the dreadful disease that brought about the world tragedy. He came to the conclusion that the trouble lay primarily in the fact that history has been the handmaid of narrow nationalisms, religious bigotry, stupid racialism, and cultural arrogance that fostered suspicions and bred hatreds; and that "there can be no common peace and prosperity without common historical ideas." Thereupon Mr. Wells determined to become the propagandist for mankind by writing a universal history from the time, about half a million years ago, when the earth was a flaring mass of matter without life, to the present day.

The *Outline* is a history with a new point of view, Mr. Wells's own. Briefly, it is this: All mankind has a common origin and heritage, has travelled along a common path, and is nearing a common goal. Being conscious of this, it has tried "to create and develop a common consciousness and a common stock of knowledge which may serve and illuminate that purpose." History in this sense becomes "the common adventure of all mankind" in search of social and international peace through a mitigation of the rights and privileges of nations and of property. Mr. Wells's history "deals with ages, and races, and nations where the ordinary history deals with reigns and pedigrees and campaigns." No people, no religion, no country, no period, is overlooked. The *Outline* is in spirit and in fact a universal history. It concerns itself with Asia and Africa no less than with Europe and America; with Buddhism and Mohammedanism no less than with Judaism and Christianity; with primitive life no less than with modern; with Hindus, Chinese, Persians, and Egyptians no less than with Englishmen, Frenchmen, and Germans.

According to Mr. Wells there have been three structural ideas in the life of mankind on which the great society of the future will be built: (1) science, first identified with Herodotus and Aristotle; (2) a universal God of righteousness, the contribution of the Semites; and (3) a system of world polity, first suggested by the empire of Alexander the Great. Mr. Wells has envisaged the path of civilization. Civilization arose as a "community of obedience," subject to priests, lords, and kings, and has progressed toward a "community of will," self-determining, democratic, free. The American Revolution, he declares, was the first great positive and successful step toward the foundation of a "community of will," for it repudiated the ancient forms of authority, king, priest, and lord. The great repudiation was of course the French Revolution.

So gigantic a task as Mr. Wells set before himself would require the industry of a Ranke, the versatility of a Leonardo da Vinci, the learning of a Mommsen, and the style of a Macaulay; in short, universal genius of the highest order. Mr. Wells, having a sense of humor, knows his limitations. He has modestly avowed them and has sought advice and assistance from many experts in various fields, the chief being Mr. Ernest Barker, Sir E. Ray Lankester, and Professor Gilbert Murray. The *Outline* is profusely illustrated with interesting and original maps, diagrams, and drawings by Mr. J. F. Horrabin. One of the unusual features of the book is the heckling, in true English fashion, of the text by the foot-notes. It is the tradition for foot-notes to murmur approval to whatever the text is pleased to say; in this history they shout defiance at the text. Mr. Wells's advisers, who wrote and signed most of the foot-notes, use this method of disagreeing with him. Sometimes he descends to the foot-notes to engage in a bout with his critics. All this is quite diverting and gay, and for once the reader will enjoy reading foot-notes.

The *Outline* contains nothing original except the point of view and method of treatment. Mr. Wells does not claim to have discovered new material or to have discredited old material. Everything in his book is accessible elsewhere. Universal histories, too, are not new; they were the fashion in the eighteenth century and even earlier. But his is the first book, and, so far as I know, the only one, that is a universal history with a distinctly modern point of view and that has utilized and has brought to bear upon its thesis the accumulated riches of modern scholarship in the related sciences of geology, biology, archæology, ethnology, sociology, comparative religions, economics, and political science.

At this point it is important to inquire on what basis Mr. Wells solved the problem of selection. Every writer of history is confronted with this vexing problem. What shall he select from the enormous mass of material that constitutes human history? What shall be excluded? What shall be emphasized? What shall be minimized? The manner in which historians react to these problems varies with their point of view, their traditions, their education, their *milieu*,* their temperament, and especially with the spirit of the age in which they live. Every age rewrites history to suit itself, because interpretation of history changes with increase of knowledge and with a better understanding of that curious being called Man. We of to-day understand the ancient Greeks far better than did Pericles because we know more of human psychology than he did. In a sense the historian may be considered a social psychoanalyst, for he brings to the surface the unconscious motives and forces that have caused profound changes in human affairs. Those who write history with the view to merely explaining the past are not historians but antiquarians. A true historian studies the past with a view primarily to explaining the present, and not infrequently does he use the present to throw light on the past. Now, what was Mr. Wells's basis of selection? In his case the question is all the more important because he had to encompass half a million years of world history in two volumes. His answer is in itself no small contribution. His purpose is to include and to emphasize only those events in the past that have a bearing on the future. Readers of Mr. Wells's books know that, in his great quest to fathom the mystery of life, his eyes have always been turned toward the future. He never tires of reiterating the sentiment that the chief business of mankind ought to be to prepare

* *Milieu*, environment, the conditions which surround one.

itself, its ideals, and its institutions for the great future that is approaching. This point of view animates and distinguishes the *Outline*.

The book possesses another unique quality, its intimacy. Mr. Wells is the one writer of history who takes the reader into his confidence and discusses with him frankly the significance of the great events of the past. History as seen through the temperament of Mr. Wells is novel, piquant, and entertaining. In reading the *Outline* one seldom gets the idea that what is narrated occurred far away and long ago. Mr. Wells has no sense of time, for he discusses events in the remote past as if they were still happening. All ages are contemporary with Mr. Wells. This gives vividness to his story and truthfulness, too; for let it not be forgotten that the dead we have always with us.

II

Book I tells the story of the origin of the world. In a style so simple and lucid that a child can understand it, he describes the Record of the Rocks, the changes of climate, the formation of the earth's surface, the first appearance of life, the origin of species, and finally the Age of Mammals. Mr. Wells's early scientific training has stood him in good stead. He has evidently read widely and deeply in this field, for he moves easily among his materials. The reader is held in breathless suspense as the thrilling tale is told of thousands of years of which the record, though so slight, is yet so significant.

Book II is, if anything, still more fascinating. It alone is worth the price of the two volumes. It tells the story of the origin and development of the human race, from our ape-like ancestor through the Heidelberg, Piltdown, Neanderthal, and Cro-Magnon types to present man. Mr. Wells possesses a scientific imagination of a high order. He reconstructs in a marvellous way the Paleolithic and Neolithic Ages with their inhabitants, tools, architecture, and art. He then tells of the origin of races, of agriculture, of herding, and of trade. Finally he reconstructs the mind of primitive man, and describes the origin of thought, of symbols, of legends, of religion, and of the various languages.

Book III, on the Dawn of History, keeps up the pace. It deals with the first civilizations, Sumerian, Assyrian, Chaldean, Egyptian, Hindu, and Chinese; with the maritime and trading people of the Ægean, the Cretans, Trojans, Phœnicians, and Homeric Greeks. There is a short but remarkably clear chapter on the origin and importance of writing. Mr. Wells traces writing through the picture, the syllable, and finally to the alphabet stage. With the coming of the written word, "verbal tradition which had hitherto changed from age to age, began to be fixed. Men separated by hundreds of miles could now communicate their thoughts. An increasing number of human beings began to share a common written knowledge and a common sense of a past and a future. Human thinking became a larger operation in which hundreds of minds in different places and different ages could react upon each other."

How the priest and king came into history is the next theme. There is a bare suggestion that the forerunner of both was the Paleolithic Old Man of the Tribe, dreaded not only in life as the master but dreaded as well after death, so that his spirit had to be propitiated. He had cared for the tribe when alive; he no doubt would care for it when dead! He was the spirit of authority. Perhaps a god! Ideas that once have lived never really die. They live on as taboos, conventions, traditions, reverences, and "sweet remembrances." Book III ends with the story of the common man. It tells the origin of castes, trades, professions, guilds, slavery, and free labor.

With Book IV, on Judea, Greece, and India, the *Outline* enters the field of history proper. Here Mr. Wells treats of familiar things in a quite unfamiliar manner. He has no great admiration for David and Solomon, both of whom are pictured as cruel, treacherous, and bloody Eastern monarchs.

Four chapters are devoted to the Greeks, whom Mr. Wells greatly admires as the first truly modern men because they were scientific and sceptical. Much valuable space is given to the struggles between the Greeks and Persians. Many trivial incidents and personalities are dwelt upon because of their picturesqueness. Crœsus gets fully six pages and Socrates only two. On the whole the chapter on Greek thought is not up to the mark. Of Alexander the Great Mr. Wells has a low opinion. Demoralized as a child by his mother, Alexander grew up to be insanely egotistical. He did nothing directly of any permanent value. As for Hellenizing the East, all he did was to wander aimlessly through the region, fighting any one who came his way and for no particular reason. Both as statesman and soldier, Alexander's father, Philip, was much his superior. Alexander is "nothing but a personal legend," his greatness an invention of historians. About the only thing that he did bequeath to posterity is the custom of shaving one's face, which he initiated because he was enamored of his own youthful loveliness. Mr. Wells has small respect for "Heroes of History," especially if they happen to be conquerors, and his opinion of Alexander, just stated, is certainly entertaining and perhaps correct.

One of the best chapters, if not the best, in the *Outline* is that on Buddhism. Strangely enough, Mr. Wells is at his best when dealing with science and religion.

The story of the life of Gautama is told with thrilling eloquence and fine appreciation. Gautama's teachings, Mr. Wells declares, are in "closest harmony with modern ideas" and are indisputably "the achievement of one of the most penetrating intelligences the world has ever known." He corrects the common misconception that Nirvana is a state of complete annihilation by explaining that it is a state of serenity of soul which comes to one who is absorbed in something greater than himself. Mr. Wells is lost in admiration for Gautama's doctrine, which he identifies with the teaching of history as presented by the *Outline*. However, Buddhism gathered corruption as it spread, so that to-day the ideals of Gautama are fairly smothered in a hideous mass of idolatry, superstition, and sacerdotalism. The teachings of a master are generally corrupted by his disciples, who are apt to be enthusiastic and undiscriminating propagandists, eager to spread the faith at all costs. "Men who would scorn to tell a lie in every-day life," writes Mr. Wells, "will become un-scrupulous cheats and liars when they have given them-selves up to propagandist work." Who has not met them these last years!

III

With the chapter on Buddhism the *Outline* reaches its high-water mark. From thence on, a startling change is noticeable. And the change is for the worse. There is no longer, as in the first volume, the sure touch and firm grasp that comes from knowledge accumulated and di-gested. Mr. Wells now moves uneasily among his ma-terials, which he has annexed from encyclopædia articles and a few simple manuals. Although he makes compara-tively few downright errors, his story of the Roman Em-pire, the Middle Ages, and Modern Times is tragically disappointing in view of the hopes he has raised in the earlier sections. The second volume is disfigured by insufficient knowledge and bad judgment, *gaucheries*,* prejudice, and even pettiness, sometimes to a degree that is positively shocking. There seems to be no rhyme or reason for the inclusion of some things and the exclusion of others except the author's whims. In short, there is no basis of selection of any kind that I can see. The various periods and countries are badly integrated, and the reader loses sight completely of the great path that humanity has travelled since its appearance on the earth.

Book V is the history of the Roman Empire. As may be expected, the children of Mars fare badly at the hands of the anti-militarist Mr. Wells. The Romans were brutal "Neanderthal men," incurious, unimaginative, and intellectually far inferior to the Greeks. The Roman Empire was "a colossally ignorant and unimaginative empire." It foresaw nothing. It had no conception of statecraft. It was a gigantic bureaucracy only, that taxed and kept the peace. Its inhabitants, both rich and poor, led dreary lives, which explains their delight in the savage conflicts of the arena. Even though one may dislike the Romans, the fact nevertheless remains that, during a period of six centuries, they did unify the Western world and did create a world polity—that thing so much desired by Mr. Wells; they did create the system of private law upon which modern jurisprudence is largely based; they did create an administrative system which functions to this day in Latin Europe.

According to Mr. Wells, the most significant fact in Roman history is the increasing use of money, making capital fluid and free. This led to speculation and the rise of a money power, which became the efficient helpmeet of the military. Mr. Wells thinks the Roman

* *Gaucheries*, awkward expressions.

system was "a crude anticipation of our own," with its machine politics and professional politicians, class conflicts, mobs, wire-pullers, "common people," reformers, political corruption, capitalism, and the "science of thwarting the common man." He tells the story of the Gracchi, and of how they were energetically massacred by the "champions of law and order." All this is highly suggestive.

Mr. Wells's judgment of famous Romans is amusing, to say the least. The picture that he draws of Cato the Censor would lead one to believe that that austere worthy fairly reeked with morals and was therefore full of hatred and all uncharitableness for the gentle and joyous things of life. Julius Cæsar's greatness, Mr. Wells firmly believes, is purely the invention of historians, who magnify and dress him up "for the admiration of careless and uncritical readers." According to our author, Cæsar was a Roman politician, rich, corrupt, and dissolute. Like Clodius and Catiline he was a vulgar schemer and conspirator, only shrewder and more crafty than they. At no time did he show any symptoms of greatness either of mind or character. At the very zenith of his power, Cæsar was much more interested in Cleopatra than in Romanizing the world. This belittling of Cæsar, as of Alexander, is due to Mr. Wells's intense dislike of conquerors and the homage that is paid them.

I was astounded to find that Mr. Wells has swallowed —hook, worm, and sinker—the legend of the "Fall" of Rome, now long exploded. He characterizes the invasion of the German barbarians as a "conquest of the Empire" which "crumpled up." He does not seem to understand that what he calls the "Fall" was a long process of decay and absorption. The cause of the "Fall," he writes, was the stupidity and "incuriousness" of the Romans. He gives us no evidence of being aware of the vast social changes that were taking place during the fourth and fifth centuries, the silent economic massacre of the lower middle classes, the sinking of the free laborers to a condition of serfdom, the race suicide—phenomena that surely offer some explanation for the decay of the Roman world.

Book VI deals with Christianity, Islam, and the Middle Ages. Naturally one is interested in what the author of *First and Last Things* has to say on the religion of his fathers and of his contemporaries. The *Outline* narrates the life of Christ in a tone that is reverent and "correct." There is no such thrilling eloquence, however, as there is in the description of Gautama.

Christianity, says Mr. Wells, diverged from the pure Gospel of Jesus of Nazareth almost from the beginning. He has severe things to say of St. Paul as a preacher "of the ancient religion of priest and altar and propitiatory bloodshed." Soon there came accretions from Mithraism and from the Isis cult of Egypt. Finally there came the dogma of the Trinity which to Mr. Wells was "a disastrous ebullition of the human mind" leading to bitter schisms that rent the Church. "Men who quarrelled over business affairs," he writes, "wives who wished to annoy their husbands, developed antagonistic views on this exalted theme." Further on in the book he goes on to say that in time "the gory forefinger of the Etruscan pontifex maximus emphasized the teachings of Jesus of Nazareth; the mental complexity of the Alexandrian Greek entangled them." So deeply hostile is Mr. Wells to Christianity that when he does say something nice about it he says something which is erroneous. He repeats the common fallacy that Christianity was opposed to slavery and brought about its abolition.

The story of Christianity's rival as a world religion, Mohammedanism, is told next. Mr. Wells's opinion of

Mohammed is that he was "vain, egotistical, tyrannous, and a self-deceiver." Although not an impostor, he was "diplomatic, treacherous, ruthless, or compromising as the occasion required." But though its founder was at once a knave and a fool, Mr. Wells assures us that Islam was superior to both Judaism and Christianity. Mr. Wells's ideas of Mohammedanism are what Alice in Wonderland would call "imaginotions." His enthusiasm for Islam is understandable, however, for its vast embrace of millions of all sorts of races and tribes marks a great step in the advance of the unity of mankind, the goal of all human history.

Mr. Wells then betakes himself to the Middle Ages. The greatness of the hero of the period, Charlemagne, another warrior-statesman, posterity has greatly exaggerated, Mr. Wells assures us. Charlemagne was the first of the imitation Cæsars of which William II was the last. Nowhere in this chapter, or in any other, is there an adequate description of feudal society; there are a few loose paragraphs about it. The Crusades, on the other hand, receive adequate treatment. Mr. Wells has a sense for movements, and he describes these romantic popular outpourings with spirit and insight.

Book VII contains two surprising chapters. The one on the Mongols is surprising because it is dull. It is the only dull chapter in the two volumes. It is a tedious recital of Tartar raids and Tartar dynasties. The other chapter deals with the Renaissance and the Protestant Revolution. It is surprising because there is so little of the Renaissance and of Protestantism in it. Petrarch, Erasmus, Sir Thomas More, and the great artists remain unhonored and unsung: for they are barely mentioned. There is a poor description of mediæval scholasticism, little or nothing of humanism, and a fairly good account of the scientific aspect of the Renaissance. I searched for the origins of Protestantism, and after a great effort I found a few lines about Martin Luther tucked away in the corner of a long dissertation on Charles V, a monarch whom Mr. Wells considers commonplace, with a "thick upper lip and long clumsy chin." Scarcely a word is to be found about Calvin, Knox, Zwingli, and Cranmer. All the space that poor Queen Elizabeth gets is that she is "among those present" in a list of Tudor monarchs. But let that good lady not worry. Shakespeare has escaped Mr. Wells's notice altogether. Much space is devoted to Machiavelli, Charles V, Francis I, and Loyola.

The reader now encounters long digressions that point in every direction. One of these is interesting and important. It is on education. Because the Roman Empire failed to establish a system of popular education, it did not develop what Mr. Wells suggestively calls "educational government"; and therefore it had to rely upon political and military government. The written word meant nothing to the average man of ancient times. Owing to this lack of popular education, ancient civilization was "a light in a dark lantern." It was Christianity that first relied successfully upon the power of the written word "to link great multitudes of diverse men together in common enterprises." Islam later imitated Christianity. By establishing schools for popular teaching the Catholic Church grasped the idea of educational government, the ideal of the future. What was lacking was the means to get knowledge and information so that this new type of government could function. That came with printing. Mr. Wells cannot overemphasize the importance of printing. In a highly interesting and instructive manner he explains how "paper liberated the human mind," causing the spread of knowledge so that "it ceased to be the privilege of a favored minority." All modern progress and all hope for the future are inevitably bound up with the printed page.

IV

Book VIII concerns itself with the period from the seventeenth century to the year 1920. The leading theme is the development of the "Great Power" idea and its evil influence upon humanity. It was, Mr. Wells believes, responsible for the dynastic wars of the seventeenth and eighteenth centuries, the English, American, and French Revolutions, the nationalistic wars of the nineteenth century, and the World War of 1914. According to Mr. Wells the modern state was a disastrous humbug that ousted Christianity as the chief religion in the Western World. At every opportunity he fires volleys of destructive criticism and withering sarcasm at the cult of nationalism, man's real, living god. A nation he defines as "in effect any assembly, mixture, or confusion of people which is either afflicted by or wishes to be afflicted by a foreign office of its own in order that it should behave collectively as if it alone constituted humanity." He denounces this "megalomaniac nationalism," and pleads for a "natural political map of the world." This should be drawn by a commission of ethnologists, geographers, and sociologists instead of by scheming and intriguing diplomats, who settle little and unsettle much. To Mr. Wells nationalism is reactionary because the idea of a world state "was already in the world two thousand years ago, never more to leave it." Mr. Wells utterly fails to see that nationalism is not an idea that one can eliminate by merely taking thought. It is a sentiment that expresses the desire of a community to live its own life in its own way, unhampered by restrictions imposed by autocrats or by outsiders. (By the way, was not Mr. Wells himself a hundred per cent Britisher during the War?) Nationalism and democracy are one and inseparable. Had there been no subject nations there would have been no nationalism. Instead of being reactionary, it was the revolutionary force of the nineteenth century; and it is one of the great progressive forces of our day. Consider India, China, Ireland, Egypt, Imperialism, the very antithesis of nationalism, is what has brought so much woe to the world.

Incomparably the worst part of the *Outline* is that which deals with the French Revolution. Being totally devoid of any knowledge or understanding of this great movement, Mr. Wells naturally turns for support to Carlyle's *French Revolution*. Six precious pages are given to Carlylian gabble about marching women, Marat-in-the-bathtub, and similar sensational episodes; and only a few paragraphs to the tremendous work of the National Assembly that completely transformed France from a feudal to a modern state. Why is Carlyle's *French Revolution* considered a great work of "literature"? I am sure that I do not know. I have tried several times to read it, but I have never got very far. This famous book is hardly more than an endless series of disconnected ejaculations, emitted by the dyspeptic philosopher who was the greatest bore in all Christendom. Mr. Wells actually says that England was a "prospective ally" of the French Revolution because of the sympathies of the English liberals with the movement, but the French lost this "prospective ally" by foolishly declaring war upon England. Could there be any poorer judgment? Of course the true cause of the French Revolution was the "Great Power" game. It would take real ability to write a chapter on the French Revolution worse than this.

Mr. Wells's description of Napoleon is the most entertaining part of the *Outline*. There is a laugh in every

line. The reader must not expect a study of the Na-
poleonic period, military, political, or social. There is
nothing there worthy of serious notice. The interest in
the chapter lies entirely in Mr. Wells's view of Napoleon
himself. He is "down on" the Man of Destiny, obviously
for the same reason that he is "down on" Alexander,
Cæsar, and Charlemagne. Napoleon was a soldier and
no soldier could possibly have been a truly great man.
Mr. Wells considers Talleyrand an abler statesman than
Napoleon; Moreau and Hoche, abler generals; Czar
Alexander I had finer imagination. Mr. Wells also opines
that Napoleon III was "a much more supple and intelligent man" than his uncle. This is too much for Ernest
Barker, who shouts from the foot-notes that "this is a
paradox to which I cannot subscribe. Please put me
down as convinced of the opposite." "Even regarded as
a pest," pursues the imperturbable Mr. Wells, "Napoleon
was not of supreme rank; he killed far fewer people than
the influenza epidemic of 1918." His victories were due
to the fact that he was "marvellously lucky" in his
"flounderings"; his diplomatic triumphs were due to
"good fortune." Napoleon's career was the "raid of an
intolerable egotist across the disordered beginning of a
new time"; "his little imitative imagination was full of
a deep cunning dream of being Cæsar all over again."
He had wonderful opportunities for creating a new world;
and "there lacked nothing to this great occasion but a
noble imagination, and failing that, Napoleon could do no
more than strut upon the crest of this great mountain of
opportunity like a cockerel on a dunghill."

V

The account of the nineteenth century opens with a
description of the Industrial Revolution which is good;

but it is not as good as might be expected from Mr. Wells, who all his life has been interested in matters social and economic. What follows this account it is hard for me to state exactly. There is little in it, political, economic, or cultural, that I recognize as nineteenth-century history. The unification of Germany and of Italy get a nonchalant page or two; the reform movements in England hardly a mention; the United States barely a page. Of France, Russia, Austria, and Spain, there is little that is worth noting; not a word of industrial Germany or England; nothing about social legislation; nothing about the relation of church and state; nothing of literature and art. For Mr. Wells, Mazzini, John Bright, and Gambetta never lived; and Bismarck, Disraeli, and Cavour barely existed. There is not a word about the woman's movement; and for this omission I leave the author of *Ann Veronica* to the tender mercies of the psychoanalysts.

What then is the chapter, a hundred pages long, about? It is all about Mr. Wells—Mr. Wells's view of this, of that, and of the other person or thing. Digressions and digressions from digressions devour most of the precious pages. As I am especially interested in the nineteenth century I was dismayed. I read the chapter over again and finally came to the conclusion that Mr. Wells did have in mind an original way of treating this period: to make a study of Darwin, Marx, and Gladstone as the truly great personalities of the century. The selection is a happy one. With these personalities as a basis he could have written a study of the scientific, the revolutionary, and the liberal movements of the period that would have been original and profound. But he fails utterly.

There is a fairly good description of the influence of Darwinism, though it is not brought up to date. For

example, Mr. Wells wholly overlooks the recent criticisms
of the doctrine of "natural selection." He shows how
Darwinism was perverted by Kiplingism; and he actually
devotes a whole page to *Stalky and Co.* to explain how
Kipling led the "children of the middle and upper class
British public back to the Jungle to learn 'the law.'"
Nothing more does the author tell us about the progress
of science during the nineteenth century.

The explanation of socialism is scrappy and totally inadequate. Mr. Wells devotes four pages to Robert Owen
and not a word to Saint-Simon or Fourier! To Karl
Marx and his ideas he devotes a page, and a very poor
page. From the *Outline* one can get almost no idea of
the meaning of Marxism, now of overshadowing interest
to the world. Mr. Wells fights shy of Marx. For a
moment he hovers over Marx's beard, and then flees,
fearful of being entangled in that vast, "uneventful"
growth.

No sooner does the *Outline* mention the name of Gladstone than the author lashes himself into a fury and falls
upon that mirror of Christian statesmanship with hammer
and tongs. He calls Gladstone a profoundly ignorant
man, who "was educated at Eton College and at Christ
Church, Oxford, and his mind never recovered from the
process." The description of Gladstone is unforgetable:
"He was a white-faced, black-haired man of incredible
energy, with eyes like an eagle's, wrath almost divine,
and the 'finest barytone voice in Europe.'" Mr. Wells
brings a strange accusation against Gladstone, namely,
that he made "nationality his guiding political principle."
In spite of the fact that, at this charge, Ernest Barker
and Gilbert Murray fire volleys of protests from the foot-
notes, Mr. Wells continues to belabor Gladstone with
undiminished zeal.

We now come to Ireland. At the hand of Mr. Wells

Ireland fares badly indeed. His treatment of the Irish Question is pervaded by a marked anti-Irish bias. Whenever Ireland comes into the *Outline* she comes in for a sound drubbing. Mr. Wells reproaches the Irish for having "a long memory for their own wrongs" and actually condones England's indifference. He slides over and even excuses Cromwell's massacres. The great loss of population in Ireland during the nineteenth century he lays to the overcultivation of the potato; and he says nothing of English landlordism with its "rack-renting" and of the savage persecution of the Irish. Now and then the readers of the *Outline* will be astonished at exhibitions of prejudice, strange indeed in a man like Mr. Wells, whose outlook is as wide as the world itself. He unmistakably dislikes the "dark whites," or Mediterranean peoples, and greatly admires the "Nordic" races, or northern Europeans. This comes out very strongly in his treatment of the Irish who, he says, are "of the dark 'Mediterranean' strain, pre-Nordic and pre-Aryan." The "dark whites" are inclined to be superstitious, but the "Nordics" are free, bold, and rational. "The English were naturally a non-sacerdotal people; they had the Northman's dislike for and disbelief in priests"; but the Irish "found the priest congenial."

At last we come to the World War. The fundamental cause was the "Great Power" game that Europe had been playing since the seventeenth century and which now culminated in universal slaughter. "All the great states of Europe before 1914," declares Mr. Wells, "were in a condition of aggressive nationalism and drifting toward war; the government of Germany did but lead in the general movement." He gives a brief and spirited account of the war, which he believes could have been ended before 1916, had the Allied army chiefs consented to use the tank sooner. "But the professional military mind is by necessity an inferior and unimaginative mind; no man of high intellectual quality would willingly imprison his gifts in such a calling." Mr. Wells's judgment of the Peace Conference follows closely that of Mr. Keynes; for the story of the Conference he relies mainly on Mr. Dillon's gossipy book.

In Book IX the historian becomes prophet. He climbs to the top of a high mountain to view the Promised Land of Future Humanity. In the distance, he sees humanity attaining its goal after the long, dreary march through the centuries. In one of the most eloquent chapters of the book, Man's Coming of Age, he describes this goal, "a world league of men," peaceful and happy. What does Mr. Wells the prophet see?

(1) A world with a common religion, neither Christianity, Islam, nor Buddhism, but "religion itself, pure and undefiled."

(2) A system of world education.

(3) A world in which there are no armies, no navies, and no unemployed.

(4) A universal organization for scientific research.

(5) A democratic world government.

(6) An economic order in which private enterprise exploits natural resources no longer as a "robber master" but as "a useful, valued, and well-rewarded servant."

(7) An honest and efficient electoral system.

(8) An honest and efficient currency system.

This world order must inevitably come, for "human history becomes more and more a race between education and catastrophe." The element in the population that will lead mankind to the World State is that between the upper and the working classes, an element "capable of being aroused to a sense not merely of wickedness but of the danger of systematic self-seeking in a strained, impoverished, and sorely tried world." This

*bourgeois éclairé** must inaugurate an educational and religious revival to enlighten all classes "by pen and per-
suasion, in schools and colleges and books, and in the
highways and byways of public life."

VI

Is Mr. Wells one of the immortals? It would hardly
be an exaggeration to say that he has been the most influential writer in English of our day. And his influence has not been merely literary. He has the power,
rare in a novelist, of affecting directly and profoundly
the political and social views of his readers. Then there
is that manner of his, that spiritual-romantic manner,
that invites you to go with him in the search for the Holy
Grail of social salvation. If ever there was a man who
viewed society as a spiritual organism, that man is Mr.
Wells. It is not surprising, therefore, that the fine spirits
among the rising generation have looked to him as the
prophet of a new and nobler order of society. And yet
I say, and I say it regretfully, that in my opinion Mr.
Wells is not an immortal. He will not pass into future
generations. My reading of the *Outline* has convinced
me of it more than ever. In this book, as in his others,
he shows his fatal weakness. The beginnings of a Wells
book are superb, wonderful, inspiring. The problem presented is a universal one, and the characters approach it
with magnificent strides. The reader feels that he is
about to see a solution of the problem worthy of its
greatness. Or perhaps Mr. Wells, like Michelangelo and
Rodin, will leave his creation superbly unfinished, because
he feels himself inadequate to express the greatness of
his concepts. But what does take place? When you
are about half-way through, there is a break; a sudden

* *Bourgeois éclairé*, enlightened middle class.

descent begins; and the book fizzles out completely in
the end. Over and over again have I had this sad experience. *Ann Veronica* is in revolt against her family
and society. She runs away from home to live her own
life, to save her own soul, to earn her own living. In
the end, she marries and lives happy ever after. Rem-
ington in *The New Machiavelli* is appalled at the human
waste and confusion of present society. In a "white
passion of statecraft" he dreams of a new statesmanship
that will end this muddle. What does he do? He establishes institutions for the Endowment of Motherhood.
Stratton in *The Passionate Friends* desires to be truly
a "world man." He goes to Africa, to Asia, to America
to study world problems in order to deal efficiently with
them. At last he finds a way. He establishes an international publishing house that sells cheap editions of good
books. Trafford in *Marriage* is a great scientist who
is driven into commercialism by the needs of an extrava-
gant wife. He is distraught, so he and his wife go to the
wilds of Labrador to think it over. There he finds that
he cares more for his wife than for anything else. He
returns home happy, and does—nothing. Lady Harman
in *The Wife of Sir Isaac Harman* resents the possessive
attitude of her wealthy husband. She has dreams of
beauty and of freedom, and falls in love with an artistic
and intellectual friend. She has several daring adventures. Suddenly her husband dies. Now she is free.
What does she do? She devotes her life to the establishment of co-operative apartments for the deserving
middle class. Job Huss in *The Undying Fire* is stricken
with misfortune. He is ill of cancer; his school burns
down; his son is reported dead. The problem of human
suffering is presented, truly a great problem. In the end
Job Huss recovers; his school is rebuilt; and his son turns
up alive. Desiring to devote his life to the cause of hu-

manity, Huss builds an Imperial Institute that will teach people history, geography, and ethnology. *The Outline of History* begins in the magnificent way that I have described. The plan of the book is given in bold strokes. It is to rewrite history so that the great purpose of the life of man on earth shall become evident. At last history has found its true use, to discover the future. And what is humanity's future, according to Mr. Wells's prophecy? It is a vague, sentimental, middle-class, middle-age, mid-Victorian vision of peace and prosperity. What is there in this vision to which Samuel Smiles would have objected! Was it for this that the hairy ape-man shambled into full humanity! Was this to be the outcome

> Of Caesar's hand and Plato's brain,
> Of Lord Christ's heart and Shakespeare's strain!

What ails Mr. Wells? What is the disease that proves him mortal? This is what I now propose to diagnose. Mr. Wells is a man of extraordinary imagination, extraordinary both for its vividness and versatility; it is poetic, scientific, religious, social, political, literary. In my opinion he is the most highly imaginative human being now living. But his intellect is not extraordinary. Toward the great problems of the world his imagination makes a magnificent stride; but his intellect cannot keep pace with it. Hence in the realm of ideas he is suggestive, not creative. He arouses, he stimulates, he throws out fine hints, he suggests new ways of looking at things; but he is utterly incapable of being the architect of any new system of thought, be it political, social, moral, or philosophical. Condemned to sterility, he becomes sentimental and half-mystical. Whenever he does succeed in giving birth to an idea, it immediately expires in a sigh. What political theories has he fashioned comparable to those of Rousseau, Locke, or Mill? What social theories, comparable to those of Comte or Saint-Simon? What interpretation of history comparable to that of Buckle or of Marx? Indeed, what characters in fiction has he created that have the immortality of Emma Bovary, Père Goriot, Pickwick, Anna Karénina, Rudin, Becky Sharp, Bergeret, Raskolnikov, Pecksniff, or Tess of the D'Urbervilles?

The *Outline*, with all its shortcomings, is nevertheless a *tour de force* such as only a remarkably versatile man like Mr. Wells could have accomplished. It gives a new model for the writing of history, with its magnificent sweep, wide range, deep sympathies, and progressive view-point. Once immersed in these volumes, students of history no less than others will gain an indelible impression of going through a great and abiding experience. To read the book is in itself a liberal education.

THE EDITORIAL ESSAY

JOSEPH ADDISON

FEMALE ORATORS

Joseph Addison (1672–1719) is the foremost figure among the essayists of the eighteenth century. He was the son of an English clergyman, in a country parish. He was sent to Oxford, and completed his education by European travel. He gained literary recognition by a poem on the battle of Blenheim, and was rewarded by various political offices. When his friend Steele began the *Tatler*, Addison contributed a number of essays to it, and in the *Spectator* the two men worked together.

The age in which they lived was a coarse one. Profane speech and bad manners were the fashion. Addison was too shrewd a man to attack these things directly, or to denounce them violently; that would only bring ridicule upon him. But if he could adroitly manage to make these things appear ridiculous, he might gain his end. So in the *Spectator* he introduces imaginary characters, and has these personages discuss the manners and follies of the day. The two essays here printed deal with conditions not peculiar to Addison's age: female orators and people who are constantly worrying about their health we have always with us.

The style of Addison has always been considered a model of English prose. Franklin in his autobiography tells how he improved his style by imitating Addison, in the same way that Stevenson describes in *A College Magazine*. Samuel Johnson said: "Whoever would attain an English style, familiar but not coarse, elegant but not ostentatious, must give his days and nights to the study of Addison."

JOSEPH ADDISON

FEMALE ORATORS

(From the *Spectator*, December 13, 1711)

We are told by some ancient authors, that Socrates was instructed in eloquence by a woman, whose name, if I am not mistaken, was Aspasia. I have indeed very often looked upon that art as the most proper for the female sex, and I think the universities would do well to consider whether they should not fill the rhetoric chairs with she professors.

It has been said in the praise of some men, that they could talk whole hours together upon anything; but it must be owned to the honor of the other sex, that there are many among them who can talk whole hours together upon nothing. I have known a woman branch out into a long extempore dissertation upon the edging of a petticoat, and chide her servant for breaking a china cup, in all the figures of rhetoric.

Were women admitted to plead in courts of judicature, I am persuaded they would carry the eloquence of the bar to greater heights than it has yet arrived at. If any one doubts this, let him but be present at those debates which frequently arise among the ladies of the British fishery.*

The first kind therefore of female orators which I shall take notice of, are those who are employed in stirring up the passions, a part of rhetoric in which Socrates

* British fishery, a playful reference to the famous fish-market at Billingsgate. The women who kept the stalls were so noted for profanity that the word billingsgate came to mean profane or scurrilous speech.

his wife * had perhaps made a greater proficiency than his above-mentioned teacher.

The second kind of female orators are those who deal in invectives, and who are commonly known by the name of the censorious. The imagination and elocution of this set of rhetoricians is wonderful. With what a fluency of invention, and copiousness of expression, will they enlarge upon every little slip in the behavior of another! With how many different circumstances, and with what variety of phrases, will they tell over the same story! I have known an old lady make an unhappy marriage the subject of a month's conversation. She blamed the bride in one place; pitied her in another; laughed at her in a third; wondered at her in a fourth; was angry with her in a fifth; and in short, wore out a pair of coach-horses in expressing her concern for her. At length, after having quite exhausted the subject on this side, she made a visit to the new-married pair, praised the wife for the prudent choice she had made, told her the unreasonable reflections which some malicious people had cast upon her, and desired that they might be better acquainted. The censure and approbation of this kind of women are therefore only to be considered as helps to discourse.

A third kind of female orators may be comprehended under the word gossips. Mrs. Fiddle Faddle is perfectly accomplished in this sort of eloquence; she launches out into descriptions of christenings, runs divisions upon an head-dress, knows every dish of meat that is served up in her neighborhood, and entertains her company a whole afternoon together with the wit of her little boy, before he is able to speak.

The coquet may be looked upon as a fourth kind of female orator. To give herself the larger field for dis-

* His wife, modern usage would be, Socrates's wife.

course, she hates and loves in the same breath, talks to her lap-dog or parrot, is uneasy in all kinds of weather, and in every part of the room: she has false quarrels and feigned obligations to all the men of her acquaintance; sighs when she is not sad, and laughs when she is not merry. The coquet is in particular a great mistress of that part of oratory which is called action, and indeed seems to speak for no other purpose, but as it gives her an opportunity of stirring a limb, or varying a feature, of glancing her eyes, or playing with her fan.

As for news-mongers, politicians, mimics, story-tellers, with other characters of that nature, which give birth to loquacity, they are as commonly found among the men as the women; for which reason I shall pass them over in silence.

I have often been puzzled to assign a cause why women should have this talent of a ready utterance in so much greater perfection than men. I have sometimes fancied that they have not a retentive power, or the faculty of suppressing their thoughts, as men have, but that they are necessitated to speak everything they think, and if so, it would perhaps furnish a very strong argument to the Cartesians, for the supporting of their doctrine that the soul always thinks. But as several are of opinion that the fair sex are not altogether strangers to the art of dissembling and concealing their thoughts, I have been forced to relinquish that opinion, and have therefore endeavored to seek after some better reason. In order to it, a friend of mine, who is an excellent anatomist, has promised me by the first opportunity to dissect a woman's tongue, and to examine whether there may not be in it certain juices which render it so wonderfully voluble or flippant, or whether the fibres of it may not be made up of a finer or more pliant thread, or whether there are not in it some particular muscles which dart it up and down by such sudden glances and vibrations; or whether in the last place, there may not be certain undiscovered channels running from the head and the heart to this little instrument of loquacity, and conveying into it a perpetual affluence of animal spirits. Nor must I omit the reason which Hudibras * has given, why those who can talk on trifles speak with the greatest fluency; namely, that the tongue is like a race-horse, which runs the faster the lesser weight it carries.

Which of these reasons soever may be looked upon as the most probable, I think the Irishman's thought was very natural, who after some hours' conversation with a female orator, told her, that he believed her tongue was very glad when she was asleep, for that it had not a moment's rest all the while she was awake.

That excellent old ballad of The Wanton Wife of Bath has the following remarkable lines:

> I think, quoth Thomas, Women's Tongues
> Of Aspen Leaves are made.

And Ovid, though in the description of a very barbarous circumstance, tells us, that when the tongue of a beautiful female was cut out, and thrown upon the ground, it could not forbear muttering even in that posture.

If a tongue would be talking without a mouth, what could it have done when it had all its organs of speech, and accomplices of sound about it? I might here mention the story of the pippin-woman, had not I some reason to look upon it as fabulous.

I must confess I am so wonderfully charmed with the music of this little instrument, that I would by no means discourage it. All that I aim at by this dissertation is, to cure it of several disagreeable notes, and in particular

---

* *Hudibras*, the title of a famous satirical poem by Samuel Butler.

of those little jarrings and dissonances which arise from anger, censoriousness, gossiping and coquetry. In short, I would always have it tuned by good nature, truth, discretion and sincerity.

JOSEPH ADDISON

LIVING IN A PAIR OF SCALES

Letters to the editor appear in almost every journal. Although the editors of the *Spectator* did not publish their names, in the first number of the paper they gave an address to which letters might be sent. These letters often provided material for an essay. Sometimes the editors wrote these letters themselves, as one might set up a straw man merely to knock him down. Such is the case with the letter in the essay that follows. In plan, the essay is typical of many of the *Spectator* papers, and indeed of the periodical essay of that period. The editor first introduces an imaginary character who is to personify some weakness of human nature; in this case it is the man who lived in a pair of scales. When he has been brought forward, and made to appear sufficiently ridiculous, the editor then dismisses him and proceeds to comment upon the trait of character shown, with advice as to a better course of conduct. Note the play of quiet humor in the essay.

JOSEPH ADDISON

LIVING IN A PAIR OF SCALES

(From the *Spectator*, March 29, 1711)

The following letter will explain itself, and needs no apology.

"*SIR*,

"I am one of that sickly tribe who are commonly known by the name of valetudinarians, and do confess to you, that I first contracted this ill habit of body, or rather of mind, by the study of physic. I no sooner began to peruse books of this nature, but I found my pulse was irregular, and scarce ever read the account of any disease that I did not fancy myself afflicted with. Dr. Sydenham's learned treatise of fevers threw me into a lingering hectic, which hung upon me all the while I was reading that excellent piece. I then applied myself to the study of several authors, who have written upon phthisical distempers, and by that means fell into a consumption, 'til at length, growing very fat, I was in a manner shamed out of that imagination. Not long after this I found in myself all the symptoms of the gout, except pain, but was cured of it by a treatise upon the gravel, written by a very ingenious author, who (as it is usual for physicians to convert one distemper into another) eased me of the gout by giving me the stone. I at length studied myself into a complication of distempers; but accidentally taking into my hand that ingenious discourse written by Sanctorius I was resolved to direct myself by a scheme of rules, which I had collected from his observations. The learned world are very well acquainted with that gentleman's invention; who, for the better carrying on of his experiments, contrived a certain mathematical chair, which was so artificially hung upon springs, that it would weigh anything as well as a pair of scales. By this means he discovered how many ounces of his food passed by perspiration, what quantity of it was turned into nourishment, and how much went away by the other channels and distributions of nature.

"Having provided myself with this chair, I used to study, eat, drink, and sleep in it; in so much that I may be said, for these three last years, to have lived in a pair of scales. I compute myself, when I am in full health, to be precisely two hundredweight, falling short of it about a pound after a day's fast, and exceeding it as much after a very full meal; so that it is my continual employment, to trim the balance between these two volatile pounds in my constitution. In my ordinary meals I fetch myself up to two hundredweight and a half pound; and if after having dined I find myself fall short of it, I drink just so much small beer, or eat such a quantity of bread, as is sufficient to make me weight. In my greatest excesses I do not transgress more than the other half pound; which, for my health's sake, I do the first Monday in every month. As soon as I find myself duly poised after dinner, I walk till I have perspired five ounces and four scruples; and when I discover, by my chair, that I am so far reduced, I fall to my books, and study away three ounces more. As for the remaining parts of the pound, I keep no account of them. I do not dine and sup by the clock, but by my chair, for when that informs me my pound of food is exhausted I conclude myself to be hungry, and lay in another with all diligence. In my days of abstinence I lose a pound and a half, and on solemn fasts am two pound lighter than on other days in the year.

"I allow myself, one night with another, a quarter of a pound of sleep within a few grains more or less; and if upon my rising I find that I have not consumed my whole quantity, I take out the rest in my chair. Upon an exact calculation of what I expended and received the last year, which I always register in a book, I find the medium to be two hundredweight, so that I cannot discover that I am impaired one ounce in my health during a whole twelve-month. And yet, Sir, notwithstanding this my great care to ballast myself equally every day, and to keep my body in its proper poise, so it is that I find myself in a sick and languishing condition. My complexion is grown very sallow, my pulse low, and my body hydropsical. Let me therefore beg you, Sir, to consider me as your patient, and to give me more certain rules to walk by than those I have already observed, and you will very much oblige

Your Humble Servant."

This letter puts me in mind of an Italian epitaph written on the monument of a valetudinarian: *Stavo ben, ma per star meglio, sto qui:** which it is impossible to translate. The fear of death often proves mortal, and sets people on methods to save their lives, which infallibly destroy them. This is a reflection made by some historians, upon observing that there are many more thousands killed in a flight than in a battle, and may be applied to those multitudes of imaginary sick persons that break their constitutions by physic, and throw themselves into the arms of death, by endeavoring to escape it. This method is not only dangerous, but below the practice of a reasonable creature. To consult the preservation of life, as the only end of it, to make our health our business, to engage in no action that is not part of a

---

* *Stavo ben,* etc. It may be freely translated thus: I was well, I would be better, and here I am.

regimen, or course of physic, are purposes so abject, so mean, so unworthy human nature, that a generous soul would rather die than submit to them. Besides that a continual anxiety for life vitiates all the relishes of it, and casts a gloom over the whole face of nature; as it is impossible we should take delight in anything that we are every moment afraid of losing.

I do not mean, by what I have here said, that I think any one to blame for taking due care of their health. On the contrary, as cheerfulness of mind and capacity for business are in a great measure the effects of a well-tempered constitution, a man cannot be at too much pains to cultivate and preserve it. But this care, which we are prompted to not only by common sense but by duty and instinct, should never engage us in groundless fears, melancholy apprehensions and imaginary distempers, which are natural to every man who is more anxious to live than how to live. In short, the preservation of life should be only a secondary concern, and the direction of it our principal. If we have this frame of mind, we shall take the best means to preserve life, without being over-solicitous about the event; and shall arrive at that point of felicity which Martial has mentioned as the perfection of happiness, of neither fearing nor wishing for death.

In answer to the gentleman who tempers his health by ounces and by scruples, and instead of complying with those natural solicitations of hunger and thirst, drowsiness or love of exercise, governs himself by the prescriptions of his chair, I shall tell him a short fable. Jupiter, says the mythologist, to reward the piety of a certain countryman promised to give him whatever he would ask. The countryman desired that he might have the management of the weather in his own estate. He obtained his request, and immediately distributed rain, snow, and sunshine, among his several fields, as he thought the nature of the soil required. At the end of the year, when he expected to see a more than ordinary crop, his harvest fell infinitely short of that of his neighbors. Upon which (says the fable) he desired Jupiter to take the weather again into his own hands, or that otherwise he should utterly ruin himself.

RICHARD STEELE
THE STAGE–COACH

The following essay belongs in the series known as the Sir Roger de Coverley papers, which appeared in the *Spectator*. Its connection with the series, however, is confined to the mention of Sir Roger in the first sentence. The real subject of the essay is behavior in public conveyances. Travellers by stage-coach were far more at the mercy of a quarrelsome or impertinent fellow passenger than are travellers to-day. In this essay Steele teaches a needed lesson, yet does it with such good humor, such touches of wit, such deft characterization, that we are pleasantly carried along, and cannot help agreeing with his conclusion. It is an excellent example of the method by which the editors of the *Spectator* set about to improve the manners of the time. For biographical sketch of Steele, see page 2.

RICHARD STEELE

THE STAGE–COACH

(From the *Spectator*, August 1, 1711)

Having notified to my good friend Sir Roger that I should set out for London the next day, his horses were ready at the appointed hour in the evening; and attended by one of his grooms, I arrived at the county town at twilight, in order to be ready for the stage-coach the day following. As soon as we arrived at the inn, the servant who waited upon me, inquired of the chamberlain in my hearing what company he had for the coach? The fellow answered, Mrs. Betty Arable, the great fortune, and the widow her mother; a recruiting officer (who took a place because they were to go); young Squire Quickset her cousin (that her mother wished her to be married to); Ephraim the Quaker, her guardian; and a gentleman that had studied himself dumb from Sir Roger de Coverley's. I observed by what he said of myself, that according to his office he dealt much in intelligence; and doubted not but there was some foundation for his reports of the rest of the company, as well as for the whimsical account he gave of me. The next morning at daybreak we were all called; and I, who know my own natural shyness, and endeavor to be as little liable to be disputed with as possible, dressed immediately, that I might make no one wait. The first preparation for our setting out was, that the captain's half-pike was placed near the coachman, and a drum behind the coach. In the meantime the drummer, the captain's equipage, was very loud, that none of the captain's things should be placed so as to be spoiled; upon which his cloak bag was fixed in the seat of the coach; and the captain himself, according to a frequent, though invidious behavior of military men, ordered his man to look sharp, that none but one of the ladies should have the place he had taken fronting to the coach box.

We were in some little time fixed in our seats, and sat with that dislike which people not too good-natured usually conceive of each other at first sight. The coach jumbled us insensibly into some sort of familiarity: and we had not moved above two miles, when the widow asked the captain what success he had in his recruiting? The officer, with a frankness he believed very graceful, told her, "That indeed he had but very little luck, and had suffered much by desertion, therefore should be glad to end his warfare in the service of her or her fair daughter. In a word," continued he, "I am a soldier, and to be plain is my character: you see me, madam, young, sound, and impudent; take me yourself, widow, or give me to her, I will be wholly at your disposal. I am a soldier of fortune, ha!" This was followed by a vain laugh of his own, and a deep silence of all the rest of the company. I had nothing left for it but to fall fast asleep, which I did with all speed. "Come," said he, "resolve upon it, we will make a wedding at the next town: we will wake this pleasant companion who is fallen asleep, to be the brideman," and giving the Quaker a clap on the knee he concluded: "This sly saint, who, I'll warrant, understands what's what as well as you or I, widow, shall give the bride as father."

The Quaker, who happened to be a man of smartness, answered: "Friend, I take it in good part that thou hast given me the authority of a father over this comely and virtuous child; and I must assure thee, that if I have the giving her. I shall not bestow her on thee. Thy mirth, friend, savoreth of folly: thou art a person of a light mind; thy drum is a type of thee, it soundeth because it is empty. Verily, it is not from thy fulness, but thy emptiness that thou hast spoken this day. Friend, friend, we have hired this coach in partnership with thee, to carry us to the great city; we cannot go any other way. This worthy mother must hear thee if thou wilt needs utter thy follies; we cannot help it, friend, I say; if thou wilt we must hear thee: but if thou wert a man of understanding, thou wouldst not take advantage of thy courageous countenance to abash us children of peace. Thou art, thou sayest, a soldier; give quarter to us, who cannot resist thee. Why didst thou fleer at our friend, who feigned himself asleep? he said nothing: but how dost thou know what he containeth? If thou speakest improper things in the hearing of this virtuous young virgin, consider it is an outrage against a distressed person that cannot get from thee. To speak indiscreetly what we are obliged to hear, by being hasped up with thee in this public vehicle, is in some degree assaulting on the highroad."

Here Ephraim paused, and the captain with an happy and uncommon impudence (which can be convicted and support itself at the same time) cried: "Faith, friend, I thank thee; I should have been a little impertinent if thou hadst not reprimanded me. Come, thou art, I see, a smoaky * old fellow, and I'll be very orderly the ensuing part of the journey. I was going to give myself airs, but, ladies, I beg pardon."

The captain was so little out of humor, and our company was so far from being soured by this little ruffle, that Ephraim and he took a particular delight in being agreeable to each other for the future; and assumed their different provinces in the conduct of the company. Our

* Smoaky, a slang phrase of the time, meaning, quick to smell out an idea.

reckonings, apartments, and accommodation, fell under Ephraim; and the captain looked to all disputes on the road, as the good behavior of our coachman, and the right we had of taking place as going to London of all vehicles coming from thence. The occurrences we met with were ordinary, and very little happened which could entertain by the relation of them. But when I considered the company we were in, I took it for no small good fortune that the whole journey was not spent in impertinences, which to one part of us might be an entertainment, to the other a suffering. What therefore Ephraim said when we were almost arrived at London, had to me an air not only of good understanding but good breeding. Upon the young lady's expressing her satisfaction in the journey, and declaring how delightful it had been to her, Ephraim declared himself as follows: "There is no ordinary part of human life which expresseth so much a good mind, and a right inward man, as his behavior upon meeting with strangers, especially such as may seem the most unsuitable companions to him; such a man, when he falleth in the way with persons of simplicity and innocence, however knowing he may be in the ways of men, will not vaunt himself thereof, but will rather hide his superiority to them, that he may not be painful unto them. My good friend," continued he, turning to the officer, "thee and I are to part by and by, and peradventure we may never meet again; but be advised by a plain man: Modes and apparel are but trifles to the real man, therefore do not think such a man as thyself terrible for thy garb, nor such a one as me contemptible for mine. When two such as thee and I meet, with affections as we ought to have toward each other, thou shouldst rejoice to see my peaceable demeanor, and I should be glad to see thy strength and ability to protect me in it."

THE REFLECTIVE ESSAY

FRANCIS BACON

STUDIES; TRUTH; TRAVEL; RICHES; GREAT PLACE; FRIENDSHIP

Francis Bacon (1561–1626) was one of the great figures of the Elizabethan age. His father was Lord Keeper of the Great Seal under Queen Elizabeth. Francis Bacon grew up in the court; he was educated at Cambridge University, and afterward studied law. He became a member of Parliament, where he was noted for his ability to say much in few words. Ben Jonson says of him: "There happened in my time one noble speaker who was full of gravity in his speaking. No man ever spake more neatly, more pressly, more weightily, or suffered less emptiness, less idleness in what he uttered. His hearers could not cough or look aside from him without loss. The fear of every man that heard him was lest he should make an end." Under James I Bacon was made Lord High Chancellor of England, the highest judicial position in the land. He was accused of receiving bribes, tried, and removed from office. He admitted receiving money from suitors, but declared that he had not allowed this to influence his decisions. The remainder of his life he spent in retirement, devoting himself to study and writing. Most of his works are written in Latin and deal with philosophy and science. His fame as an English writer rests upon his essays. They are marked by clearness and conciseness of style, depth of thought, and occasional beauty of imagery. They are full of quotable sentences. To use his own words, some books "are to be tasted, others to be swallowed, and some few to be chewed and digested." His essays are among the books to be chewed and digested.

FRANCIS BACON

OF STUDIES

(This and the five following essays are from *Essays, or Counsels, Civil and Moral.*)

Studies serve for delight, for ornament, and for ability. Their chief use for delight is in privateness and retiring; for ornament is in discourse; and for ability is in the judgment and disposition of business. For expert men can execute, and perhaps judge of particulars, one by one; but the general counsels, and the plots and marshalling of affairs, come best from those that are learned. To spend too much time in studies is sloth, to use them too much for ornament is affectation, to make judgment only by their rules is the humor of a scholar. They perfect nature, and are perfected by experience. For natural abilities are like natural plants, that need pruning by study; and studies themselves do give forth directions too much at large, except they be bounded in by experience. Crafty men contemn studies, simple men admire them, and wise men use them; for they teach not their own use, but that is a wisdom without them and above them, won by observation.

Read not to contradict and confute, nor to believe and take for granted, nor to find talk and discourse, but to weigh and consider. Some books are to be tasted, others to be swallowed, and some few to be chewed and digested; that is, some books are to be read only in parts; others to be read, but not curiously; and some few to be read wholly, and with diligence and attention. Some books also may be read by deputy, and extracts made of them by others; but that would be only in the less important arguments and the meaner sort of books; else distilled books are like common distilled waters, flashy things. Reading maketh a full man, conference a ready man, and writing an exact man. And therefore if a man write little, he had need have a great memory; if he confer little, he had need have a present wit; and if he read little, he had need have much cunning to seem to know that he doth not.

Histories make men wise, poets witty, the mathematics subtile, natural philosophy deep, moral grave, logic and rhetoric able to contend. "Abeunt studia in mores."* Nay, there is no stond † or impediment in the wit but may be wrought out by fit studies, like as diseases of the body may have appropriate exercises. Bowling is good for the stone and reins, shooting for the lungs and breast, gentle walking for the stomach, riding for the head, and the like. So if a man's wit be wandering, let him study the mathematics; for in demonstrations, if his wit be called away never so little, he must begin again. If his wit be not apt to distinguish or find differences, let him study the schoolmen, for they are *cymini sectores*.‡ If he be not apt to beat over matters, and to call up one thing to prove and illustrate another, let him study the lawyers' cases. So every defect of the mind may have a special receipt.

OF TRUTH

"What is truth?" said jesting Pilate;§ and would not stay for an answer. Certainly there be that delight in giddiness; and count it a bondage to fix a belief; affecting free will in thinking, as well as in acting. And

---

* *Abeunt*, etc., studies pass over into habits.
† Stond, an obsolete form of stand, here used to mean a halt.
‡ *Cymini sectores*, splitters of hairs.
§ Pilate. See *New Testament*, John, xviii, 38.

though the sects of philosophers of that kind be gone, yet there remain certain discoursing wits which are of the same veins, though there be not so much blood in them as was in those of the ancients. But it is not only the difficulty and labor which men take in finding out of truth; nor again, that when it is found it imposeth upon men's thoughts, that doth bring lies in favor; but a natural though corrupt love of the lie itself. One of the later school of the Grecians examineth the matter, and is at a stand to think what should be in it that men should love lies, where neither they make for pleasure, as with poets; nor for advantage, as with the merchant; but for the lie's sake. But I cannot tell; this same truth is a naked and open daylight, that doth not show the masks, and mummeries, and triumphs of the world half so stately and daintily as candle-lights. Truth may perhaps come to the price of a pearl, that showeth best by day; but it will not rise to the price of a diamond or carbuncle, that showeth best in varied lights. A mixture of a lie doth ever add pleasure. Doth any man doubt, that if there were taken out of men's minds vain opinions, flattering hopes, false valuations, imaginations as one would, and the like, but it would leave the minds of a number of men poor shrunken things, full of melancholy and indisposition, and unpleasing to themselves? One of the Fathers,* in great severity, called poesy *vinum dæmonum*,† because it filleth the imagination, and yet it is but with the shadow of a lie. But it is not the lie that passeth through the mind, but the lie that sinketh in, and settleth in it, that doth the hurt; such as we spake of before.

But howsoever these things are thus in men's depraved judgments and affections, yet truth, which only doth judge itself, teacheth that the inquiry of truth, which is

* Fathers, St. Augustine, in his *Confessions*.
† *Vinum dæmonum*, the wine of demons.

the love-making or wooing of it; the knowledge of truth, which is the presence of it; and the belief of truth, which is the enjoying of it—is the sovereign good of human na-ture. The first creature of God, in the works of the days, was the light of the sense; the last was the light of reason; and his Sabbath work ever since is the illumination of his Spirit. First he breathed light upon the face of the matter, or chaos; then he breathed light into the face of man; and still he breatheth and inspireth light into the face of his chosen. The poet * that beautified the sect that was otherwise inferior to the rest, saith yet excellently well: "It is a pleasure to stand upon the shore, and to see ships tossed upon the sea; a pleasure to stand in the window of a castle, and to see a battle, and the adventures thereof below; but no pleasure is comparable to the standing upon the vantage ground of truth" (a hill not to be commanded, and where the air is always clear and serene) "and to see the errors, and wanderings, and mists, and tempests, in the vale below"; so always, that this prospect be with pity, and not with swelling or pride. Certainly, it is heaven upon earth to have a man's mind move in charity, rest in providence, and turn upon the poles of truth.

To pass from theological and philosophical truth to the truth of civil business, it will be acknowledged, even by those that practise it not, that clear and round dealing is the honor of man's nature; and that mixture of falsehood is like alloy in coin of gold and silver; which may make the metal work the better, but it embaseth it. For these winding and crooked courses are the goings of the serpent, which goeth basely upon the belly, and not upon the feet. There is no vice that doth so cover a man with shame as to be found false and perfidious.

* The poet, Lucretius, a Roman poet, of the "sect" of the Epicureans.

And therefore Montaigne saith prettily, when he inquired the reason why the word of the lie should be such a disgrace, and such an odious charge; saith he: "If it be well weighed, to say that a man lieth is as much as to say that he is brave toward God and a coward toward men." For a lie faces God, and shrinks from man. Surely the wickedness of falsehood, and breach of faith, cannot possibly be so highly expressed as in that it shall be the last peal to call the judgments of God upon the generations of men; it being foretold that when Christ cometh "He shall not find faith upon the earth." *

OF TRAVEL

Travel, in the younger sort, is a part of education; in the elder, a part of experience. He that travelleth into a country before he hath some entrance into the language, goeth to school, and not to travel. That young men travel under some tutor or grave servant, I allow well; so that he be such a one that hath the language and hath been in the country before, whereby he may be able to tell them what things are worthy to be seen in the country where they go, what acquaintances they are to seek, what exercises or discipline the place yieldeth. For else young men shall go hooded, and look abroad little.

It is a strange thing that in sea voyages, where there is nothing to be seen but sky and sea, men should make diaries; but in land travel, wherein so much is to be observed, for the most part they omit it; as if chance were fitter to be registered than observation. Let diaries therefore be brought in use.

The things to be seen and observed are: the courts of princes, specially when they give audience to ambassadors; the courts of justice, while they sit and hear

* Quoted from Luke, xviii, 8.

causes; and so of consistories ecclesiastic; the churches and monasteries, with the monuments which are therein extant; the walls and fortifications of cities and towns, and so the havens and harbors; antiquities and ruins; libraries, colleges, disputations, and lectures, where any are; shipping and navies; houses and gardens of state and pleasure near great cities, armories, arsenals, magazines, exchanges, burses, warehouses; exercises of horsemanship, fencing, training of soldiers, and the like; comedies, such whereunto the better sort of persons do resort; treasuries of jewels and robes, cabinets and rarities; and, to conclude, whatsoever is memorable in the places where they go: after all which the tutors or servants ought to make diligent inquiry. As for triumphs, masques, feasts, weddings, funerals, capital executions, and such shows, men need not to be put in mind of them; yet are they not to be neglected.

If you will have a young man to put his travel into a little room, and in short time to gather much, this you must do: first, as was said, he must have some entrance into the language before he goeth. Then he must have such a servant or tutor as knoweth the country, as was likewise said. Let him carry with him also some card or book describing the country where he travelleth, which will be a good key to his inquiry. Let him keep also a diary. Let him not stay long in one city or town; more or less as the place deserveth, but not long. Nay, when he stayeth in one city or town, let him change his lodging from one end and part of the town to another, which is a great adamant of acquaintance. Let him sequester himself from the company of his countrymen, and diet in such places where there is good company of the nation where he travelleth. Let him, upon his removes from one place to another, procure recommendation to some person of quality residing in the place whither he removeth, that he may use his favor in those things he desireth to see or know. Thus he may abridge his travel with much profit.

As for the acquaintance which is to be sought in travel, that which is most of all profitable is acquaintance with the secretaries and employed men of ambassadors; for so in travelling in one country he shall suck the experience of many. Let him also see and visit eminent persons in all kinds which are of great name abroad, that he may be able to tell how the life agreeth with the fame. For quarrels, they are with care and discretion to be avoided. They are commonly for mistresses, healths, place, and words. And let a man beware how he keepeth company with choleric and quarrelsome persons, for they will engage him into their own quarrels. When a traveller returneth home, let him not leave the countries where he hath travelled altogether behind him, but maintain a correspondence by letters with those of his acquaintance which are of most worth. And let his travel appear rather in his discourse than in his apparel or gesture; and in his discourse let him be rather advised in his answers than forward to tell stories. And let it appear that he doth not change his country manners for those of foreign parts, but only prick in some flowers of that he hath learned abroad, into the customs of his own country.

OF RICHES

I cannot call riches better than the baggage of virtue. The Roman word is better, "impedimenta," for as the baggage is to an army so is riches to virtue. It cannot be spared, nor left behind, but it hindereth the march; yea, and the care of it sometimes loseth or disturbeth the victory.

Of great riches there is no real use, except it be in the

distribution; the rest is but conceit. So saith Solomon, "Where much is, there are many to consume it; and what hath the owner but the sight of it with his eyes?"* The personal fruition in any man cannot reach to feel great riches: there is a custody of them, or a power of dole and donative of them, or a fame of them, but no solid use to the owner. Do you not see what feigned prices are set upon little stones and rarities? And what works of ostentation are undertaken, because there might seem to be some use of great riches? But then, you will say, they may be of use to buy men out of dangers or troubles. As Solomon saith: "Riches are as a stronghold in the imagination of the rich man."† But this is excellently expressed, that it is in imagination, and not always in fact. For certainly great riches have sold more men than they have bought out.

Seek not proud riches, but such as thou mayest get justly, use soberly, distribute cheerfully, and leave contentedly. Yet have no abstract nor friarly contempt of them; but distinguish, as Cicero saith well of Rabirius Posthumas, "in studio rei amplificandæ apparebat, non avaritiæ prædam, sed instrumentum bonitati quæri."‡ Hearken also to Solomon, and beware of hasty gathering of riches: "Qui festinat ad divitas, non erit insons." § The poets feign that when Plutus, which is riches, is sent from Jupiter, he limps, and goes slowly, but when he is sent from Pluto, he runs, and is swift of foot; meaning, that riches gotten by good means and just labor pace slowly, but when they come by the death of others, as by the course of inheritance, testaments, and the like,

---

* From Ecclesiastes, v, 11.   † From Proverbs, xviii, 11.

‡ *In studio*, etc. In the endeavor to increase his estate, it was evident that he sought, not the plunder of avarice, but the means of doing good.

§ *Qui festinat*, etc. He that makes waste to be rich shall not be innocent. Proverbs, xxviii, 22.

they come tumbling upon a man. But it might be applied likewise to Pluto, taking him for the devil. For when riches come from the devil, as by fraud, and oppression, and unjust means, they come upon speed.

The ways to enrich are many, and most of them foul. Parsimony is one of the best, and yet is not innocent, for it withholdeth men from works of liberality and charity. The improvement of the ground is the most natural obtaining of riches, for it is our great mother's blessing, the earth's; but it is slow. And yet, where men of great wealth do stoop to husbandry, it multiplieth riches exceedingly. I knew a nobleman in England that had the greatest audits of any man in my time: a great grazier, a great sheep master, a great timber man, a great collier, a great corn master, a great lead man, and so of iron, and a number of the like points of husbandry; so as the earth seemed a sea to him, in respect of the perpetual importation. It was truly observed by one, that himself came very hardly to a little riches, and very easily to great riches. For when a man's stock is come to that, that he can expect the prime of markets, and overcome those bargains which, for their greatness, are few men's money, and be partner in the industries of younger men, he cannot but increase mainly.

The gains of ordinary trades and vocations are honest, and furthered by two things chiefly, by diligence, and by a good name for good and fair dealing. But the gains of bargains are of a more doubtful nature, when men shall wait upon others' necessity; broke* by servants and instruments to draw them on; put off others cunningly that would be better chapmen†; and the like practices, which are crafty and naught. As for the chopping of bargains,—when a man buys, not to hold, but to sell over again,—that commonly grindeth double, both upon the

---

* Broke, negotiate.　　　　　　　† Chapmen, buyers.

seller and upon the buyer. Sharings do greatly enrich, if the hands be well chosen that are trusted. Usury is the certainest means of gain, though one of the worst, as that whereby a man doth eat his bread "in sudore vultus alieni,* and besides, doth plough upon Sundays. But yet, certain though it be, it hath flaws; for that the scriveners and brokers do value unsound men, to serve their own turn.

The fortune in being the first in an invention, or in a privilege, doth cause sometimes a wonderful overgrowth in riches, as it was with the first sugarman in the Canaries. Therefore, if a man can play the true logician, to have as well judgment as invention, he may do great matters, especially if the times be fit. He that resteth upon gains certain, shall hardly grow to great riches; and he that puts all upon adventures, doth oftentimes break, and come to poverty; it is good therefore to guard adventures with certainties that may uphold losses. Monopolies, and coemption of wares for resale, where they are not restrained, are great means to enrich; especially if the party have intelligence what things are like to come into request, and to store himself beforehand. Riches gotten by service, though it be of the best rise, yet when they are gotten by flattery, feeding humors, and other servile conditions, they may be placed amongst the worst. As for fishing for testaments and executorships (as Tacitus saith of Seneca, "Testamenta et orbos tanquam indagine capi"†), it is yet worse; by how much men submit themselves to meaner persons than in service.

Believe not much them that seem to despise riches, for they despise them that despair of them; and none worse

---

* *In sudore*, in the sweat of another's brow.

† *Testamenta*, etc. Wills and trusteeships were pulled in by him as if with a net.

when they come to them. Be not penny-wise; riches have wings, and sometimes they fly away of themselves, sometimes they must be set flying to bring in more.

Men leave their riches either to their kindred, or to the public; and moderate portions prosper best in both. A great estate left to an heir is as a lure to all the birds of prey round about to seize on him, if he be not the better stablished in years and judgment. Likewise glorious gifts and foundations are like sacrifices without salt; and but the painted sepulchres of alms, which soon will putrefy and corrupt inwardly. Therefore measure not thine advancements by quantity, but frame them by measure. And defer not charities till death; for certainly, if a man weigh it rightly, he that doth so, is rather liberal of another man's than of his own.

OF GREAT PLACE

Men in great place are thrice servants: servants of the sovereign or state, servants of fame, and servants of business; so as they have no freedom, neither in their persons, nor in their actions, nor in their times. It is a strange desire to seek power and to lose liberty; or to seek power over others and to lose power over a man's self. The rising unto place is laborious, and by pains men come to greater pains; and it is sometimes base, and by indignities men come to dignities. The standing is slippery, and the regress is either a downfall or at least an eclipse, which is a melancholy thing. "Cum non sis qui fueris, non esse cur velis vivere." * Nay, retire men cannot when they would, neither will they when it were reason, but are impatient of privateness, even in age and sickness, which require the shadow; like old townsmen

* *Cum non*, etc. Since you are not what you were, there is no reason why you should wish to live.

that will be still sitting at their street door, though thereby they offer age to scorn. Certainly, great persons had need to borrow other men's opinions to think themselves happy, for if they judge by their own feeling they cannot find it; but if they think with themselves what other men think of them, and that other men would fain be as they are, then they are happy as it were by report, when perhaps they find the contrary within. For they are the first that find their own griefs, though they be the last that find their own faults. Certainly, men in great fortunes are strangers to themselves, and while they are in the puzzle of business they have no time to tend their health either of body or mind. "Illi mors gravis incubat, qui notus nimis omnibus, ignotus moritur sibi." *

In place there is license to do good and evil, whereof the latter is a curse; for in evil the best condition is not to will, the second not to can. But power to do good is the true and lawful end of aspiring. For good thoughts, though God accept them, yet toward men are little better than good dreams, except they be put in act; and that cannot be without power and place, as the vantage and commanding ground. Merit and good works is the end of man's motion, and conscience of the same is the accomplishment of man's rest. For if a man can be partaker of God's theatre, he shall likewise be partaker of God's rest. "Et conversus Deus, ut aspiceret opera, quæ fecerunt manus suæ, vidit quod omnia essent bona nimis,"† and then the Sabbath.

In the discharge of thy place set before thee the best examples, for imitation is a globe of precepts. And after

---

* *Illi*, etc. Death presses heavily upon him who, well known to all others, dies unknown to himself.

† *Et conversus*, etc. And God turned to behold the works which his hands had wrought, and he saw that everything was very good. Genesis, i, 31.

a time set before thee thine own example, and examine thyself strictly, whether thou didst not best at first. Neglect not also the examples of those that have carried themselves ill in the same place, not to set off thyself by taxing their memory, but to direct thyself what to avoid. Reform, therefore, without bravery or scandal of former times and persons; but yet set it down to thyself, as well to create good precedents as to follow them. Reduce things to the first institution, and observe wherein and how they have degenerated; but yet ask counsel of both times: of the ancient time what is best, and of the latter time what is fittest. Seek to make thy course regular, that men may know beforehand what they may expect; but be not too positive and peremptory, and express thyself well when thou digressest from thy rule. Preserve the right of thy place, but stir not questions of jurisdiction; and rather assume thy right in silence and *de facto*,* than voice it with claims and challenges. Preserve likewise the rights of inferior places, and think it more honor to direct in chief than to be busy in all. Embrace and invite helps and advices touching the execution of thy place, and do not drive away such as bring thee information, as meddlers, but accept of them in good part.

The vices of authority are chiefly four: delays, corruption, roughness, and facility. For delays: give easy access, keep times appointed, go through with that which is in hand, and interlace not business but of necessity. For corruption: do not only bind thine own hands, or thy servants' hands, from taking, but bind the hands of suitors also from offering. For integrity used doth the one; but integrity professed, and with a manifest detestation of bribery, doth the other. And avoid not only the fault but the suspicion. Whosoever is found variable, and changeth manifestly without manifest cause, giveth

* *De facto*, as a matter of course.

suspicion of corruption. Therefore always when thou changest thine opinion or course, profess it plainly, and declare it, together with the reasons that move thee to change, and do not think to steal it. A servant or a favorite, if he be inward, and no other apparent cause of esteem, is commonly thought but a byway to close corruption. For roughness: it is a needless cause of discontent; severity breedeth fear, but roughness breedeth hate. Even reproofs from authority ought to be grave, and not taunting. As for facility,* it is worse than bribery. For bribes come but now and then; but if importunity or idle respects lead a man, he shall never be without. As Solomon saith: "To respect persons is not good; for such a man will transgress for a piece of bread." †

It is most true that was anciently spoken, "A place showeth the man"; and it showeth some to the better and some to the worse. "Omnium consensu, capax imperii, nisi imperasset,"‡ saith Tacitus of Galba; but of Vespasian he saith, "Solus imperantium Vespasianus mutatus in melius." § Though the one was meant of sufficiency, the other of manners and affection. It is an assured sign of a worthy and generous spirit, whom honor amends. For honor is, or should be, the place of virtue: and as in nature things move violently to their place, and calmly in their place; so virtue in ambition is violent, in authority settled and calm.

All rising to great place is by a winding stair, and, if there be factions, it is good to side a man's self whilst he is in the rising, and to balance himself when he is placed. Use the memory of thy predecessor fairly and tenderly;

* Facility, being too easy of access.

† Proverbs, xxviii, 21.

‡ *Omnium*, etc. By the consent of all he was fit to govern, if he had not governed.

§ *Solus*, etc. Of all the emperors, Vespasian alone changed for the better after he came to the throne.

for if thou dost not, it is a debt will sure be paid when thou art gone. If thou have colleagues, respect them, and rather call them when they look not for it, than exclude them when they have reason to look to be called. Be not too sensible or too remembering of thy place in conversation and private answers to suitors; but let it rather be said, "When he sits in place he is another man."

OF FRIENDSHIP

It had been hard for him that spake it to have put more truth and untruth together in few words than in that speech, "Whosoever is delighted in solitude is either a wild beast or a god." For it is most true that a natural and secret hatred and aversation toward society in any man hath somewhat of the savage beast; but it is most untrue that it should have any character at all of the divine nature, except it proceed, not out of a pleasure in solitude, but out of a love and desire to sequester a man's self for a higher conversation: such as is found to have been falsely and feignedly in some of the heathen, as Epimenides* the Candian, Numa the Roman, Empedocles the Sicilian, and Apollonius of Tyana; and truly and really in divers of the ancient hermits and holy fathers of the Church. But little do men perceive what solitude is, and how far it extendeth; for a crowd is not company, and faces are but a gallery of pictures, and talk but a tinkling cymbal, where there is no love. The Latin adage meeteth with it a little, "Magna civitas, magna solitudo"†; because in a great town friends are scattered, so that there is not that fellowship, for the most part,

* Epimenides is said to have fallen into a sleep which lasted fifty-seven years; Numa pretended that he was instructed by a divine nymph; Empedocles declared himself to be immortal; Apollonius professed to be able to perform miracles.

† *Magna*, etc. A great city is a great solitude.

which is in less neighborhoods. But we may go further, and affirm most truly that it is a mere and miserable solitude to want true friends, without which the world is but a wilderness. And even in this sense also of solitude, whosoever in the frame of his nature and affections is unfit for friendship, he taketh it of the beast, and not from humanity.

A principal fruit of friendship is the ease and discharge of the fulness and swellings of the heart, which passions of all kinds do cause and induce. We know diseases of stoppings and suffocations are the most dangerous in the body, and it is not much otherwise in the mind; you may take sarza to open the liver, steel to open the spleen, flour of sulphur for the lungs, castoreum for the brain, but no receipt openeth the heart but a true friend, to whom you may impart griefs, joys, fears, hopes, suspicions, counsels, and whatsoever lieth upon the heart to oppress it, in a kind of civil shrift or confession.

It is a strange thing to observe how high a rate great kings and monarchs do set upon the fruit of friendship whereof we speak; so great as they purchase it many times at the hazard of their own safety and greatness. For princes, in regard of the distance of their fortune from that of their subjects and servants, cannot gather this fruit except, to make themselves capable thereof, they raise some persons to be, as it were, companions and almost equals to themselves, which many times sorteth to inconvenience. The modern languages give unto such persons the name of favorites or privadoes, as if it were matter of grace or conversation; but the Roman name attaineth the true use and cause thereof, naming them "participes curarum," * for it is that which tieth the knot. And we see plainly that this hath been done, not by weak and passionate princes only, but by the wisest and most

* Sharers of cares.

politic that ever reigned; who have oftentimes joined to themselves some of their servants, whom both themselves have called friends, and allowed others likewise to call them in the same manner, using the word which is received between private men.

L. Sylla, when he commanded Rome, raised Pompey, after surnamed the Great, to that height that Pompey vaunted himself for Sylla's overmatch. For when he had carried the consulship for a friend of his against the pursuit of Sylla, and that Sylla did a little resent thereat, and began to speak great, Pompey turned upon him again, and in effect bade him be quiet, "for that more men adored the sun rising than the sun setting." With Julius Cæsar, Decimus Brutus had obtained that interest, as he set him down in his testament for heir in remainder after his nephew. And this was the man that had power with him to draw him forth to his death. For when Cæsar would have discharged the senate, in regard of some ill presages, and especially a dream of Calpurnia, this man lifted him gently by the arm out of his chair, telling him he hoped he would not dismiss the senate till his wife had dreamed a better dream. And it seemeth his favor was so great as Antonius, in a letter which is recited verbatim in one of Cicero's Philippics, calleth him "venefica," witch, as if he had enchanted Cæsar. Augustus raised Agrippa, though of mean birth, to that height as, when he consulted with Mæcenas about the marriage of his daughter Julia, Mæcenas took the liberty to tell him, "That he must either marry his daughter to Agrippa or take away his life; there was no third way, he had made him so great." With Tiberius Cæsar, Sejanus had ascended to that height as they two were termed and reckoned as a pair of friends. Tiberius in a letter to him saith: "Hæc pro amicitia nostra non occultavi"*; and the whole senate

* *Hæc*, etc. These things, by reason of our friendship, I have not concealed from you.

dedicated an altar to friendship, as to a goddess, in respect of the great dearness of friendship between them two. The like or more was between Septimius Severus and Plautianus. For he forced his eldest son to marry the daughter of Plautianus, and would often maintain Plautianus in doing affronts to his son; and did write also in a letter to the senate by these words: "I love the man so well as I wish he may overlive me." Now, if these princes had been as a Trajan, or a Marcus Aurelius, a man might have thought that this had proceeded of an abundant goodness of nature; but being men so wise, of such strength and severity of mind, and so extreme lovers of themselves, as all these were, it proveth most plainly that they found their own felicity, though as great as ever happened to mortal men, but as a half-piece, except they might have a friend to make it entire. And yet, which is more, they were princes which had wives, sons, nephews; and yet all these could not supply the comfort of friendship.

It is not to be forgotten what Comineus observeth of his first master, Duke Charles the Hardy; namely, that he would communicate his secrets with none, and least of all those secrets which troubled him most. Whereupon he goeth on, and saith that toward his latter time "that closeness did impair, and a little perish his understanding." Surely Comineus might have made the same judgment also, if it had pleased him, of his second master, Louis XI, whose closeness was indeed his tormentor. The parable of Pythagoras is dark but true: "Cor ne edito," eat not the heart. Certainly, if a man would give it a hard phrase, those that want friends to open themselves unto are cannibals of their own hearts. But one thing is most admirable (wherewith I will conclude this first-fruit of friendship), which is, that this communicating of a man's self to his friend works two contrary effects: for it redoubleth joys, and cutteth griefs in halves. For there is no man that imparteth his joys to his friend, but he joyeth the more; and no man that imparteth his griefs to his friend, but he grieveth the less. So that it is, in truth, of operation upon a man's mind, of like virtue as the alchemists used to attribute to their stone for man's body, that it worketh all contrary effects, but still to the good and benefit of nature. But yet, without praying in aid of alchemists, there is a manifest image of this in the ordinary course of nature. For in bodies, union strengtheneth and cherisheth any natural action, and, on the other side, weakeneth and dulleth any violent impression; and even so is it of minds.

The second fruit of friendship is healthful and sovereign for the understanding, as the first is for the affections. For friendship maketh indeed a fair day in the affections from storm and tempests; but it maketh daylight in the understanding out of darkness and confusion of thoughts. Neither is this to be understood only of faithful counsel, which a man receiveth from his friend; but before you come to that, certain it is, that whosoever hath his mind fraught with many thoughts, his wits and understanding do clarify and break up in the communicating and discoursing with another: he tosseth his thoughts more easily, he marshalleth them more orderly, he seeth how they look when they are turned into words; finally, he waxeth wiser than himself, and that more by an hour's discourse than by a day's meditation. It was well said by Themistocles to the King of Persia, "That speech was like cloth of Arras, opened and put abroad, whereby the imagery doth appear in figure; whereas in thoughts they lie but as in packs." Neither is this second fruit of friendship, in opening the understanding, restrained only to such friends as are able to give a man counsel; they indeed are best, but even without that, a man learneth of himself, and bringeth his own thoughts to light, and whetteth his wits as against a stone, which itself cuts not. In a word, a man were better relate himself to a statue or picture, than to suffer his thoughts to pass in smother.

Add now, to make this second fruit of friendship complete, that other point which lieth more open, and falleth within vulgar observation: which is faithful counsel from a friend. Heraclitus saith well on one of his enigmas, "Dry light is ever the best." And certain it is, that the light that a man receiveth by counsel from another is drier and purer than that which cometh from his own understanding and judgment, which is ever infused and drenched in his affections and customs. So as there is as much difference between the counsel that a friend giveth, and that a man giveth himself, as there is between the counsel of a friend and of a flatterer. For there is no such flatterer as is a man's self; and there is no such remedy against flattery of a man's self as the liberty of a friend. Counsel is of two sorts: the one concerning manners, the other concerning business. For the first, the best preservative to keep the mind in health is the faithful admonition of a friend. The calling of a man's self to a strict account is a medicine sometimes too piercing and corrosive. Reading good books of morality is a little flat and dead. Observing our faults in others is sometimes unproper for our case. But the best receipt (best, I say, to work, and best to take) is the admonition of a friend. It is a strange thing to behold what gross errors and extreme absurdities many, especially of the greater sort, do commit for want of a friend to tell them of them; to the great damage both of their fame and fortune. For, as St. James saith, they are as men "that look sometimes into a glass, and presently forget their own shape and favor." * As for business, a man may

* James, i, 23

think if he will that two eyes see no more than one; or
that a gamester seeth always more than a looker-on; or
that a man in anger is as wise as he that hath said over
the four-and-twenty letters; or that a musket may be
shot off as well upon the arm as upon a rest; and such
other fond and high imaginations, to think himself all in
all. But when all is done, the help of good counsel is that
which setteth business straight. And if any man think
that he will take counsel, but it shall be by pieces; asking
counsel in one business of one man, and in another business of another man; it is well (that is to say, better perhaps than if he asked none at all), but he runneth two
dangers. One, that he shall not be faithfully counselled:
for it is a rare thing, except it be from a perfect and entire
friend, to have counsel given, but such as shall be bowed
and crooked to some ends which he hath that giveth it.
The other, that he shall have counsel given, hurtful and
unsafe, though with good meaning, and mixed partly of
mischief and partly of remedy. Even as if you would
call a physician that is thought good for the cure of the
disease you complain of, but is unacquainted with your
body; and therefore may put you in way for a present
cure, but overthroweth your health in some other kind,
and so cure the disease and kill the patient. But a friend
that is wholly acquainted with a man's estate will beware
by furthering any present business how he dasheth upon
other inconvenience. And, therefore, rest not upon scattered counsels; they will rather distract and mislead than
settle and direct.

After these two noble fruits of friendship (peace in the
affections, and support of the judgment) followeth the
last fruit, which is like the pomegranate, full of many
kernels: I mean aid, and bearing a part in all actions and
occasions. Here the best way to represent to life the
manifold use of friendship, is to cast and see how many

things there are which a man cannot do himself; and then it will appear that it was a sparing speech of the ancients to say, "That a friend is another himself"; for that a friend is far more than himself. Men have their time, and die many times in desire of some things which they principally take to heart,—the bestowing of a child, the finishing of a work, or the like. If a man have a true friend, he may rest almost secure that the care of those things will continue after him. So that a man hath, as it were, two lives in his desires. A man hath a body, and that body is confined to a place; but where friendship is, all offices of life are, as it were, granted to him and his deputy, for he may exercise them by his friend. How many things are there which a man cannot, with any face or comeliness say or do himself! A man can scarce allege his own merits with modesty, much less extol them; a man cannot sometimes brook to supplicate or beg; and a number of the like. But all these things are graceful in a friend's mouth, which are blushing in a man's own. So again, a man's person hath many proper relations which he cannot put off. A man cannot speak to his son, but as a father; to his wife but as a husband; to his enemy but upon terms; whereas a friend may speak as the case requires, and not as it sorteth with the person. But to enumerate these things were endless. I have given the rule where a man cannot fitly play his own part: if he have not a friend, he may quit the stage.

THOMAS CARLYLE

THE INFLUENCE OF BOOKS

Thomas Carlyle (1795–1881) is noted as a historian and essayist. He was the son of a Scotch stone-mason of Ecclefechan. When, at fourteen, he was ready to enter college, he walked the eighty miles to Edinburgh to enter the university there. Most of his life was spent in London, and it was given entirely to literature, resulting in a long row of volumes. His first book, *Sartor Resartus* (The Tailor Re-tailored), was a curious setting forth of his philosophy of life, written in such an unusual style that it found few readers. His next book, *The French Revolution*, made him famous. For vivid description, picturesque characterization, and dramatic narrative, it stands alone among historical works. He also wrote biographies of Cromwell, of John Sterling, and of Frederick the Great, and contributed to magazines a number of critical essays, including a famous paper on Burns. He delivered a course of lectures on great men, which was published under the title *Heroes and Hero-Worship*. This book and his *French Revolution* are the best known of his works. The selection here given is from *Heroes and Hero-Worship*, being a part of the lecture on "The Hero as Man of Letters." It shows the vigor of Carlyle's style, the intense earnestness of the man, and the originality of his thought.

THOMAS CARLYLE

THE INFLUENCE OF BOOKS

(From *Heroes and Hero-Worship*, Lecture V)

Complaint is often made, in these times, of what we call the disorganized condition of society: how ill many arranged forces of society fulfil their work; how many powerful forces are seen working in a wasteful, chaotic, altogether unarranged manner. It is too just a complaint, as we all know. But perhaps if we look at this of Books and the Writers of Books, we shall find here, as it were, the summary of all other disorganization;—a sort of *heart*, from which, and to which, all other confusion circulates in the world! Considering what Book-writers do in the world, and what the world does with Book-writers, I should say, it is the most anomalous thing the world at present has to show.—We should get into a sea far beyond sounding, did we attempt to give account of this: but we must glance at it for the sake of our subject.

Our pious Fathers, feeling well what importance lay in the speaking of man to men, founded churches, made endowments, regulations; everywhere in the civilized world there is a Pulpit, environed with all manner of complex dignified appurtenances and furtherances, that therefrom a man with the tongue may, to best advantage, address his fellow men. They felt that this was the most important thing; that without this there was no good thing. It is a right pious work, that of theirs; beautiful to behold! But now with the art of Writing, with the

283

art of Printing, a total change has come over that business. The Writer of a Book, is not he a Preacher preaching not to this parish or that, on this day or that, but to all men in all times and places? Surely it is of the last importance that *he* do his work right, whoever do it wrong;—that the *eye* report not falsely, for then all the other members are astray! Well; how he may do his work, whether he do it right or wrong, or do it at all, is a point which no man in the world has taken the pains to think of. To a certain shopkeeper, trying to get some money for his books, if lucky, he is of some importance; to no other man of any. Whence he came, whither he is bound, by what ways he arrived, by what he might be furthered on his course, no one asks. He is an accident in society. He wanders like a wild Ishmaelite, in a world of which he is as the spiritual light, either the guidance or the misguidance!

Certainly the art of Writing is the most miraculous of all things man has devised. Odin's *Runes* * were the first form of the work of a Hero; *Books*, written words, are still miraculous *Runes*, the latest form! In Books lies the *soul* of the whole Past Time; the articulate audible voice of the Past, when the body and material substance of it has altogether vanished like a dream. Mighty fleets and armies, harbors and arsenals, vast cities, high-domed, many-engined,—they are precious, great: but what do they become? Agamemnon, the many Agamemnons, Pericleses, and their Greece; all is gone now to some ruined fragments, dumb mournful wrecks and blocks: but the Books of Greece! There Greece, to every thinker, still very literally lives; can be called up again into life. No magic *Rune* is stranger than a Book. All that Mankind has done, thought, gained or been: it is lying as in

---

* *Runes*, a name given to the ancient Scandinavian alphabet, which according to tradition was given to mankind by the god Odin.

magic preservation in the pages of Books. They are the chosen possession of men.

Do not Books still accomplish *miracles*, as *Runes* were fabled to do? They persuade men. Not the wretchedest circulating-library novel, which foolish girls thumb and con in remote villages, but will help to regulate the actual practical weddings and households of those foolish girls. So "Celia" felt, so "Clifford" acted: the foolish Theorem of Life, stamped into those young brains, comes out as a solid Practice one day. Consider whether any *Rune* in the wildest imagination of Mythologist ever did such wonders as, on the actual firm Earth, some Books have done! What built St. Paul's Cathedral? Look at the heart of the matter, it was that divine Hebrew Book, —the word partly of the man Moses, an outlaw tending his Midianitish herds, four thousand years ago, in the wildernesses of Sinai! It is the strangest of things, yet nothing is truer. With the art of Writing, of which Printing is a simple, an inevitable and comparatively insignificant corollary, the true reign of miracles for mankind commenced. It related, with a wondrous new contiguity and perpetual closeness, the Past and Distant with the Present in time and place; all times and all places with this our actual Here and Now. All things were altered for men; all modes of important work of men: teaching, preaching, governing, and all else.

To look at Teaching, for instance. Universities are a notable, respectable product of the modern ages. Their existence too is modified, to the very basis of it, by the existence of Books. Universities arose while there were yet no Books procurable; while a man, for a single Book, had to give an estate of land. That, in those circumstances, when a man had some knowledge to communicate, he should do it by gathering the learners round him, face to face, was a necessity for him. If you wanted to

know what Abelard knew, you must go and listen to
Abelard. Thousands, as many as thirty thousand, went
to hear Abelard and that metaphysical theology of his.
And now for any other teacher who had also something
of his own to teach, there was a great convenience opened:
so many thousands eager to learn were already assembled yonder; of all places the best place for him was that.
For any third teacher it was better still; and grew ever
the better, the more teachers there came. It only needed
now that the King took notice of this new phenomenon;
combined or agglomerated the various schools into one
school; gave it edifices, privileges, encouragements, and
named it *Universitas*, or School of all Sciences: the University of Paris, in its essential characters, was there.
The model of all subsequent Universities; which down
even to these days, for six centuries now, have gone on to
found themselves. Such, I conceive, was the origin of
Universities.

It is clear, however, that with this simple circumstance,
facility of getting Books, the whole conditions of the business from top to bottom were changed. Once invent
Printing, you metamorphosed all Universities, or super-
seded them! The Teacher needed not now to gather
men personally round him, that he might *speak* to them
what he knew: print it in a Book, and all learners far and
wide, for a trifle, had it each at his own fireside, much
more effectually to learn it!—Doubtless there is still
peculiar virtue in Speech; even Writers of Books may still,
in some circumstances, find it convenient to speak also,
—witness our present meeting here! * There is, one would
say, and must ever remain while man has a tongue, a
distinct province for Speech as well as for Writing and
Printing. In regard to all things this must remain; to
Universities among others. But the limits of the two

* This was originally given as a lecture.

have nowhere yet been pointed out, ascertained; much less put in practice; the University which would completely take in that great new fact, of the existence of Printed Books, and stand on a clear footing for the Nineteenth Century as the Paris one did for the Thirteenth, has not yet come into existence. If we think of it, all that a University, or final highest School can do for us, is still but what the first School began doing,—teach us to *read*. We learn to *read*, in various languages, in various sciences; we learn the alphabet and letters of all manner of Books. But the place where we are to get knowledge, even theoretic knowledge, is the Books themselves! It depends on what we read, after all manner of Professors have done their best for us. The true University of these days is a Collection of Books.

But to the Church itself, as I hinted already, all is changed, in its preaching, in its working, by the introduction of Books. The Church is the working recognized Union of our Priests or Prophets, of those who by wise teaching guide the souls of men. While there was no Writing, even while there was no Easy-writing or *Printing*, the preaching of the voice was the natural sole method of performing this. But now with Books!—He that can write a true Book, to persuade England, is not he the Bishop and Archbishop, the Primate of England and of All England? I many a time say, the writers of Newspapers, Pamphlets, Poems, Books, these *are* the real working effective Church of a modern country. Nay, not only our preaching, but even our worship, is not it too accomplished by means of Printed Books? The noble sentiment which a gifted soul has clothed for us in melodious words, which brings melody into our hearts,—is not this essentially, if we will understand it, of the nature of worship? There are many, in all countries, who, in this confused time, have no other method of worship.

He who, in any way, shows us better than we knew before that a lily of the fields is beautiful, does he not show it us as an effluence of the Fountain of all Beauty; as the *handwriting*, made visible there, of the great Maker of the Universe? He has sung for us, made us sing with him, a little verse of a sacred Psalm. Essentially so. How much more he who sings, who says, or in any way brings home to our heart the noble doings, feelings, darings and endurances of a brother man! He has verily touched our hearts as with a live coal *from the altar*. Perhaps there is no worship more authentic.

Literature, so far as it is Literature, is an "apocalypse of Nature," a revealing of the "open secret." It may well enough be named, in Fichte's style, a "continuous revelation" of the Godlike in the Terrestrial and Common. The Godlike does ever, in very truth, endure there; is brought out, now in this dialect, now in that, with various degrees of clearness: all true gifted Singers and Speakers are, consciously or unconsciously, doing so. The dark stormful indignation of a Byron, so wayward and perverse, may have touches of it; nay the withered mockery of a French sceptic,—his mockery of the False, a love and worship of the True. How much more the sphere-harmony of a Shakspeare, of a Goethe; the cathedral music of a Milton! They are something too, those humble genuine lark notes of a Burns,—skylark, starting from the humble furrow, far overhead into the blue depths, and singing to us so genuinely there! For all true singing is of the nature of worship; as indeed all true *working* may be said to be,—whereof such *singing* is but the record, and fit melodious representation, to us. Fragments of a real "Church Liturgy" and "Body of Homilies," strangely disguised from the common eye, are to be found weltering in that huge froth-ocean of Printed Speech we loosely call Literature! Books are our Church too.

Or turning now to the Government of men. Witena-gemote, old Parliament, was a great thing. The affairs of the nation were there deliberated and decided; what we were to *do* as a nation. But does not, though the name Parliament subsists, the parliamentary debate go on now, everywhere and at all times, in a far more comprehensive way, *out* of Parliament altogether? Burke said there were Three Estates in Parliament; but, in the Reporters' Gallery yonder, there sat a *Fourth Estate* more important far than they all. It is not a figure of speech, or a witty saying; it is a literal fact,—very momentous to us in these times. Literature is our Parliament too. Printing, which comes necessarily out of Writing, I say often, is equivalent to Democracy: invent Writing, Democracy is inevitable. Writing brings Printing; brings universal everyday extempore Printing as we see at present. Whoever can speak, speaking now to the whole nation, becomes a power, a branch of government, with inalienable weight in lawmaking, in all acts of authority. It matters not what rank he has, what revenues or garnitures: the requisite thing is, that he have a tongue which others will listen to; this and nothing more is requisite. The nation is governed by all that has tongue in the nation: Democracy is virtually *there*. Add only, that whatsoever power exists will have itself, by and by, organized; working secretly under bandages, obscurations, obstructions, it will never rest till it get to work free, unencumbered, visible to all. Democracy virtually extant will insist on becoming palpably extant.

On all sides, are we not driven to the conclusion that, of the things which man can do or make here below, by far the most momentous, wonderful and worthy are the things we call Books! Those poor bits of rag-paper with black ink on them;—from the Daily Newspaper to the sacred Hebrew Book, what have they not done, what are they not doing!—For indeed, whatever be the outward form of the thing (bits of paper, as we say, and black ink), is it not verily, at bottom, the highest act of man's faculty that produces a Book?   It is the *Thought* of man; the true thaumaturgic virtue; by which man works all things whatsoever.   All that he does, and brings to pass, is the vesture of a Thought.   This London City, with all its houses, palaces, steam-engines, cathedrals, and huge immeasurable traffic and tumult, what is it but a Thought, but millions of Thoughts made into One;—a huge, immeasurable Spirit of Thought, embodied in brick, in iron, smoke, dust, Palaces, Parliaments, Hackney Coaches, Catherine Docks, and the rest of it!   Not a brick was made but some man had to *think* of the making of that brick.—The thing we called "bits of paper with traces of black ink," is the *purest* embodiment of a Thought man can have.   No wonder it is, in all ways, the activest and noblest.

All this, of the importance and supreme importance of the Man of Letters in modern Society, and how the Press is to such a degree superseding the Pulpit, the Senate, the *Senatus Academicus* and much else, has been admitted for a good while; and recognized often enough, in late times, with a sort of sentimental triumph and wonderment.   It seems to me, the Sentimental by and by will have to give place to the Practical.   If Men of Letters *are* so incalculably influential, actually performing such work for us from age to age, and even from day to day, then I think we may conclude that Men of Letters will not always wander like unrecognized unregulated Ishmaelites among us!   Whatsoever thing, as I said above, has virtual unnoticed power will cast off its wrappages, bandages, and step forth one day with palpably articulated, universally visible power.   That one man wear the clothes and take the wages of a function which is done by quite another: there can be no profit in this; this is not right, it is wrong. And yet, alas, the *making* of it right,—what a business, for long times to come! Sure enough, this that we call Organization of the Literary Guild is still a great way off, encumbered with all manner of complexities. If you asked me what were the best possible organization for the Men of Letters in modern society; the arrangement of furtherance and regulation, grounded the most accurately on the actual facts of their position and of the world's position,—I should beg to say that the problem far exceeded my faculty! It is not one man's faculty; it is that of many successive men turned earnestly upon it, that will bring out even an approximate solution. What the best arrangement were, none of us could say. But if you ask, Which is the worst? I answer: This which we now have, that Chaos should sit umpire in it; this is the worst. To the best, or any good one, there is yet a long way.

RALPH WALDO EMERSON

SELF-RELIANCE

Ralph Waldo Emerson (1803–1882), one of the famous New England group of writers, was the son of a Boston minister. He attended the Boston Latin School and Harvard College, where he waited on table for his board. After graduation he taught school for a time, preached for a time, and then found his real vocation as lecturer and writer. His home was in Concord, a village near Boston. Here he spent his days quietly, the mornings in reading and writing, the afternoons in long walks, usually alone; the evenings with his family. At this time nearly every small town had its "lyceum," or course of lectures, every winter, and Emerson was much in demand as a lecturer. He gave courses on science, on biography, and on literature. Gradually his subjects became more general, such as Compensation, Heroism, Self-Reliance, Spiritual Laws. Then he began to publish the substance of these lectures as books. In 1847 he was invited to England to lecture. Here he met Carlyle, Coleridge, Wordsworth, Tennyson, Dickens, Thackeray, and other notable people. His impressions of England were published under the title *English Traits*. His other writings are: *Nature, Essays, First and Second Series, Poems, Representative Men, Conduct of Life, Society and Solitude, Letters and Social Aims*. His prose works are practically all essays, and are of the reflective type. They contain the mature wisdom of one who had read carefully and thought deeply. They are not easy reading; the thought is close-packed, and often the connection between one idea and the next is not evident, but one who reads slowly and attentively will be richly repaid.

RALPH WALDO EMERSON

SELF-RELIANCE

(From *Essays, First Series*)

Ne te quæsiveris extra.*

Man is his own star; and the soul that can
Render an honest and a perfect man,
Commands all light, all influence, all fate;
Nothing to him falls early or too late.
Our acts our angels are, or good or ill,
Our fatal shadows that walk by us still.

—*Epilogue to Beaumont and Fletcher's Honest Man's Fortune.*

Cast the bantling on the rocks,
Suckle him with the she-wolf's teat,
Wintered with the hawk and fox,
Power and speed be hands and feet.

—EMERSON.

I read the other day some verses written by an eminent painter which were original and not conventional. Always the soul hears an admonition in such lines, let the subject be what it may. The sentiment they instil is of more value than any thought they may contain. To believe your own thought, to believe that what is true for you in your private heart is true for all men,—that is genius. Speak your latent conviction, and it shall be the universal sense; for always the inmost becomes the outmost—and our first thought is rendered back to us by the trumpets of the Last Judgment. Familiar as the voice of the mind is to each, the highest merit we ascribe to Moses, Plato,

* Do not seek beyond thyself.

and Milton is that they set at naught books and traditions, and spoke not what men, but what they thought.
A man should learn to detect and watch that gleam of
light which flashes across his mind from within, more
than the lustre of the firmament of bards and sages.
Yet he dismisses without notice his thought, because it
is his. In every work of genius we recognize our own
rejected thoughts; they come back to us with a certain
alienated majesty. Great works of art have no more
affecting lesson for us than this. They teach us to abide
by our spontaneous impression with good-humored in-
flexibility then most when the whole cry of voices is on
the other side. Else to-morrow a stranger will say with
masterly good sense precisely what we have thought and
felt all the time, and we shall be forced to take with
shame our own opinion from another.

There is a time in every man's education when he arrives at the conviction that envy is ignorance; that imitation is suicide; that he must take himself for better for
worse as his portion; that though the wide universe is
full of good, no kernel of nourishing corn can come to him
but through his toil bestowed on that plot of ground
which is given to him to till. The power which resides
in him is new in nature, and none but he knows what
that is which he can do, nor does he know until he has
tried. Not for nothing one face, one character, one fact,
makes much impression on him, and another none. It
is not without pre-established harmony, this sculpture
in the memory. The eye was placed where one ray
should fall, that it might testify of that particular ray.
Bravely let him speak the utmost syllable of his concession. We but half express ourselves, and are ashamed of
that divine idea which each of us represents. It may be
safely trusted as proportionate and of good issues, so it
be faithfully imparted, but God will not have his work

made manifest by cowards. It needs a divine man to exhibit anything divine. A man is relieved and gay when he has put his heart into his work and done his best; but what he has said or done otherwise shall give him no peace. It is a deliverance which does not deliver. In the attempt his genius deserts him; no muse befriends; no invention, no hope.

Trust thyself: every heart vibrates to that iron string. Accept the place the divine providence has found for you, the society of your contemporaries, the connection of events. Great men have always done so, and confided themselves childlike to the genius of their age, betraying their perception that the Eternal was stirring at their heart, working through their hands, predominating in all their being. And we are now men, and must accept in the highest mind the same transcendent destiny; and not minors and invalids in a protected corner, not cowards fleeing before a revolution, but redeemers and benefactors, pious aspirants to be noble clay; under the Almighty effort let us advance on Chaos and the Dark.

What pretty oracles nature yields us on this text in the face and behavior of children, babes, and even brutes. That divided and rebel mind, that distrust of a sentiment because our arithmetic has computed the strength and means opposed to our purpose, these have not. Their mind being whole, their eye is as yet unconquered, and when we look in their faces, we are disconcerted. Infancy conforms to nobody; all conform to it; so that one babe commonly makes four or five out of the adults who prattle and play to it. So God has armed youth and puberty and manhood no less with its own piquancy and charm, and made it enviable and gracious and its claims not to be put by, if it will stand by itself. Do not think the youth has no force, because he cannot speak to you and me. Hark! in the next room who spoke so clear and

emphatic? It seems he knows how to speak to his contemporaries. Good Heaven! it is he! it is that very
lump of bashfulness and phlegm which for weeks has done
nothing but eat when you were by, and now rolls out
these words like bell strokes. It seems he knows how to
speak to his contemporaries. Bashful or bold then, he
will know how to make us seniors very unnecessary.

The nonchalance of boys who are sure of a dinner, and
would disdain as much as a lord to do or say aught to
conciliate one, is the healthy attitude of human nature.
How is a boy the master of society; independent, irre-
sponsible, looking out from his corner on such people and
facts as pass by, he tries and sentences them on their
merits, in the swift, summary way of boys, as good, bad,
interesting, silly, eloquent, troublesome. He cumbers
himself never about consequences, about interests; he
gives an independent, genuine verdict. You must court
him; he does not court you. But the man is as it were
clapped into jail by his consciousness. As soon as he
has once acted or spoken with éclat he is a committed
person, watched by the sympathy or the hatred of hundreds, whose affections must now enter into his account.
There is no Lethe * for this. Ah, that he could pass again
into his neutral, godlike independence! Who can thus
lose all pledge and, having observed, observe again from
the same unaffected, unbiassed, unbribable, unaffrighted
innocence, must always be formidable, must always engage the poet's and the man's regards. Of such an immortal youth the force would be felt. He would utter
opinions on all passing affairs, which being seen to be
not private but necessary, would sink like darts into the
ear of men and put them in fear.

These are the voices which we hear in solitude, but

---

* Lethe. In Greek mythology, Lethe was a river in Hades. Those
who drank of its waters lost all memory of their past lives.

they grow faint and inaudible as we enter into the world. Society everywhere is in conspiracy against the manhood of every one of its members. Society is a joint-stock company, in which the members agree, for the better securing of his bread to each shareholder, to surrender the liberty and culture of the eater. The virtue in most request is conformity. Self-reliance is its aversion. It loves not realities and creators, but names and customs.

Whoso would be a man, must be a nonconformist. He who would gather immortal palms must not be hindered by the name of goodness, but must explore if it be goodness. Nothing is at last sacred but the integrity of our own mind. Absolve you to yourself, and you shall have the suffrage of the world. I remember an answer which when quite young I was prompted to make to a valued adviser who was wont to importune me with the dear old doctrines of the church. On my saying, What have I to do with the sacredness of traditions, if I live wholly from within? my friend suggested, —"But these impulses may be from below, not from above." I replied, "They do not seem to me to be such, but if I am the devil's child, I will live then from the devil." No law can be sacred to me but that of my nature. Good and bad are but names very readily transferable to that or this; the only right is what is after my constitution; the only wrong what is against it. A man is to carry himself in the presence of all opposition as if everything were titular and ephemeral but he. I am ashamed to think how easily we capitulate to badges and names, to large societies and dead institutions. Every decent and well-spoken individual affects and sways me more than is right! I ought to go upright and vital, and speak the rude truth in all ways. If malice and vanity wear the coat of philanthropy, shall that pass? If an angry bigot assumes this bountiful cause of Abolition, and comes to me with his last

news from Barbadoes,* why should I not say to him, "Go
love thy infant; love thy wood-chopper; be good-natured
and modest; have that grace; and never varnish your
hard, uncharitable ambition with this incredible tenderness for black folk a thousand miles off. Thy love afar
is spite at home." Rough and graceless would be such
greeting, but truth is handsomer than the affectation of
love. Your goodness must have some edge to it,—else
it is none. The doctrine of hatred must be preached, as
the counteraction of the doctrine of love, when that pules
and whines. I shun father and mother and wife and
brother when my genius calls me. I would write on the
lintels of the door post, *Whim*. I hope it is somewhat
better than whim at last, but we cannot spend the day
in explanation. Expect me not to show cause why I
seek or why I exclude company. Then, again, do not
tell me, as a good man did to-day, of my obligation to
put all poor men in good situations. Are they *my* poor?
I tell thee, thou foolish philanthropist, that I grudge the
dollar, the dime, the cent I give to such men as do not
belong to me and to whom I do not belong. There is a
class of persons to whom by all spiritual affinity I am
bought and sold; for them I will go to prison if need be;
but your miscellaneous popular charities; the education
at college of fools; the building of meeting-houses to the
vain end to which many now stand; alms to sots, and the
thousandfold Relief Societies;—though I confess with
shame I sometime succumb and give the dollar, it is a
wicked dollar, which by and by I shall have the manhood
to withhold.

Virtues are, in the popular estimate, rather the exception than the rule. There is the man *and* his virtues.
Men do what is called a good action, as some piece of

---

* At the time this was written, slavery still existed in the British
West Indies.

courage or charity, much as they would pay a fine in expiation of daily non-appearance on parade. Their works are done as an apology or extenuation of their living in the world,—as invalids and the insane pay a high board. Their virtues are penances. I do not wish to expiate, but to live. My life is not an apology, but a life. It is for itself and not for a spectacle. I much prefer that it should be of a lower strain, so it be genuine and equal, than that it should be glittering and unsteady. I wish it to be sound and sweet, and not to need diet and bleeding. My life should be unique; it should be an alms, a battle, a conquest, a medicine. I ask primary evidence that you are a man, and refuse this appeal from the man to his actions. I know that for myself it makes no difference whether I do or forbear those actions which are reckoned excellent. I cannot consent to pay for a privilege where I have intrinsic right. Few and mean as my gifts may be, I actually am, and do not need for my own assurance or the assurance of my fellows any secondary testimony.

What I must do is all that concerns me, not what the people think. This rule, equally arduous in actual and in intellectual life, may serve for the whole distinction between greatness and meanness. It is the harder because you will always find those who think they know what is your duty better than you know it. It is easy in the world to live after the world's opinion; it is easy in solitude to live after our own; but the great man is he who in the midst of the crowd keeps with perfect sweetness the independence of solitude.

The objection to conforming to usages that have become dead to you is that it scatters your force. It loses your time and blurs the impression of your character. If you maintain a dead church, contribute to a dead Bible Society, vote with a great party either for the Government or against it, spread your table like base house-keepers,—under all these screens I have difficulty to detect the precise man you are. And of course so much force is withdrawn from your proper life. But do your thing, and I shall know you. Do your work, and you shall reinforce yourself. A man must consider what a blindman's buff is this game of conformity. If I know your sect I anticipate your argument. I hear a preacher announce for his text and topic the expediency of one of the institutions of his church. Do I not know beforehand that not possibly can he say a new and spontaneous word? Do I not know that with all this ostentation of examining the grounds of the institution he will do no such thing? Do I not know that he is pledged to himself not to look but at one side, the permitted side, not as a man, but as a parish minister? He is a retained attorney, and these airs of the bench are the emptiest affectation. Well, most men have bound their eyes with one or another handkerchief, and attached themselves to some one of these communities of opinion. This conformity makes them not false in a few particulars, authors of a few lies, but false in all particulars. Their every truth is not quite true. Their two is not the real two, their four not the real four: so that every word they say chagrins us and we know not where to begin to set them right. Meantime nature is not slow to equip us in the prison uniform of the party to which we adhere. We come to wear one cut of face and figure, and acquire by degrees the gentlest asinine expression. There is a mortifying experience in particular, which does not fail to wreak itself also in the general history; I mean "the foolish face of praise," the forced smile which we put on in company where we do not feel at ease, in answer to conversation which does not interest us. The muscles, not spontaneously moved but moved by a low usurping wilfulness, grow tight about the outline of the face, and make the most disagreeable sensation; a sensation of rebuke and warning which no brave young man will suffer twice.

For non-conformity the world whips you with its displeasure. And therefore a man must know how to estimate a sour face. The bystanders look askance on him in the public street or in the friend's parlor. If this aversation had its origin in contempt and resistance like his own he might well go home with a sad countenance; but the sour faces of the multitude, like their sweet faces, have no deep cause—disguise no god, but are put on and off as the wind blows and a newspaper directs. Yet is the discontent of the multitude more formidable than that of the senate and the college. It is easy enough for a firm man who knows the world to brook the rage of the cultivated classes. Their rage is decorous and prudent, for they are timid, as being very vulnerable themselves. But when to their feminine rage the indignation of the people is added, when the ignorant and the poor are aroused, when the unintelligent brute force that lies at the bottom of society is made to growl and mow, it needs the habit of magnanimity and religion to treat it godlike as a trifle of no concernment.

The other terror that scares us from self-trust is our consistency; a reverence for our past act or word because the eyes of others have no other data for computing our orbit than our past acts, and we are loath to disappoint them.

But why should you keep your head over your shoulder? Why drag about this monstrous corpse of your memory, lest you contradict somewhat you have stated in this or that public place? Suppose you should contradict yourself; what then? It seems to be a rule of wisdom never to rely on your memory alone, scarcely even in acts of pure memory, but to bring the past for judgment into the thousand-eyed present, and live ever in a new day. Trust your emotion. In your metaphysics you have denied personality to the Deity, yet when the devout motions of the soul come, yield to them heart and life, though they should clothe God with shape and color. Leave your theory, as Joseph his coat in the hand of the harlot, and flee.

A foolish consistency is the hobgoblin of little minds, adored by little statesmen and philosophers and divines. With consistency a great soul has simply nothing to do. He may as well concern himself with his shadow on the wall. Out upon your guarded lips! Sew them up with packthread, do. Else if you would be a man speak what you think to-day in words as hard as cannon-balls, and to-morrow speak what to-morrow thinks in hard words again, though it contradict everything you said to-day. Ah, then, exclaim the aged ladies, you shall be sure to be misunderstood! Misunderstood! It is a right fool's word. Is it so bad then to be misunderstood? Pythagoras* was misunderstood, and Socrates, and Jesus, and Luther, and Copernicus, and Galileo, and Newton, and every pure and wise spirit that ever took flesh. To be great is to be misunderstood.

I suppose no man can violate his nature. All the sallies of his will are rounded in by the law of his being, as the inequalities of Andes and Himmaleh are insignificant in the curve of the sphere. Nor does it matter how you gauge and try him. A character is like an acrostic or Alexandrian† stanza;—read it forward, backward, or

* Pythagoras and Socrates were Greek philosophers; one was banished; the other was unjustly sentenced to death. Copernicus and Galileo were famous astronomers. Copernicus established the theory that the earth revolved about the sun, but for fear of persecution dared not announce his discovery; Galileo was imprisoned for publishing his discoveries.

† Alexandrian stanza, a line of twelve syllables. Emerson probably meant the palindrome, which reads the same backward or forward, as "Madam, I'm Adam."

across, it still spells the same thing. In this pleasing con-
trite wood life which God allows me, let me record day
by day my honest thought without prospect or retrospect,
and, I cannot doubt, it will be found symmetrical, though
I mean it not and see it not. My book should smell of
pines and resound with the hum of insects. The swallow
over my window should interweave that thread or straw
he carries in his bill into my web also. We pass for what
we are. Character teaches above our wills. Men imagine
that they communicate their virtue or vice only by overt
actions, and do not see that virtue or vice emit a breath
every moment.

Fear never but you shall be consistent in whatever
variety of actions, so they be each honest and natural in
their hour. For of one will, the actions will be harmoni-
ous, however unlike they seem. These varieties are lost
sight of when seen at a little distance, at a little height of
thought. One tendency unites them all. The voyage
of the best ship is a zigzag line of a hundred tacks. This
is only microscopic criticism. See the line from a sufficient distance, and it straightens itself to the average
tendency. Your genuine action will explain itself and
will explain your other genuine actions. Your conformity
explains nothing. Act singly, and what you have already
done singly will justify you now. Greatness always ap-
peals to the future. If I can be great enough now to do
right and scorn eyes, I must have done so much right before as to defend me now. Be it how it will, do right now.
Always scorn appearances and you always may. The
force of character is cumulative. All the foregone days
of virtue work their health into this. What makes the
majesty of the heroes of the senate and the field, which
so fills the imagination? The consciousness of a train
of great days and victories behind. There they all stand
and shed an united light on the advancing actor. He is

attended as by a visible escort of angels to every man's eye. That is it which throws thunder into Chatham's voice, and dignity into Washington's port, and America into Adams's eye. Honor is venerable to us because it is no ephemeris. It is always ancient virtue. We worship it to-day because it is not of to-day. We love it and pay it homage because it is not a trap for our love and homage, but is self-dependent, self-derived, and therefore of an old immaculate pedigree, even if shown in a young person.

I hope in these days we have heard the last of conformity and consistency. Let the words be gazetted and ridiculous henceforward. Instead of the gong for dinner, let us hear a whistle from the Spartan fife. Let us bow and apologize nevermore. A great man is coming to eat at my house. I do not wish to please him: I wish that he should wish to please me. I will stand here for humanity, and though I would make it kind, I would make it true. Let us affront and reprimand the smooth mediocrity and squalid contentment of the times, and hurl in the face of custom and trade and office, the fact which is the upshot of all history, that there is a great responsible Thinker and Actor moving wherever moves a man; that a true man belongs to no other time or place, but is the centre of things. Where he is, there is nature. He measures you and all men and all events. You are constrained to accept his standard. Ordinarily, everybody in society reminds us of somewhat else, or of some other person. Character, reality, reminds you of nothing else; it takes place of the whole creation. The man must be so much that he must make all circumstances indifferent—put all means into the shade. This all great men are and do. Every true man is a cause, a country, and an age; requires infinite spaces and numbers and time fully to accomplish his thought;—and posterity seem to follow his steps as a procession. A man Cæsar is born,

and for ages after we have a Roman Empire. Christ is
born, and millions of minds so grow and cleave to his
genius that he is confounded with virtue and the possible
of man. An institution is the lengthened shadow of one
man; as, the Reformation, of Luther; Quakerism, of Fox;
Methodism, of Wesley; Abolition, of Clarkson. Scipio,
Milton called "the height of Rome"; and all history re-
solves itself very easily into the biography of a few stout
and earnest persons.

Let a man then know his worth, and keep things under
his feet. Let him not peep or steal, or skulk up and down
with the air of a charity boy, a bastard, or an interloper
in the world which exists for him. But the man in the
street, finding no worth in himself which corresponds to
the force which built a tower or sculptured a marble god,
feels poor when he looks on these. To him a palace, a
statue, or a costly book have an alien and forbidding air,
much like a gay equipage, and seem to say like that,
"Who are you, sir?" Yet they all are his, suitors for his
notice, petitioners to his faculties that they will come out
and take possession. The picture waits for my verdict;
it is not to command me, but I am to settle its claim to
praise. That popular fable* of the sot who was picked
up dead drunk in the street, carried to the duke's house,
washed and dressed and laid in the duke's bed, and, on
his waking, treated with all obsequious ceremony like the
duke, and assured that he had been insane—owes its
popularity to the fact that it symbolizes so well the state
of man, who is in the world a sort of sot, but now and
then wakes up, exercises his reason and finds himself a
true prince.

Our reading is mendicant and sycophantic. In history

---

* The story is in the *Arabian Nights*, under the title "Abou Hassan, or the Sleeper Awakened." It is also used by Shakespeare in
the Induction to *The Taming of the Shrew*.

our imagination makes fools of us, plays us false.   Kingdom and lordship, power and estate, are a gaudier vocabulary than private John and Edward in a small house
and common day's work: but the things of life are the
same to both: the sum total of both is the same.   Why
all this deference to Alfred and Scanderberg* and Gustavus? † Suppose they were virtuous; did they wear out
virtue? As great a stake depends on your private act to-
day as followed their public and renowned steps.   When
private men shall act with original views, the lustre will
be transferred from the actions of kings to those of gentlemen.

The world has indeed been instructed by its kings, who
have so magnetized the eyes of nations.   It has been
taught by this colossal symbol the mutual reverence that
is due from man to man.   The joyful loyalty with which
men have everywhere suffered the king, the noble, or
the great proprietor to walk among them by a law of
his own, make his own scale of men and things and reverse theirs, pay for benefits not with money but with
honor, and represent the Law in his person, was the
hieroglyphic by which they obscurely signified their consciousness of their own right and comeliness, the right of
every man.

The magnetism which all original action exerts is explained when we inquire the reason of self-trust.   Who
is the Trustee? What is the aboriginal Self, on which a
universal reliance may be grounded? What is the nature
and power of that science-baffling star, without parallax,‡

* Scanderberg, an Albanian leader of the fifteenth century who
successfully defended his country against Turkey.

† Gustavus, Gustavus Adolphus of Sweden, who defeated Russia
in the Thirty Years' War.

‡ Parallax, a reference to the method of calculating the distance
of the stars. A star without parallax would be so remote that its
distance could not be calculated.

without calculable elements, which shoots a ray of beauty even into trivial and impure actions, if the least mark of independence appear? The inquiry leads us to that source, at once the essence of genius, the essence of virtue, and the essence of life, which we call Spontaneity or Instinct. We denote this primary wisdom as Intuition, whilst all later teachings are tuitions. In that deep force, the last fact behind which analysis cannot go, all things find their common origin. For the sense of being which in calm hours rises, we know not how, in the soul, is not diverse from things, from space, from light, from time, from man, but one with them and proceedeth obviously from the same source whence their life and being also proceedeth. We first share the life by which things exist, and afterward see them as appearances in nature and forget that we have shared their cause. Here is the fountain of action and the fountain of thought. Here are the lungs of that inspiration which giveth man wisdom, of that inspiration of man which cannot be denied without impiety and atheism. We lie in the lap of immense intelligence, which makes us organs of its activity and receivers of its truth. When we discern justice, when we discern truth, we do nothing of ourselves, but allow a passage to its beams. If we ask whence this comes, if we seek to pry into the soul that causes,—all metaphysics, all philosophy is at fault. Its presence or its absence is all we can affirm. Every man discerns between the voluntary acts of his mind and his involuntary perceptions. And to his involuntary perceptions he knows a perfect respect is due. He may err in the expression of them, but he knows that these things are so, like day and night, not to be disputed. All my wilful actions and acquisitions are but roving;—the most trivial revery, the faintest native emotion, are domestic and divine. Thoughtless people contradict as readily the statement of perceptions as of opinions, or rather much more readily; for they do not distinguish between perception and notion. They fancy that I choose to see this or that thing. But perception is not whimsical, but fatal.* If I see a trait, my children will see it after me, and in course of time all mankind,—although it may chance that no one has seen it before me. For my perception of it is as much a fact as the sun.

The relations of the soul to the divine spirit are so pure that it is profane to seek to interpose helps. It must be that when God speaketh he should communicate, not one thing, but all things; should fill the world with his voice; should scatter forth light, nature, time, souls, from the centre of the present thought; and new date and new create the whole. Whenever a mind is simple and receives a divine wisdom, then old things pass away,— means, teachers, texts, temples fall; it lives now, and absorbs past and future into the present hour. All things are made sacred by relation to it,—one thing as much as another. All things are dissolved to their centre by their cause, and in the universal miracle petty and particular miracles disappear. This is and must be. If therefore a man claims to know and speak of God and carries you backward to the phraseology of some old mouldered nation in another country, in another world, believe him not. Is the acorn better than the oak which is its fulness and completion? Is the parent better than the child into whom he has cast his ripened being? Whence then this worship of the past? The centuries are conspirators against the sanity and majesty of the soul. Time and space are but physiological colors which the eye maketh, but the soul is light; where it is, is day; where it was, is night; and history is an impertinence and an injury if it be anything more than a cheerful apologue or parable of my being and becoming.

* Fatal, here meaning ordained by fate.

Man is timid and apologetic; he is no longer upright; he dares not say "I think," "I am," but quotes some saint or sage. He is ashamed before the blade of grass or the blowing rose. These roses under my window make no reference to former roses or to better ones; they are for what they are; they exist with God to-day. There is no time to them. There is simply the rose; it is perfect in every moment of its existence. Before a leaf-bud has burst, its whole life acts; in the full-blown flower there is no more; in the leafless root there is no less. Its nature is satisfied and it satisfies nature in all moments alike. There is no time to it. But man postpones or remembers; he does not live in the present, but with reverted eye laments the past, or, heedless of the riches that surround him, stands on tiptoe to foresee the future. He cannot be happy and strong until he too lives with nature in the present, above time.

This should be plain enough. Yet see what strong intellects dare not yet hear God himself unless he speak the phraseology of I know not what David, or Jeremiah, or Paul. We shall not always set so great a price on a few texts, on a few lives. We are like children who repeat by rote the sentences of grandames and tutors, and, as they grow older, of the men of talents and character they chance to see,—painfully recollecting the exact words they spoke; afterward, when they come into the point of view which those had who uttered these sayings, they understand them and are willing to let the words go; for at any time they can use words as good when occasion comes. So was it with us, so will it be, if we proceed. If we live truly, we shall see truly. It is as easy for the strong man to be strong, as it is for the weak to be weak. When we have new perception, we shall gladly disburthen the memory of its hoarded treasures as old rubbish. When a man lives with God, his voice shall be as sweet as the murmur of the brook and the rustle of the corn.

And now at last the highest truth on this subject remains unsaid; probably cannot be said; for all that we say is the far-off remembering of the intuition. That thought, by what I can now nearest approach to say it, is this. When good is near you, when you have life in yourself,—it is not by any known or appointed way; you shall not discern the footprints of any other; you shall not see the face of man; you shall not hear any name;— the way, the thought, the good, shall be wholly strange and new. It shall exclude all other being. You take the way from man, not to man. All persons that ever existed are its fugitive ministers. There shall be no fear in it. Fear and hope are alike beneath it. It asks nothing. There is somewhat low even in hope. We are then in vision. There is nothing that can be called gratitude, nor properly joy. The soul is raised over passion. It seeth identity and eternal causation. It is a perceiving that Truth and Right are. Hence it becomes a Tranquillity out of the knowing that all things go well. Vast spaces of nature; the Atlantic Ocean, the South Sea; vast intervals of time, years, centuries, are of no account. This which I think and feel underlay that former state of life and circumstances, as it does underlie my present and will always all circumstances, and what is called life and what is called death.

Life only avails, not the having lived. Power ceases in the instant of repose; it resides in the moment of transition from a past to a new state, in the shooting of the gulf, in the darting to an aim. This one fact the world hates, that the soul *becomes;* for that forever degrades the past; turns all riches to poverty, all reputation to a shame; confounds the saint with the rogue; shoves Jesus and Judas equally aside. Why then do we prate of self-reliance? Inasmuch as the soul is present there will be power not confident but agent. To talk of reliance is a poor external way of speaking. Speak rather of that which relies because it works and is. Who has more soul than I masters me, though he should not raise his finger. Round him I must revolve by the gravitation of spirits. Who has less I rule with like facility. We fancy it rhetoric when we speak of eminent virtue. We do not yet see that virtue is Height, and that a man or a company of men, plastic and permeable to principles, by the law of nature must overpower and ride all cities, nations, kings, rich men, poets, who are not.

This is the ultimate fact which we so quickly reach on this, as on every topic, the resolution of all into the ever-blessed ONE. Virtue is the governor, the creator, the reality. All things real are so by so much virtue as they contain. Hardship, husbandry, hunting, whaling, war, eloquence, personal weight, are somewhat, and engage my respect as examples of the soul's presence and impure action. I see the same law working in nature for conservation and growth. The poise of a planet, the bended tree recovering itself from the strong wind, the vital resources of every animal and vegetable, are also demonstrations of the self-sufficing and therefore self-relying soul. All history, from its highest to its trivial passages is the various record of this power.

Thus all concentrates; let us not rove; let us sit at home with the cause. Let us stun and astonish the intruding rabble of men and books and institutions by a simple declaration of the divine fact. Bid them take the shoes from off their feet, for God is here within. Let our simplicity judge them, and our docility to our own law demonstrate the poverty of nature and fortune beside our native riches.

But now we are a mob. Man does not stand in awe of man, nor is the soul admonished to stay at home, to put itself in communication with the internal ocean, but it goes abroad to beg a cup of water of the urns of men. We must go alone. Isolation must precede true society. I like the silent church before the service begins better than any preaching. How far off, how cool, how chaste the persons look, begirt each one with a precinct or sanctuary. So let us always sit. Why should we assume the faults of our friend, or wife, or father, or child, because they sit around our hearth, or are said to have the same blood? All men have my blood and I have all men's. Not for that will I adopt their petulance or folly, even to the extent of being ashamed of it. But your isolation must not be mechanical, but spiritual, that is, must be elevation. At times the whole world seems to be in conspiracy to importune you with emphatic trifles. Friend, client, child, sickness, fear, want, charity, all knock at once at thy closet door and say, "Come out unto us."— Do not spill thy soul; do not all descend; keep thy state; stay at home in thine own heaven; come not for a moment into their facts, into their hubbub of conflicting appearances, but let in the light of thy law on their confusion. The power men possess to annoy me I give them by a weak curiosity. No man can come near me but through my act. "What we love, that we have; but by desire we bereave ourselves of the love."

If we cannot at once rise to the sanctities of obedience and faith, let us at least resist our temptations, let us enter into the state of war and wake Thor and Woden, courage and constancy, in our Saxon breasts. This is to be done in our smooth times by speaking the truth. Check this lying hospitality and lying affection. Live no longer to the expectation of these deceived and deceiving people with whom we converse. Say to them, O father, O mother, O wife, O brother, O friend, I have lived with you after appearances hitherto. Henceforward I am the truth's. Be it known unto you that hence-

forward I obey no law less than the eternal law. I will
have no covenants but proximities. I shall endeavor to
nourish my parents, to support my family, to be the
chaste husband of one wife,—but these relations I must
fill after a new and unprecedented way. I appeal from
your customs. I must be myself. I cannot break myself any longer for you, or you. If you can love me for
what I am, we shall be happier. If you cannot, I will
still seek to deserve that you should. I must be myself.
I will not hide my tastes or aversions. I will so trust
that what is deep is holy, that I will do strongly before
the sun and moon whatever inly rejoices me and the
heart appoints. If you are noble, I will love you; if you
are not, I will not hurt you and myself by hypocritical
attentions. If you are true, but not in the same truth
with me, cleave to your companions; I will seek my own.
I do this not selfishly but humbly and truly. It is alike
your interest, and mine, and all men's, however long we
have dwelt in lies, to live in truth. Does this sound
harsh to-day? You will soon love what is dictated by
your nature as well as mine, and if we follow the truth
it will bring us out safe at last.—But so may you give
these friends pain. Yes, but I cannot sell my liberty and
my power, to save their sensibility. Besides, all persons
have their moments of reason, when they look out into
the region of absolute truth; then will they justify me and
do the same thing.

The populace think that your rejection of popular
standards is a rejection of all standard, and mere antinomianism;* and the bold sensualist will use the name of
philosophy to gild his crimes. But the law of consciousness abides. There are two confessionals, in one or the
other of which we must be shriven. You may fulfil

* Antinomianism, the doctrine that one may be saved by faith,
regardless of his disobedience of the moral law.

your round of duties by clearing yourself in the *direct*, or in the *reflex* way. Consider whether you have satisfied your relations to father, mother, cousin, neighbor, town, cat and dog; whether any of these can upbraid you. But I may also neglect this reflex standard and absolve me to myself. I have my own stern claims and perfect circle. It denies the name of duty to many offices that are called duties. But if I can discharge its debts it enables me to dispense with the popular code. If any one imagines that this law is lax, let him keep its commandment one day.

And truly it demands something godlike in him who has cast off the common motives of humanity and has ventured to trust himself for a taskmaster. High be his heart, faithful his will, clear his sight, that he may in good earnest be doctrine, society, law, to himself, that a simple purpose may be to him as strong as iron necessity is to others.

If any man consider the present aspects of what is called by distinction *society*, he will see the need of these ethics. The sinew and heart of man seem to be drawn out, and we are become timorous desponding whimperers. We are afraid of truth, afraid of fortune, afraid of death, and afraid of each other. Our age yields no great and perfect persons. We want men and women who shall renovate life and our social state, but we see that most natures are insolvent; cannot satisfy their own wants, have an ambition out of all proportion to their practical force, and so do lean and beg day and night continually. Our housekeeping is mendicant, our arts, our occupations, our marriages, our religion we have not chosen, but society has chosen for us. We are parlor soldiers. The rugged battle of fate, where strength is born, we shun.

If our young men miscarry in their first enterprises they lose all heart. If the young merchant fails, men say he is *ruined*. If the finest genius studies at one of our colleges, and is not installed in an office within one year afterward, in the cities or suburbs of Boston or New York, it seems to his friends and to himself that he is right in being disheartened and in complaining the rest of his life. A sturdy lad from New Hampshire or Vermont, who in turn tries all the professions, who *teams it, farms it, peddles*, keeps a school, preaches, edits a newspaper, goes to Congress, buys a township, and so forth, in successive years, and always like a cat falls on his feet, is worth a hundred of these city dolls. He walks abreast with his days and feels no shame in not "studying a profession," for he does not postpone his life, but lives already. He has not one chance, but a hundred chances. Let a stoic arise who shall reveal the resources of man and tell men they are not leaning willows, but can and must detach themselves; that with the exercise of self-trust, new powers shall appear; that a man is the word made flesh, born to shed healing to the nations, that he should be ashamed of our compassion, and that the moment he acts from himself, tossing the laws, the books, idolatries and customs out of the window,—we pity him no more but thank and revere him;—and that teacher shall restore the life of man to splendor and make his name dear to all History.

It is easy to see that a greater self-reliance—a new respect for the divinity in man—must work a revolution in all the offices and relations of men; in their religion; in their education; in their pursuits; their modes of living; their association; in their property; in their speculative views.

1. In what prayers do men allow themselves! That which they call a holy office is not so much as brave and manly. Prayer looks abroad and asks for some foreign addition to come through some foreign virtue, and loses itself in endless mazes of natural and supernatural, and

mediatorial and miraculous. Prayer that craves a particular commodity—anything less than all good, is vicious. Prayer is the contemplation of the facts of life from the highest point of view. It is the soliloquy of a beholding and jubilant soul. It is the spirit of God pronouncing his works good. But prayer as a means to effect a private end is theft and meanness. It supposes dualism and not unity in nature and consciousness. As soon as the man is at one with God, he will not beg. He will then see prayer in all action. The prayer of the farmer kneeling in his field to weed it, the prayer of the rower kneeling with the stroke of his oar, are true prayers heard throughout nature, though for cheap ends. Caratach, in Fletcher's *Bonduca*, when admonished to inquire the mind of the god Audate, replies,

> His hidden meaning lies in our endeavors;
> Our valors are our best gods.

Another sort of false prayers are our regrets. Discontent is the want of self-reliance: it is infirmity of will. Regret calamities if you can thereby help the sufferer; if not, attend your own work and already the evil begins to be repaired. Our sympathy is just as base. We come to them who weep foolishly and sit down and cry for company, instead of imparting to them truth and health in rough electric shocks, putting them once more in communication with the soul. The secret of fortune is joy in our hands. Welcome evermore to gods and men is the self-helping man. For him all doors are flung wide. Him all tongues greet, all honors crown, all eyes follow with desire. Our love goes out to him and embraces him because he did not need it. We solicitously and apologetically caress and celebrate him because he held on his way and scorned our disapprobation. The gods love him because men hated him. "To the persevering mortal," said Zoroaster, "the blessed Immortals are swift."

As men's prayers are a disease of the will, so are their creeds a disease of the intellect. They say with those foolish Israelites, "Let not God speak to us, lest we die. Speak thou, speak any man with us, and we will obey." * Everywhere I am bereaved of meeting God in my brother, because he has shut his own temple doors and recites fables merely of his brother's, or his brother's brother's God. Every new mind is a new classification. If it prove a mind of uncommon activity and power, a Locke,† a Lavoisier, a Hutton, a Bentham, a Spurzheim, it imposes its classification on other men, and lo! a new system. In proportion always to the depth of the thought, and so to the number of the objects it touches and brings within reach of the pupil, is his complacency. But chiefly is this apparent in creeds and churches, which are also classifications of some powerful mind acting on the great elemental thought of Duty and man's relation to the Highest. Such is Calvinism, Quakerism, Swedenborgianism. The pupil takes the same delight in subordinating everything to the new terminology that a girl does who has just learned botany in seeing a new earth and new seasons thereby. It will happen for a time that the pupil will feel a real debt to the teacher—will find his intellectual power has grown by the study of his writings. This will continue until he has exhausted his master's mind. But in all unbalanced minds the classification is idolized, passes for the end and not for a speedily exhaustible means, so that the walls of the system blend to their eye in the remote horizon with the walls of the uni-

* Exodus, 20, 19.

† Locke and Bentheim were English philosophers; Lavoisier a French chemist who discovered the composition of water; Hutton was a Scotch geologist; Spurzheim, a German who put forth the system of phrenology.

verse; the luminaries of heaven seem to them hung on the arch their master built. They cannot imagine how you aliens have any right to see—how you can see; "It must be somehow that you stole the light from us." They do not yet perceive that light, unsystematic, indomitable, will break into any cabin, even into theirs. Let them chirp awhile and call it their own. If they are honest and do well, presently their neat new pinfold will be too strait and low, will crack, will lean, will rot and vanish, and the immortal light, all young and joyful, million-orbed, million-colored, will beam over the universe as on the first morning.

2. It is for want of self-culture that the idol of Travelling, the idol of Italy, of England, of Egypt, remains for all educated Americans. They who made England, Italy, or Greece venerable in the imagination, did so not by rambling round creation as a moth round a lamp, but by sticking fast where they were, like an axis of the earth. In manly hours we feel that duty is our place and that the merry men of circumstance should follow as they may. The soul is no traveller: the wise man stays at home with the soul, and when his necessities, his duties, on any occasion call him from his house, or into foreign lands, he is at home still and is not gadding abroad from himself, and shall make men sensible by the expression of his countenance that he goes the missionary of wisdom and virtue, and visits cities and men like a sovereign and not like an interloper or a valet.

I have no churlish objection to the circumnavigation of the globe for the purposes of art, of study, and benevolence, so that the man is first domesticated, or does not go abroad with the hope of finding somewhat greater than he knows. He who travels to be amused or to get somewhat which he does not carry, travels away from himself and grows old even in youth among old things.

In Thebes, in Palmyra, his will and mind have become old and dilapidated as they. He carries ruins to ruins.

Travelling is a fool's paradise. We owe to our first journeys the discovery that place is nothing. At home I dream that at Naples, at Rome, I can be intoxicated with beauty and lose my sadness. I pack my trunk, embrace my friends, embark on the sea and at last wake up in Naples, and there beside me is the stern Fact, the sad self, unrelenting, identical, that I fled from. I seek the Vatican and the palaces. I affect to be intoxicated with sights and suggestions, but I am not intoxicated. My giant goes with me wherever I go.

3. But the rage of travelling is itself only a symptom of a deeper unsoundness affecting the whole intellectual action. The intellect is vagabond, and the universal system of education fosters restlessness. Our minds travel when our bodies are forced to stay at home. We imitate; and what is imitation but the travelling of the mind? Our houses are built with foreign taste; our shelves are garnished with foreign ornaments; our opinions, our tastes, our whole minds, lean, and follow the Past and the Distant, as the eyes of a maid follow her mistress. The soul created the arts wherever they have flourished. It was in his own mind that the artist sought his model. It was an application of his own thought to the thing to be done and the conditions to be observed. And why need we copy the Doric or the Gothic model? Beauty, convenience, grandeur of thought and quaint expression are as near to us as to any, and if the American artist will study with hope and love the precise thing to be done by him, considering the climate, the soil, the length of the day, the wants of the people, the habit and form of the government, he will create a house in which all these will find themselves fitted, and taste and sentiment will be satisfied also.

Insist on yourself; never imitate. Your own gift you can present every moment with the cumulative force of a whole life's cultivation; but of the adopted talent of another you have only an extemporaneous half-possession. That which each can do best, none but his Maker can teach him. No man yet knows what it is, nor can, till that person has exhibited it. Where is the master who could have taught Shakspeare? Where is the master who could have instructed Franklin, or Washington, or Bacon, or Newton? Every great man is an unique. The Scipionism of Scipio is precisely that part he could not borrow. If anybody will tell me whom the great man imitates in the original crisis when he performs a great act, I will tell him who else than himself can teach him. Shakspeare will never be made by the study of Shakspeare. Do that which is assigned thee and thou canst not hope too much or dare too much. There is at this moment, there is for me an utterance bare and grand as that of the colossal chisel of Phidias, or trowel of the Egyptians, or the pen of Moses or Dante, but different from all these. Not possibly will the soul, all rich, all eloquent, with thousand-cloven tongue, deign to repeat itself; but if I can hear what these patriarchs say, surely I can reply to them in the same pitch of voice; for the ear and the tongue are two organs of one nature. Dwell up there in the simple and noble regions of thy life, obey thy heart and thou shalt reproduce the Foreworld again.

4. As our Religion, our Education, our Art look abroad, so does our spirit of society. All men plume themselves on the improvement of society, and no man improves.

Society never advances. It recedes as fast on one side as it gains on the other. Its progress is only apparent, like the workers of a treadmill. It undergoes continual changes; it is barbarous, it is civilized, it is christianized, it is rich, it is scientific; but this change is not amelioration. For everything that is given something is taken. Society acquires new arts and loses old instincts. What a contrast between the well-clad, reading, writing, thinking American, with a watch, a pencil and a bill of exchange in his pocket, and the naked New Zealander, whose property is a club, a spear, a mat and an undivided twentieth of a shed to sleep under. But compare the health of the two men and you shall see that his aboriginal strength the white man has lost. If the traveller tell us truly, strike the savage with a broadax and in a day or two the flesh shall unite and heal as if you struck the blow into soft pitch, and the same blow shall send the white to his grave.

The civilized man has built a coach, but has lost the use of his feet. He is supported on crutches, but lacks so much support of muscle. He has got a fine Geneva watch, but he has lost the skill to tell the hour by the sun. A Greenwich nautical almanac he has, and so being sure of the information when he wants it, the man in the street does not know a star in the sky. The solstice he does not observe; the equinox he knows as little; and the whole bright calendar of the year is without a dial in his mind. His note-books impair his memory: his libraries overload his wit; the insurance-office increases the number of accidents; and it may be a question whether machinery does not encumber; whether we have not lost by refinement some energy, by a Christianity intrenched in establishments and forms, some vigor of wild virtue. For every Stoic was a Stoic; but in Christendom where is the Christian?

There is no more deviation in the moral standard than in the standard of height or bulk. No greater men are now than ever were. A singular equality may be observed between the great men of the first and of the last ages; nor can all the science, art, religion, and philosophy of the nineteenth century avail to educate greater men than Plutarch's* heroes, three or four and twenty centuries ago. Not in time is the race progressive. Phocion, Socrates, Anaxagoras, Diogenes, are great men, but they leave no class. He who is really of their class will not be called by their name, but be wholly his own man, and in his turn the founder of a sect. The arts and inventions of each period are only its costume and do not invigorate men. The harm of the improved machinery may compensate its good. Hudson and Behring accomplished so much in their fishing-boats as to astonish Parry and Franklin, whose equipment exhausted the resources of science and art. Galileo, with an opera-glass, discovered a more splendid series of facts than any one since. Columbus found the New World in an undecked boat. It is curious to see the periodical disuse and perishing of means and machinery which were introduced with loud laudation a few years or centuries before. The great genius returns to essential man. We reckoned the improvements of the art of war among the triumphs of science, and yet Napoleon conquered Europe by the bivouac, which consisted of falling back on naked valor and disencumbering it of all aids. The Emperor held it impossible to make a perfect army, says Las Cases, "without abolishing our arms, magazines, commissaries and carriages, until, in imitation of the Roman custom, the soldier should receive his supply of corn, grind it in his handmill and bake his bread himself."

Society is a wave. The wave moves onward, but the water of which it is composed does not. The same particle does not rise from the valley to the ridge. Its unity

---

* Plutarch, a Greek historian who wrote the lives of illustrious Greeks and Romans. The names following are those of great statesmen and philosophers of whom he wrote.

is only phenomenal. The persons who make up a nation to-day, next year die, and their experience dies with them.

And so the reliance on Property, including the reliance on governments which protect it, is the want of self-reliance. Men have looked away from themselves and at things so long that they have come to esteem what they call the soul's progress, namely, the religious, learned and civil institutions, as guards of property, and they deprecate assaults on these, because they feel them to be assaults on property. They measure their esteem of each other by what each has, and not by what each is. But a cultivated man becomes ashamed of his property, ashamed of what he has, out of new respect for his being. Especially he hates what he has if he see that it is accidental, came to him by inheritance, or gift, or crime; then he feels that it is not having; it does not belong to him, has no root in him, and merely lies there because no revolution or no robber takes it away. But that which a man is, does always by necessity acquire, and what the man acquires, is permanent and living property, which does not wait the beck of rulers, or mobs, or revolutions, or fire, or storm, or bankruptcies, but perpetually renews itself wherever the man is put. "Thy lot or portion of life," said the Caliph Ali, "is seeking after thee; therefore be at rest from seeking after it." Our dependence on these foreign goods leads us to our slavish respect for numbers. The political parties meet in numerous conventions; the greater the concourse and with each new uproar of announcement, The delegation from Essex! The Democrats from New Hampshire! The Whigs of Maine! the young patriot feels himself stronger than before by a new thousand of eyes and arms. In like manner the reformers summon conventions and vote and resolve in multitude. But not so O friends! will the God deign to enter and inhabit you, but by a method precisely the reverse. It is only as a man puts off from himself all external support and stands alone that I see him to be strong and to prevail. He is weaker by every recruit to his banner. Is not a man better than a town? Ask nothing of men, and, in the endless mutation, thou only firm column must presently appear the upholder of all that surrounds thee. He who knows that power is in the soul, that he is weak only because he has looked for good out of him and elsewhere, and, so perceiving, throws himself unhesitatingly on his thought, instantly rights himself, stands in the erect position, commands his limbs, works miracles; just as a man who stands on his feet is stronger than a man who stands on his head.

So use all that is called Fortune. Most men gamble with her, and gain all, and lose all, as her wheel rolls. But do thou leave as unlawful these winnings, and deal with Cause and Effect, the chancellors of God. In the Will work and acquire, and thou hast chained the wheel of Chance, and shalt always drag her after thee. A political victory, a rise of rents, the recovery of your sick or the return of your absent friend, or some other quite external event raises your spirits, and you think good days are preparing for you. Do not believe it. It can never be so. Nothing can bring you peace but yourself. Nothing can bring you peace but the triumph of principles.

JOHN GALSWORTHY

AMERICAN AND BRITON

John Galsworthy (1867———), one of the most significant of English writers of to-day, was born at Coombe, Surrey, of an old English family, and was educated at Harrow and at Oxford. After several years spent in travel, he returned to England and began his literary work. He is noted as a novelist, dramatist, and essayist. His novels deal with contemporary English life; the best known of these are *The Man of Property*, *Fraternity*, *The Dark Flower*, *The Freelands*, and *Saint's Progress*. He visited America in 1918, delivering lectures on literature, which were published as *Addresses in America*. He is among the successful dramatists of to-day. His plays often present some problem of the time, as *Strife*, which dramatizes the conflict between employer and employee, with a strike as the chief incident; or *Justice*, which deals with our methods of punishment. Other plays are: *The Silver Box*, *Joy*, *The Little Dream*, *The Pigeon*, *The Eldest Son*, *The Fugitive*, *The Mob*, *A Bit o' Love*, *The Skin Game*. Many of these have been produced in America. His essays include four volumes, *A Motley*, *The Inn of Tranquillity*, *A Sheaf*, and *Another Sheaf*.

JOHN GALSWORTHY

AMERICAN AND BRITON

(From *Another Sheaf*)

On the mutual understanding of each other by Britons and Americans the future happiness of nations depends more than on any other world cause.

I have never held a whole-hearted brief for the British character. There is a lot of good in it, but much which is repellent. It has a kind of deliberate unattractiveness, setting out on its journey with the words: "Take me or leave me." One may respect a person of this sort, but it is difficult either to know or to like him. I am told that an American officer said recently to a British staff officer in a friendly voice: "So we're going to clean up Brother Boche together!" and the British staff officer replied "Really!" No wonder Americans sometimes say: "I've got no use for those fellows."

The world is consecrate to strangeness and discovery, and the attitude of mind concreted in that "Really!" seems unforgivable, till one remembers that it is manner rather than matter which divides the hearts of American and Briton.

In a huge, still half-developed country, where every kind of national type and habit comes to run a new thread into the rich tapestry of American life and thought, people must find it almost impossible to conceive the life of a little old island where traditions persist generation after generation without anything to break them up; where blood remains undoctored by new strains; demeanor becomes crystallized for lack of contrasts· and

manner gets set like a plaster mask. The English manner of to-day, of what are called the classes, is the growth
of only a century or so. There was probably nothing at
all like it in the days of Elizabeth or even of Charles II.
The English manner was still racy when the inhabitants
of Virginia, as we are told, sent over to ask that there
might be despatched to them some hierarchical assistance
for the good of their souls, and were answered: "D——n
your souls, grow tobacco!" The English manner of
to-day could not even have come into its own when that
epitaph of a lady, quoted somewhere by Gilbert Murray,
was written: "Bland, passionate, and deeply religious,
she was second cousin to the Earl of Leitrim; of such are
the Kingdom of Heaven." About that gravestone motto
was a certain lack of the self-consciousness which is now
the foremost characteristic of the English manner.

But this British self-consciousness is no mere fluffy
gaucherie,* it is our special form of what Germans would
call "Kultur." Behind every manifestation of thought
or emotion the Briton retains control of self, and is thinking: "That's all I'll let them see"; even: "That's all I'll
let myself feel." This stoicism is good in its refusal to
be foundered; bad in that it fosters a narrow outlook;
starves emotion, spontaneity, and frank sympathy; de-
stroys grace and what one may describe roughly as the
lovable side of personality. The English hardly ever say
just what comes into their heads. What we call "good
form," the unwritten law which governs certain classes of
the Briton, savors of the dull and glacial; but there lurks
within it a core of virtue. It has grown up like callous
shell round two fine ideals—suppression of the ego lest
it trample on the corns of other people, and exaltation of
the maxim: "Deeds before words." Good form, like any
other religion, starts well with some ethical truth, but

* *Gaucherie*, awkwardness, stiffness.

soon gets commonized and petrified till we can hardly trace its origin, and watch with surprise its denial and contradiction of the root idea.

Without doubt good form had become a kind of disease in England. A French friend told me how he witnessed in a Swiss hotel the meeting between an Englishwoman and her son, whom she had not seen for two years; she was greatly affected—by the fact that he had not brought a dinner jacket. The best manners are no "manners," or at all events no mannerisms; but many Britons who have even attained to this perfect purity are yet not free from the paralytic effects of "good form"; are still self-conscious in the depths of their souls, and never do or say a thing without trying not to show what they are feeling. All this guarantees a certain decency in life; but in intimate intercourse with people of other nations who have not this particular cult of suppression, we English disappoint, and jar, and often irritate. Nations have their differing forms of snobbery. At one time the English all wanted to be second cousins to the Earl of Leitrim, like that lady bland and passionate. Nowadays it is not so simple. The Earl of Leitrim has become etherealized. We no longer care how a fellow is born so long as he be-haves as the Earl of Leitrim would have, never makes himself conspicuous or ridiculous, never shows too much what he's really feeling, never talks of what he's going to do, and always "plays the game." The cult is centred in our public schools* and universities.

At a very typical and honored old public school the writer of this essay passed on the whole a happy time; but what a curious life, educationally speaking! We lived rather like young Spartans; and were not encour-

* Public school, in England, means a private school where the sons of the well-to-do and the nobility prepare for college. They corre-spond to Lawrenceville, Exeter, and other academies in America.

aged to think, imagine, or see anything that we learned in relation to life at large. It's very difficult to teach boys, because their chief object in life is not to be taught anything, but I should say we were crammed, not taught at all. Living as we did the herd-life of boys with little or no intrusion from our elders, and they men who had been brought up in the same way as ourselves, we were debarred from any real interest in philosophy, history, art, literature and music, or any advancing notions in social life or politics. I speak of the generality, not of the few black swans among us. We were reactionaries almost to a boy. I remember one summer term Gladstone came down to speak to us, and we repaired to the Speech Room with white collars and dark hearts, muttering what we would do to that Grand Old Man if we could have our way. But he contrived to charm us, after all, till we cheered him vociferously. In that queer life we had all sorts of unwritten rules of suppression. You must turn up your trousers; must not go out with your umbrella rolled. Your hat must be worn tilted forward; you must not walk more than two abreast till you reached a certain form, nor be enthusiastic about anything, except such a supreme matter as a drive over the pavilion at cricket, or a run the whole length of the ground at football. You must not talk about yourself or your home people, and for any punishment you must assume complete indifference.

I dwell on these trivialities because every year thousands of British boys enter these mills which grind exceeding small, and because these boys constitute in after-life the great majority of the official, military, academic, professional, and a considerable proportion of the business classes of Great Britain. They become the Englishmen who say: "Really!" and they are for the most part the Englishmen who travel and reach America. The great defense I have always heard put up for our public schools is that they form character. As oatmeal is supposed to form bone in the bodies of Scotsmen, so our public schools are supposed to form good, sound moral fibre in British boys. And there is much in this plea. The life does make boys enduring, self-reliant, good-tempered and honorable, but it most carefully endeavors to destroy all original sin of individuality, spontaneity, and engaging freakishness. It implants, moreover, in the great majority of those who have lived it the mental attitude of that swell, who when asked where he went for his hats, replied: "Blank's, of course. Is there another fellow's?"

To know all is to excuse all—to know all about the bringing up of English public school boys makes one excuse much. The atmosphere and tradition of those places is extraordinarily strong, and persists through all modern changes. Thirty-seven years have gone since I was a new boy, but cross-examining a young nephew who left not long ago, I found almost precisely the same features and conditions. The war, which has changed so much of our social life, will have some, but no very great, effect on this particular institution. The boys still go there from the same kind of homes and preparatory schools and come under the same kind of masters. And the traditional unemotionalism, the cult of a dry and narrow stoicism, is rather fortified than diminished by the times we live in.

Our universities, on the other hand, are now mere ghosts of their old selves. At a certain old college in Oxford, last term, they had only two English students. In the chapel under the Joshua Reynolds window, through which the sun was shining, hung a long "roll of honor," a hundred names and more. In the college garden an open-air hospital was ranged under the old city wall, where we used to climb and go wandering in the early summer mornings after some all-night spree. Down on the river the empty college barges lay void of life. From the top of one of them an aged custodian broke into words: "Ah! Oxford'll never be the same again in my time. Why, who's to teach 'em rowin'? When we do get undergrads again, who's to teach 'em? All the old ones gone, killed, wounded and that. No! Rowin'll never be the same again—not in my time." That was *the* tragedy of the war for him. Our universities will recover faster than he thinks, and resume the care of our particular "Kultur," and cap the products of our public schools with the Oxford accent and the Oxford manner.

An acute critic tells me that Americans reading such deprecatory words as these by an Englishman about his country's institutions would say that this is precisely an instance of what an American means by the Oxford manner. Americans whose attitude toward their own country is that of a lover to his lady or a child to its mother, cannot—he says—understand how Englishmen can be critical of their own country, and yet love her. Well, the Englishman's attitude to his country is that of a man to himself, and the way he runs her down is but a part of that special English bone-deep self-consciousness. Englishmen (the writer amongst them) love their country as much as the French love France and the Americans America; but she is so much a part of them that to speak well of her is like speaking well of themselves, which they have been brought up to regard as "bad form." When Americans hear Englishmen speaking critically of their own country, let them note it for a sign of complete identification with that country rather than of detachment from it. But on the whole it must be admitted that English universities have a broadening influence on the material which comes to them so set and narrow.

They do a little to discover for their children that there are many points of view, and much which needs an open mind in this world. They have not precisely a democratic influence, but taken by themselves they would not be inimical to democracy. And when the war is over they will surely be still broader in philosophy and teaching. Heaven forbid that we should see vanish all that is old, and has, as it were, the virginia-creeper, the wistaria bloom of age upon it; there is a beauty in age and a health in tradition, ill dispensed with. What is hateful in age is its lack of understanding and of sympathy; in a word—its intolerance. Let us hope this wind of change may sweep out and sweeten the old places of our country, sweep away the cobwebs and the dust, our narrow ways of thought, our mannikinisms. But those who hate intolerance dare not be intolerant with the foibles of age; we should rather see them as comic, and gently laugh them out. I pretend to no proper knowledge of the American people; but, though amongst them there are doubtless pockets of fierce prejudice, I have on the whole the impression of a wide and tolerant spirit. To that spirit one would appeal when it comes to passing judgment on the educated Briton. He may be self-sufficient, but he has grit; and at bottom grit is what Americans appreciate more than anything. If the motto of the old Oxford college, "Manners makyth man," were true, one would often be sorry for the Briton. But his manners do not make him; they mar him. His goods are all absent from the shop-window; he is not a man of the world in the wider meaning of that expression. And there is, of course, a particularly noxious type of travelling Briton, who does his best, unconsciously, to deflower his country wherever he goes. Selfish, coarse-fibred, loud-voiced, —the sort which thanks God he is a Briton—I suppose because nobody else will do it for him.

We live in times when patriotism is exalted above all other virtues, because there happen to lie before the patriotic tremendous chances for the display of courage and self-sacrifice. Patriotism ever has that advantage, as the world is now constituted; but patriotism and provincialism are sisters under the skin, and they who can only see bloom on the plumage of their own kind, who prefer the bad points of their countrymen to the good points of foreigners, merely write themselves down blind of an eye, and panderers to herd feeling. America is advantaged in this matter. She lives so far away from other nations that she might well be excused for thinking herself the only people in the world; but in the many strains of blood which go to make up America there is as yet a natural corrective to the narrower kind of patriotism. America has vast spaces and many varieties of type and climate, and life to her is still a great adventure. Americans have their own form of self-absorption, but seem free as yet from the special competitive self-centrement which has been forced on Britons through long centuries by countless continental rivalries and wars. Insularity was driven into the very bones of our people by the generation-long wars of Napoleon. A distinguished French writer, André Chevrillon, whose book* may be commended to any one who wishes to understand British peculiarities, used these words in a recent letter: "You English are so strange to us French, you are so utterly different from any other people in the world." Yes! We are a lonely race. Deep in our hearts, I think, we feel that only the American people could ever really understand us. And being extraordinarily self-conscious, perverse, and proud, we do our best to hide from Americans that we have any such feeling. It would distress the average Briton to confess that he wanted to be under-

*England and the War. Hodder & Stoughton.

stood, had anything so natural as a craving for fellowship
or for being liked. We are a weird people, though we
seem so commonplace. In looking at photographs of
British types among photographs of other European na-
tionalities, one is struck by something which is in no
other of those races—exactly as if we had an extra skin;
as if the British animal had been tamed longer than the
rest. And so he has. His political, social, legal life was
fixed long before that of any other Western country.
He was old, though not mouldering, before the *Mayflower* touched American shores and brought there ava-
tars, grave and civilized as ever founded nation. There
is something touching and terrifying about our character,
about the depth at which it keeps its real yearnings, about
the perversity with which it disguises them, and its in-
ability to show its feelings. We are, deep down, under
all our lazy mentality, the most combative and competitive race in the world, with the exception, perhaps, of the
American. This is at once a spiritual link with America,
and yet one of the great barriers to friendship between
the two peoples. We are not sure whether we are better
men than Americans. Whether we are really better than
French, Germans, Russians, Italians, Chinese, or any
other race is, of course, more than a question; but those
peoples are all so different from us that we are bound, I
suppose, secretly to consider ourselves superior. But
between Americans and ourselves, under all differences,
there is some mysterious deep kinship which causes us to
doubt and makes us irritable, as if we were continually
being tickled by that question: Now am I really a better
man than he? Exactly what proportion of American
blood at this time of day is British, I know not; but
enough to make us definitely cousins—always an awkward
relationship. We see in Americans a sort of image of
ourselves; feel near enough, yet far enough, to criticise

and carp at the points of difference. It is as though a man went out and encountered, in the street, what he thought for the moment was himself, and, wounded in his *amour propre*,* instantly began to disparage the appearance of that fellow. Probably community of language rather than of blood accounts for our sense of kinship, for a common means of expression cannot but mould thought and feeling into some kind of unity. One can hardly overrate the intimacy which a common literature brings. The lives of great Americans, Washington and Franklin, Lincoln and Lee and Grant, are unsealed for us, just as to Americans are the lives of Marlborough and Nelson, Pitt and Gladstone and Gordon. Longfellow and Whittier and Whitman can be read by the British child as simply as Burns and Shelley and Keats. Emerson and William James are no more difficult to us than Darwin and Spencer to Americans. Without an effort we rejoice in Hawthorne and Mark Twain, Henry James and Howells, as Americans can in Dickens and Thackeray, Meredith and Thomas Hardy. And, more than all, Americans own with ourselves all literature in the English tongue before the *Mayflower* sailed; Chaucer and Spenser and Shakespeare, Raleigh, Ben Jonson, and the authors of the English Bible Version are their spiritual ancestors as much as ever they are ours. The tie of language is all-powerful—for language is the food formative of minds. A volume could be written on the formation of character by literary humor alone. The American and Briton, especially the British townsman, have a kind of bone-deep defiance of Fate, a readiness for anything which may turn up, a dry wry smile under the blackest sky, and an individual way of looking at things which nothing can shake. Americans and Britons both, we must and will think for ourselves, and know why we do a thing before

* *Amour propre*, self-love, vanity.

we do it. We have that ingrained respect for the individual conscience which is at the bottom of all free institutions. Some years before the war an intelligent and cultivated Austrian, who had lived long in England, was asked for his opinion of the British. "In many ways," he said, "I think you are inferior to us; but one great thing I have noticed about you which we have not. You think and act and speak for yourselves." If he had passed those years in America instead of in England he must needs have pronounced the same judgment of Americans. Free speech, of course, like every form of freedom, goes in danger of its life in war-time. The other day, in Russia, an Englishman came on a street meeting shortly after the first revolution had begun. An extremist was addressing the gathering and telling them that they were fools to go on fighting, that they ought to refuse and go home, and so forth. The crowd grew angry, and some soldiers were for making a rush at him; but the chairman, a big, burly peasant, stopped them with these words: "Brothers, you know that our country is now a country of free speech. We must listen to this man, we must let him say anything he will. But, brothers, when he's finished, we'll bash his head in!"

I cannot assert that either Britons or Americans are incapable in times like these of a similar interpretation of "free speech." Things have been done in our country, and will be done in America, which should make us blush. But so strong is the free instinct in both countries that some vestiges of it will survive even this war, for democracy is a sham unless it means the preservation and development of this instinct of thinking for oneself throughout a people. "Government of the people, by the people, for the people" means nothing unless individuals keep their consciences unfettered and think freely. Accustom people to be nose-led and spoon-fed, and democracy is a mere pretense. The measure of democracy is the measure of the freedom and sense of individual responsibility in its humblest citizens. And democracy— I say it with solemnity—has yet to prove itself.

A scientist, Dr. Spurrell, in a recent book, *Man and His Forerunners*, diagnoses the growth of civilizations somewhat as follows: A civilization begins with the enslavement by some hardy race of a tame race living a tame life in more congenial natural surroundings. It is built up on slavery, and attains its maximum vitality in conditions little removed therefrom. Then, as individual freedom gradually grows, disorganization sets in and the civilization slowly dissolves away in anarchy. Dr. Spurrell does not dogmatize about our present civilization, but suggests that it will probably follow the civilizations of the past into dissolution. I am not convinced of that, because of certain factors new to the history of man. Recent discoveries are unifying the world; such old isolated swoops of race on race are not now possible. In our great industrial states, it is true, a new form of slavery has arisen, but not of man by man, rather of man by machines. Moreover, all past civilizations have been more or less Southern, and subject to the sapping influence of the sun. Modern civilization is essentially Northern. The individualism, however, which, according to Dr. Spurrell, dissolved the empires of the past, exists already, in a marked degree, in every modern state; and the problem before us is to discover how democracy and liberty of the subject can be made into enduring props rather than dissolvents. It is the problem of making democracy genuine. And certainly, if that cannot be achieved and perpetuated, there is nothing to prevent democracy drifting into anarchism and dissolving modern states, till they are the prey of pouncing dictators, or of states not so far gone in dissolution. What, for instance, will happen to Russia if she does not succeed in making her democracy genuine? A Russia which remains anarchic must very quickly become the prey of her neighbors on west and east.

Ever since the substantial introduction of democracy nearly a century and a half ago with the American War of Independence, Western civilization has been living on two planes or levels—the autocratic plane, with which is bound up the idea of nationalism, and the democratic, to which has become conjoined the idea of internationalism. Not only little wars, but great wars such as this, come because of inequality in growth, dissimilarity of political institutions between states; because this state or that is basing its life on different principles from its neighbors. The decentralization, delays, critical temper, and importance of home affairs prevalent in democratic countries make them at once slower, weaker, less apt to strike, and less prepared to strike than countries where bureaucratic brains subject to no real popular check devise world policies which can be thrust, prepared to the last button, on the world at a moment's notice. The free and critical spirit in America, France, and Britain has kept our democracies comparatively unprepared for anything save their own affairs.

We fall into glib usage of words like democracy and make fetiches of them without due understanding. Democracy is inferior to autocracy from the aggressively national point of view; it is not necessarily superior to autocracy as a guarantee of general well-being; it may even turn out to be inferior unless we can improve it. But democracy is the rising tide; it may be dammed or delayed, but cannot be stopped. It seems to be a law in human nature that where, in any corporate society, the idea of self-government sets foot it refuses to take that foot up again. State after state, copying the American example, has adopted the democratic principle; the world's face is that way set. And civilization is now so of a pattern that the Western world may be looked on as one state and the process of change therein from autocracy to democracy regarded as though it were taking place in a single old-time country such as Greece or Rome. If throughout Western civilization we can secure the single democratic principle of government, its single level of state morality in thought and action, we shall be well on our way to unanimity throughout the world; for even in China and Japan the democratic virus is at work. It is my belief that only in a world thus uniform, and freed from the danger of pounce by autocracies, have states any chance to develop the individual conscience to a point which shall make democracy proof against anarchy and themselves proof against dissolution; and only in such a world can a League of Nations to enforce peace succeed.

But even if we do secure a single plane for Western civilization and ultimately for the world, there will be but slow and difficult progress in the lot of mankind. And unless we secure it, there will be only a march backward.

For this advance to a uniform civilization the solidarity of the English-speaking races is vital. Without that there will be no bottom on which to build.

The ancestors of the American people sought a new country because they had in them a reverence for the individual conscience; they came from Britain, the first large state in the Christian era to build up the idea of political freedom. The instincts and ideals of our two races have ever been the same. That great and lovable people, the French, with their clear thought and expression, and their quick blood, have expressed those ideals more vividly than either of us. But the phlegmatic and

the dry tenacity of our English and American temperaments has ever made our countries the most settled
and safe homes of the individual conscience, and of its
children—Democracy, Freedom and Internationalism.
Whatever their faults—and their offenses cry aloud to
such poor heaven as remains of chivalry and mercy—the
Germans are in many ways a great race, but they possess
two qualities dangerous to the individual conscience—
unquestioning obedience and exaltation. When they
embrace the democratic idea they may surpass us all in
its logical development, but the individual conscience
will still not be at ease with them. We must look to our
two countries to guarantee its strength and activity, and
if we English-speaking races quarrel and become dis-
united, civilization will split up again and go its way to
ruin. We are the ballast of the new order.

I do not believe in formal alliances or in grouping nations to exclude and keep down other nations. Friend-
ships between countries should have the only true reality
of common sentiment, *and be animated by desire for the
general welfare of mankind.* We need no formal bonds,
but we have a sacred charge in common, to let no petty
matters, differences of manner, or divergencies of material interest, destroy our spiritual agreement. Our
pasts, our geographical positions, our temperaments make
us, beyond all other races, the hope and trustees of mankind's advance along the only line now open—democratic
internationalism. It is childish to claim for Americans
or Britons virtues beyond those of other nations, or to
believe in the superiority of one national culture to another; they are different, that is all. It is by accident
that we find ourselves in this position of guardianship to
the main line of human development; no need to pat
ourselves on the back about it. But we are at a great and
critical moment in the world's history—how critical none

of us alive will ever realize. The civilization slowly built since the fall of Rome has either to break up and dissolve into jagged and isolated fragments through a century of wars; or, unified and reanimated by a single idea, to move forward on one plane and attain greater height and breadth.

Under the pressure of this war there is, beneath the lip-service we pay to democracy, a disposition to lose faith in it because of its undoubted weakness and inconvenience in a struggle with states autocratically governed; there is even a sort of secret reaction to autocracy. On those lines there is no way out of a future of bitter rivalries, chicanery and wars, and the probable total failure of our civilization. The only cure which I can see lies in democratizing the whole world and removing the present weaknesses and shams of democracy by education of the individual conscience in every country. Good-by to that chance if Americans and Britons fall foul of each other, refuse to pool their thoughts and hopes, and to keep the general welfare of mankind in view. They have got to stand together, not in aggressive and jealous policies, but in defense and championship of the self-helpful, self-governing, "live and let live" philosophy of life.

The house of the future is always dark. There are few corner-stones to be discerned in the temple of our fate. But of these few one is the brotherhood and bond of the English-speaking races, not for narrow purposes, but that mankind may yet see faith and good-will enshrined, yet breathe a sweeter air, and know a life where Beauty passes, with the sun on her wings.

We want in the lives of men a "Song of Honor," as in Ralph Hodgson's poem:

> "The song of men all sorts and kinds,
> As many tempers, moods and minds
> As leaves are on a tree,

As many faiths and castes and creeds,
As many human bloods and breeds,
　As in the world may be."

In the making of that song the English-speaking races will assuredly unite. What made this world we know not; the principle of life is inscrutable and will forever be; but we know that Earth is yet on the up-grade of existence, the mountain top of man's life not reached, that many centuries of growth are yet in front of us before Nature begins to chill this planet till it swims, at last, another moon, in space. In the climb to that mountain top of a happy life for mankind our two great nations are as guides who go before, roped together in perilous ascent. On their nerve, loyalty, and wisdom the adventure now hangs. What American or British knife will sever the rope?

He who ever gives a thought to the life of man at large, to his miseries and disappointments, to the waste and cruelty of existence, will remember that if American or Briton fail himself, or fail the other, there can but be for us both, and for all other peoples, a hideous slip, a swift and fearful fall into an abyss, whence all shall be to begin over again.

We shall not fail—neither ourselves, nor each other. Our comradeship will endure.

1917.

HENRY VAN DYKE

IS THE WORLD GROWING BETTER?

Henry van Dyke (1852——), one of the eminent men of letters of to-day, was born at Germantown, near Philadelphia. He prepared for college at the Brooklyn Polytechnic Institute, and was graduated from Princeton in 1873. He next took a course in the Theological Seminary, followed by study at the University of Berlin. He entered the Presbyterian ministry, serving as pastor of the Brick Presbyterian Church in New York City. His work as a literary critic having given him a reputation, he was offered and accepted a position as professor of literature at Princeton. In 1913-17 he served as United States minister to the Netherlands, and during the World War his writings were of great value, both as interpreting Europe to America and America to Europe. He has received degrees from many universities; he is a commander in the Legion of Honor, and has served as president of the National Institute of Arts and Sciences.

His published works include a score of volumes, the most important of which are a book of essays on *The Poetry of Tennyson;* several volumes of poems, published in collected form in 1911; two books of short stories, *The Blue Flower* and *The Ruling Passion,* and several volumes of essays and sketches with such attractive titles as *Fisherman's Luck, Little Rivers,* and *Days Off.* Another volume, *Essays in Application,* deals with deeper themes; it is from this that the essay, "Is the World Growing Better?" is taken.

His writing is characterized by finish of style, breadth of outlook, and ripe and serene wisdom.

HENRY VAN DYKE

IS THE WORLD GROWING BETTER?

(From *Essays in Application*)

No man knows, of a certainty, the answer to this question.

If it were an inquiry into the condition of the world's pocketbook, or farm, or garden, or machine house, or library, or schoolroom, the answer would be easy. Six million more spindles whirling in the world's workshop in 1903 than in 1900; eight hundred million more bushels of wheat in the world's grain-fields than in 1897; an average school attendance gaining 145 per cent between 1840 and 1888, while the population of Europe increased only 33 per cent. So the figures run in every department. No doubt the world is busier, richer, better fed, and probably it knows more, than ever before.

I am not one of those highly ethereal and supercilious people who can find nothing in this to please them, and who cry lackadaisically: "What is all this worth?" I am honest enough to confess to a sense of satisfaction when my little vegetable garden rewards my care with an enlarged crop, or when my children bring home a good report from school. Why should not a common-sense philanthropy lead us to feel in the same way about the improved condition and the better reports of the big world to which we belong? Of course our satisfaction is checked and shadowed, often very darkly shadowed, by the remembrance of those who are left behind in the march of civilization—the retarded races, the benighted classes, the poor relations, of the world. But our sympathy with them is much more likely to be helpful if it is hopeful, than if it is despairing. I do not think it necessary to cultivate melancholy or misanthropy as a preparation for beneficence.

A generous man ought to find something cheerful and encouraging to his own labors, in the knowledge that the world is growing "better off."

But is it growing better? That's another question, and a far more important one. What is happening to the world itself, the owner of all this gear, the prosperous old adventurer whose wealth, according to Mr. Gladstone, increased twice as much during the first seventy years of the nineteenth century as it had done during the eighteen hundred years preceding? Is this marvellous increase of goods beneficial to the character of the race? Or is it injurious? Or has it, perhaps, no deep or definite influence one way or the other?

You know how hard it is to come to a clear and just conclusion on such points as these, even in the case of an individual man. Peter Silvergilt's wealth has grown from nothing to three hundred million dollars during the last fifty years; but are you sure that Peter's personality is better, finer, nobler, more admirable than it was when he was a telegraph-boy earning ten dollars a week? William Wiseman has a world-wide fame as a scholar; it is commonly reported that he has forgotten more than most men ever knew; but can you trust William more implicitly to be fair and true and generous than when he was an obscure student just beginning to work for a degree in philosophy?

When we try to apply such questions, not to a single person, but to the world at large, positive and mathematical answers are impossible. The field of inquiry is too vast. The facts of racial character are too secret and subtle.

But a provisional estimate of the general condition of

the world from the point of view of goodness, comparing the present with the past—a probable guess at the direction in which the race is moving morally—this is something that we may fairly make. Indeed, if you think and care much about your brother men you can hardly help making it, and upon the color of this guess the tone of your philosophy depends. If the color is dark, you belong among the pessimists, who cannot be very happy, though they may sometimes be rather useful. If the color is bright, you are what men call an optimist, though I think George Eliot's word, "meliorist," would be a more fitting name.

For what is it, after all, that we can venture to claim for this old world of ours, at most? Certainly not that it is altogether good, nor even that it is as good as it might be and therefore ought to be. Police stations and prisons and wars are confessions that some things are wrong and need correction. The largest claim that a cheerful man who is also a thoughtful man—a child of hope with his eyes open—dares to make for the world is that it is better than it used to be, and that it has a fair prospect of further improvement. This is meliorism, the philosophy of actual and possible betterment; not a high-stepping, trumpet-blowing, self-flattering creed, immediately available for advertising purposes; but a modest and sober faith, useful for consolation in those hours of despondency and personal disappointment when the grasshopper and the critic both become a burden, and for encouragement to more earnest effort in those hours of cheer when a high tide of the spirit fills us with good-will to our fellow men.

I asked John Friendly the other day: "Do you think the world is growing better?"

"Certainly," said he, with a smile like sunrise on his honest face, "I haven't the slightest doubt of it."

"But what makes you so sure of it?"

"Why, it must be so! Look at all the work that is being done to-day to educate people and help them into better ways of living. All this effort must count for something. The wagon must move with so many horses pulling at it. The world can't help growing better!"

Then he left me, to go down to a meeting of his "Citizens' Committee for the Application of the Social Boycott to Political Offenders" (which frequently adjourns without a quorum). Immediately afterward I passed the door of the "Michael T. Moriarty Republi-cratic Club"—wide open and crowded. On my way up the avenue I saw a liquor-saloon on every block—and all busy. The news-stands were full of placards announcing articles in the magazines—"Graft in Chicago," "The Criminal Calendar of Millionaires," "St. Louis, the Bribers' Paradise," "The Plunder of Philadelphia." Head-lines in the yellow jour-nals told of "Immense Slaughter in Manchuria," "Russia Ripe for Revolution," "The Black Hand Terror in the Bronx," "Gilded Gambling-Dens of the Four Hundred," "Diamonds and Divorce."

John Friendly's cheerful *a priori** confidence in the bet-terment of the world seemed to need reinforcement. Some of the horses are pulling his way, no doubt, but a good many appear to be pulling the other way. Under such conditions the wagon might stick fast, or go backward. Possibly it might be pulled to pieces. Who can measure, in the abstract, the comparative strength of the good and the evil forces? Who can tell beforehand which way the tug-of-war must go?

The only sound and satisfactory method is to bring out the foot rule of fact and apply it to the tracks of the wagon. Has it moved? How fast, how far, which way? "Growing better" is a phrase about which a company

* *A priori*, reasoning from cause to effect.

of college professors would probably have a long preliminary dispute; but plain people understand it well enough for practical purposes. There are three factors in it. When we say that a man grows better, we mean that, in the main, he is becoming more just, and careful to do the right thing; more kind, and ready to do the helpful thing; more self-controlled, and willing to sacrifice his personal will to the general welfare. Is the world growing better in this sense? Is there more justice, more kindness, more self-restraint, among the inhabitants of earth than in the days of old?

Of course, when we consider a question like this, before even a modest guess at the answer is possible, we must be willing to take a long view and a wide view. The world, like the individual man, has its moods and its vagaries, its cold fits and its hot fits, its backslidings and its repentances, its reactions and its revivals. An advance made in one century may be partly lost in the next, and regained with interest in a later century. One nation may be degenerating, under local infections of evil, while others are improving. There may be years, or regions, of short harvest in the field of morals, just as there are in the cotton-field or the corn-field. The same general conditions that work well for the development of most men, may prove unfavorable to certain races. Civilization seems to oppress and demoralize some tribes to the point of extinction. Liberty is a tonic too strong for certain temperaments; it intoxicates them. But what we have to look at is not the local exception, nor the temporary reaction: it is the broad field as far as we can see it, the general movement as far as we can trace it. And as I try to look at the question in this way, clearly and steadily, it seems to me that the world is really growing better: not in every eddy, but in the main current of its life; not in a straight line, but with a winding course; not in every respect, but in at least two of the three main points of goodness; not swiftly, but slowly, surely, really growing better.

Take the matter of justice. The world's sense of equity, its desire to act fairly and render to every man his due, is expressed most directly in its laws. Who can fail to see a process of improvement in the spirit and temper of legislation, a conscientious effort to make the law more efficient in the protection of human rights and more just in the punishment of offenses?

In Shakespeare's time, for example, a woman's existence, in the eye of the law, was merged in that of her husband. A man could say of his wife: "She is my goods, my chattels; she is my house, my household stuff, my field, my barn, my horse, my ox, my anything." The very presents which he gave her were still his property. He could beat her. He could deprive her of the guardianship of her children. It was not until the end of the seventeenth century that the law secured her right to the separate use of her property, and not until the middle of the nineteenth century that the legislation of Great Britain and America began to recognize and protect her as a person, entitled to work and receive wages, to dispose of her own earnings, to have an equal share with her husband in the guardianship of their children. Surely it is an immense gain in justice that woman should be treated as a human being.

This gain is most evident, of course, in those nations which are leading the march of civilization. But I think we can see traces of it elsewhere. The abolition of child-marriage and the practical extinction of the *suttee** in India, the decline of the cruelly significant fashion of

* *Suttee*, the custom among Hindoo wives of casting themselves into the funeral pyre where the body of the husband was being burned.

"foot-binding" in China, the beginning of the education of girls in Egypt, are hints that even the heathen world is learning to believe that woman may have a claim to justice.

In the same way we must interpret the laws for the protection of the young against cruelty, oppression, and injustice. Beginning with the Factory Act of 1833 and the Mines and Collieries Act of 1842 in England, there has been a steadily increasing effort to diminish and prevent the degradation of the race by the enslavement of childhood to labor. Even the parent's right of control, says the modern world, must be held in harmony with the child's right to life and growth, mental, moral, and physical. The law itself must recognize the injustice of dealing with young delinquents as if they were old and hardened criminals. No more herding of children ten and twelve years old in the common jail! Juvenile courts and probation officers, asylums and reformatories: an intelligent and systematic effort to reclaim the young life before it has fallen into hopeless bondage to crime: this is the spirit of civilized legislation to-day. In 1903 no less than ten of the American states enacted special statutes with this end in view.

The great change for the better in modern criminal law is another proof that the world is growing more just. Brutal and degrading methods of execution, such as crucifixion, burying alive, impaling, disembowelling, breaking on the wheel: the judicial torture of prisoners and unwilling witnesses by the thumb-screw, the strappado, and the rack: cruel and agonizing penalties of various kinds have been abolished, not merely by way of concession to humanity, but with the purpose of maintaining justice in purity and dignity.

The world has been learning to discriminate more carefully between the degrees of crime. In the eighteenth century men were condemned to death for forgery; for stealing from a shop to the value of five shillings or from a house to the value of forty shillings; for malicious injury to trees, cattle, or fish-ponds; for the cutting of hop-bands from the poles in a plantation. Within eighty years capital punishment has been inflicted in England for sheep-stealing and for robbery from a house. The laws of Pennsylvania at the time of the Revolution enumerated twenty crimes punishable with death; in Virginia and Kentucky there were twenty-seven. Modern legislation recognizes the futility as well as the fundamental injustice of such crass and indiscriminate retribution, and reserves the final penalty for the supreme crime against the life of the individual or the state.

At the same time there has been a twofold rectification of the scope of the criminal law. Some of the offenses most severely punished in old times have ceased to be grounds of prosecution: for example, heresy, witchcraft, religious nonconformity. On the other hand, misdeeds which formerly were disregarded have been made punishable. It was not until 1833 that the English law began to treat drunkenness as a crime, rather than a misfortune. In 1857 a fraud on the part of a trustee, and in 1875 the falsification of accounts, were declared to be criminal. The laws of various States are recognizing and defining a vast number of new misdemeanors, such as the adulteration of foods, gambling, violation of laws in restraint of the liquor traffic, selling cigarettes to children, tapping electric wires, disfiguring the landscape with advertisements or printing them on the American flag, making combinations in restraint of trade, sleeping in a public bakery, spitting on the floor of a street-car. I do not say that all of these offenses are wisely defined or fairly punished; but I do say that the process of modern legislation in regard to such matters indicates a growing desire among men that justice shall prevail in the community.

A large part of what appears to be the increase of crime in recent years (according to statistics), is due to this new definition of misdemeanors. There are more offenders in the most peaceful and well-governed states, because there are more offenses defined. Another part comes from the greater efficiency in the execution of laws and the greater completeness in the tabulation of reports. The remaining part comes from a cause on which I will touch later. But in spite of this apparent increase of crime, no sensible man believes that the actual amount of violence and disorder among men is as great as it used to be. Pike's *History of Crime in England* estimates that in the fourteenth century murders were at least sixteen times as frequent as in our own day.

I pass by such notorious and splendid triumphs of the world's moral sense as the abolition of the slave-trade, and the establishment of international law, to mention two humble, concrete illustrations of what I mean by the advance of justice. The purchase by the American Government of the lands of the Spanish friars in the Philippines was a just way of accomplishing what would have been done a century ago by confiscation. The passage by the Congress of the United States of an act granting copyright to foreigners was a recognition, resisted by selfishness and ignorance for fifty years, of the fundamental principles of righteousness and fair dealing.

I know there are many items, and some of them most grievous, to be set down on the other side. There are still wars of conquest; corruptions and delays in legislation; oppressions and inequalities in government; robberies and cruelties which go unpunished. But these are not new things; they are as old as sin; evils not yet shaken off. I do not dream that the world is already quite just.

But by the light that comes from the wiser, fairer laws of many lands, I guess that the world is growing more just.

In regard to the increase of kindness in the human race, the evidence is even more clear and strong. There are more people in the world who love mercy, and they are having better success in making their spirit prevail. More is being done to-day to prevent and mitigate human suffering, to shelter and protect the weak and helpless, to minister wisely to the sick and wounded in body and in mind, than ever before in the history of mankind. Part of the evidence of this lies in some of the facts already noted in connection with the humanizing of the law, and in the extraordinary story of the work begun by John Howard, a hundred and thirty years ago, which has cleansed away so much of the shame of a cruel, filthy, and irrational prison system. But there is evidence, also, of a more direct and positive sort, going beyond the removal of ancient evils and manifesting a spirit of creative kindness eager to find new ways of helping others.

Since the middle of the nineteenth century, says the best authority on statistics, charity has grown twice as fast as wealth in England, three times as fast in France. In the United States the amount of the larger gifts ($5,000 or more) rose from $29,000,000, in 1893, to $107,000,000, in 1901. The public and private charities of New York alone (excluding the money spent on buildings) are estimated at $50,000,000 a year.

With all this increase of money comes an equal increase of care and thought in regard to the best way of using it for the real benefit of mankind. Reckless almsgiving is recognized as an amiable but idiotic form of self-indulgence. The penny dropped into the beggar's hat gives place to an inquiry into the beggar's condition. This costs more, but it is worth more. Waste in money given is no more virtuous than waste in money earned. Schools of philanthropy are established to study and teach the economy of generosity. Asylums are investigated and supervised. Relief funds are intrusted to responsible committees, who keep books and render accounts. Men and women are trying to take the head into partnership with the heart in beneficence. A rich father and mother lose their child by scarlet fever: they give a million dollars to endow an institution for the study and prevention of infectious diseases. An excursion steamboat is burned in New York harbor and a thousand people, most of them poor, lose their lives; within two weeks $125,000 is given for relief; it is not thrown away with open hands, but administered by a committee with as much care as they would bestow on their own affairs; every dollar is accounted for, and a balance of $17,000 is left, to meet future calls, or to be devoted to some kindred purpose. These are illustrations of intelligent mercy.

Consider the advance in the general spirit of kindness which is indicated by such a fact as the founding and successful operation of the system of Working Men's Insurance in Germany. A certain sum of money is set aside for each workman every week (the employer and the employee each contributing half), and the Government adds a supplement of twelve dollars on each pension. Ten million workmen are thus insured against sickness; seventeen million against accident; ten million against disability from old age. Six hundred and seventy thousand persons receive the benefit of this fund in yearly pensions. Incidentally there has been an immense benefit in the increase of precautions to prevent accidents and to reduce dangerous occupations. The employer who is not yet willing to protect his workmen, for kindness' sake, will do it to escape heavier taxes. And the community which silently compels him to do this, the community which says to the laboring man, "If you will perform your

duty, you shall not starve when you are sick and old,"
is certainly growing more kind as well as more just.

Look at the broad field of what we may call international mercy. It has been estimated that since the days
when the failure of the harvest drove Abraham from Pal-
estine down to Egypt to seek food for his starving people,
there have been three hundred and fifty great famines in
various parts of the world. How many of the hungry
nations received help from the outside world before the
nineteenth century began? But now, within a week after
the distress is known, money, food, and help of all kinds
begin to flow in from all quarters of the globe. The
famine in India in 1900–1901 called forth contributions
from Great Britain, Germany, France, America, to the
amount of $72,000,000. The greater part came from
England, of course, but the whole world stood ready to
aid her.

After the great fire of London in 1666, and the Lisbon
earthquake in 1755, there was some outside assistance
given, it is true. But in the main, the stricken cities had
to suffer alone and help themselves. When the little city
of Galveston, Texas, was swept by flood in 1900, within
three weeks $750,000 was poured in for its relief, and
the whole fund amounted to nearly a million and a
half.

Turn again to look at the effort which the world is
making to get rid of the hell of war, or, if that be not
possible, at least to mitigate its horrors and torments.
The High Tribunal of Arbitration at The Hague is a
mile-stone on the world's path of progress toward the
peaceful method of solving international disputes. Each
year sees some new advance in that direction. Since
1903 Great Britain and France, Holland and Denmark,
France and Spain, Great Britain and Italy, France and
Holland, Great Britain and Spain, Italy and France, have

made treaties by which they pledge themselves to refer all differences of certain kinds which may arise between them to this tribunal for settlement. During the same time at least seven international questions have been referred to special arbitrators.

True, war has not yet been eliminated from the programme of the race. Great armaments are maintained at incredible expense, and nations insist, as Ruskin said, that it is good policy to purchase terror of one another at the cost of hundreds of millions every year. Some of the honest friends of peace are not yet reasonable enough to see the folly of this arrangement. A peace which depends upon fear is nothing but a suppressed war. Every now and then the restraining fear gives way, in one place or another, and thousands of men are dressed in uniform and marshalled with music to blow one another's brains out. But, in spite of all this, the growth of the spirit of mercy in the world makes itself known in the application of more humane rules to the inhumanity of war. Private wars, prevalent in the Middle Ages, and piracy, tolerated until the nineteenth century, have been abolished. The slaughter, torture, and enslavement of prisoners of war, which was formerly practised by even Christian nations, gave place in the middle of the seventeenth century to the custom of releasing all prisoners at the close of the war without ransom. Even Mahometan nations agreed by treaty that they would no longer subject their captives to bondage or torture. Persia and Turkey, in 1828, pledged themselves to the exchange of prisoners.

There has been a steady advance in the strictness and efficiency of the rules protecting the life and property of non-combatants, an immense decrease in the atrocities inflicted by conquering armies upon the peaceful inhabitants of vanquished countries. Let any man read the story of the siege and sack of a town in Holland by the

Spanish soldiers as it is given in Motley's *Dutch Republic*, and compare it with the story of the capture of Paris in 1870, or even the taking of Pekin in 1900, and he will understand that war itself has felt the restraining touch of mercy. Let him reflect upon the significance of the work of the Red Cross Society, with its pledge of kindly succor to all who are wounded in battle, "treating friend and foe alike"; let him consider the remarkable fact that this society in Japan has a service as perfectly organized as any in the world, with a million members, and an annual income of more than $1,500,000, and he cannot but acknowledge that the spirit of pity and compassion has gained ground since the days of Charlemagne and Barbarossa and Napoleon—yes, even since the days of Libby Prison and Elmira. And if none of these things are enough to comfort or encourage him, let him take in the meaning of the simple fact that not one of the great nations of the world to-day would dare to proclaim a war in the name of Religion. By this blessed change alone, I should make bold to guess that the world is surely growing better.

But how is it with the third factor of real betterment: self-restraint, the willingness to sacrifice one's own passion and pleasure for the good of others? Here, I confess, my guessing is confused and troubled. There was a vast improvement from the fourteenth to the nineteenth century, no doubt. But whether the twentieth century is carrying on the advance seems uncertain.

It may be that on this point we have entered into a period of reaction. The theory of individual liberty threatens to assert itself in dangerous forms. Literature and art are throwing their enchantments about the old lie that life's highest value is found in moments of intense self-gratification. Speed is glorified, regardless of direction. Strength is worshipped at the expense of reason. Success is deified as the power to do what one likes. Gilding covers a multitude of sins.

On the one hand, we have a so-called "upper class," which says: "The world was made to amuse me; nothing else matters." On the other hand, we have an apparent increase of the criminal class, which lives at war with the social order. Corporations and labor unions engage in a struggle so fierce that the rights and interests of the community are forgotten by both parties. In our own country lynching, which is organized murder for unproved offenses, grows more common; divorces increase to 60,000 in one year; and there is an epidemic of shocking accidents and disasters, greater than any hitherto recorded, and due apparently to the spirit of unrestraint and recklessness which is sweeping furiously in its motor-car along the highways of modern life.

Is this selfish and headlong spirit growing? Will it continue to accelerate the pace at which men live, and diminish the control by which they are guided? Will it weaken more and more the bonds of reverence, and mutual consideration, and household fidelity, and civic virtue, until the states which have been civilized by the sanctions of love and the convictions of duty are whirled backward, by the passion of self-indulgence, into the barbarism of luxurious pleasure or the anarchy of social strife?

These are the questions that rise to trouble us in our moments of despondency and foreboding. But I think that it is neither wise nor brave to give them an answer of despair. Two are stronger than one. The growth of justice and of kindness, I guess, will in the long run prevail over the decline of self-restraint, and the selfish, reckless spirit will be overcome.

At all events, when Christmas comes I shall sit down with John Friendly to enjoy its cheer, rather than with any sour pessimist. For one thing is sure. The hope of humanity lies in the widening, deeping influence of that blessed Life which was born nineteen hundred years ago in Bethlehem. The Lesson which that Life teaches us is that the only way to make the world better is for each man to do his best.

Christmas, 1904!

THE GREAT RELAPSE

Christmas, 1920! Sixteen years have passed since the foregoing pages were written. Between them and now what dread disaster has befallen our too cheerful hopes, what hideous war-clouds have shadowed the world and drenched it with blood and tears!

Whence came this tempest of wrath? Out of the depths of human nature, not yet delivered from the lusts and passions that war within us and make wars around us: out of the reckless greed of our civilization centering its efforts on material riches and luxury and neglecting the discipline of the mind and heart: and especially out of the violent "will to power" of the German Empire, ready to set fire to the world in order to gain its dominion. These were the sources of the vast world-war of 1914–1918, whose after-flames still burn along the borders and whose ashes cover the face of the earth.

How immense the cost of that conflagration! Eight million human lives swiftly blotted out in battle, and as many more slowly devoured by misery and heart-break, disease and starvation; two hundred billion dollars' worth of world-wealth squandered in destruction or desperately spent in defense; fair cities and famous temples laid in ruin, fertile lands left bare and desolate; the health of the race impaired by pestilence and famine; the mind of millions poisoned by wild hatreds, shaken by swift tumults of unrest, shell-shocked into a state of dull suspicion, anxious fear, and sudden anger that comes near insanity,—what a frightful price mankind has had to pay! And for what? For nothing, absolutely nothing; unless,—*unless indeed it was for liberty and a lesson.* Liberty to begin again, trying to make the world better: the lesson that it never can be done until to a clearer ideal of justice and a deeper impulse of mercy, mankind shall join a greater power of self-control.

That was the point at which the slow progress of the race,—a real advance by small degrees, though far from perfection,—that was the point where the process of peaceful development broke down in 1914, and the world was plunged into the awful pit of strife and the red mire of slaughter. I was wrong in saying that "two are stronger than one." My calculation that because the sense of justice and the motive of kindness were increasing all must go well, was too hasty, too easy, too absolute. At a given hour, for a certain time, one may be stronger than two.

> *"Yet all these fences and their whole array*
> *One cunning bosom-sin blows quite away."*

It was the lack of self-control in German ambition, it was the reckless and ruthless urge of self-aggrandizement and the lust of mondial dominion, that swept away the restraints of righteousness and silenced the scruples of compassion and made Germany will war to win world-power. "Upon the heads of her diplomats and princes are the blood and guilt of it." But the burden and the sorrow and the calamity of it press heavily upon all the nations.

Yet in our dejection and the revulsion of our minds, in our shock of dismay that such a thing could happen in the twentieth century, we must beware of falling into the dark exaggerations of despair. This latest war was indeed the largest, but I do not believe it was the most terrible, cruel, and barbarous known to history. Let us be sane in our judgments and seek not to claim a false pre-eminence for our own time even in evil things. Much that mankind has gained through the centuries in mitigation of the concomitant horrors of warfare was forfeited to the Teutonic theory of *Schrecklichkeit*, and the Allies themselves were not free from reproach in their methods of reprisal. Poison-gas, submarines, aerial bombardments are indiscriminate and horrible weapons. But after all there were some things in ancient warfare which were not practised, for very shame, in this great conflict of arms.

Prisoners of war were not chained in the galleys, nor decapitated by thousands. Wicked things were done in Louvain and Dinant and Lille and elsewhere. But rich captured cities were not given over to death and destruction. When Sulla took Athens the massacre of the inhabitants was so fierce that the blood filled the market-place like a pool and ran out of the city gate. When Titus destroyed Jerusalem, when the Goths sacked Rome, nothing was spared. When "The Spanish Fury" fell on Antwerp in 1576, eight thousand people were murdered in three days. Nothing comparable with that happened in Belgium or Northern France in the late war. It was bad, unspeakably bad, but it was not as bad as in the olden time. If it had been, half the population of Europe would have perished.

International law, though often broken and evaded by the Germans, was never wholly denied. They even promised to make good their transgressions when they had won their victory! The blackest page of the whole history was the massacre of the Armenians by the Turks, —the unforgetable crime of an unpardonable despotism.

Through all this long and ghastly strife the Red Cross went calmly and bravely on its errands of mercy to friend and foe, ministering to the sick and wounded, seeking with a divine inconsistency to help with one hand of civilization those whom the other had smitten down.

Nor may we forget, amid our natural abhorrence of the repulsive realities of war, that there was a real and essential difference between the two sides of the combat. Germany was the actual assailant,—she attacked, she invaded, fighting for the extension of her empire, for "a place in the sun," which she claimed as needful for her fuller self-realization. The Allies were on the defensive. They fought on their own soil to maintain their liberties, their rights, their honor, and their life.

Now it is profoundly unreasonable to ignore the vital difference between these two kinds of war, and so to put them on a level, either in the same condemnation. Even those who hold the absolute pacifist theory that physical resistance to evil is never permissible, must still admit that the aggressor has a far deeper guilt than the man who withstands aggression. On the other hand, we who believe that the gift of strength carries an obligation to use it for the protection of assaulted virtue, imperilled freedom, and justice endangered or openly attacked, must hold that men who take arms in such a cause are soldiers of the right, "thrice-armed" because they "have their quarrel just." Believing this, I regard the victory of the Allies and America in the late war as in the main, (and despite all minor drawbacks and delinquencies,) a great moral victory and a proof that the world *is* growing better. If any one doubts this let him consider the alternative; let him read the programmes which the Lords of Potsdam issued before and during their mad adventure; let him think carefully what the triumph of the German Empire would have meant to the rest of mankind. Seeing that this great disaster did not come to pass, let us thank God and take courage.

But these considerations are only rays of light gilding the cloud of danger, distress, and apprehension that still hangs over us. Will the world ever be much better unless we get rid of the anachronism of war as the arbiter of disputes between nations? May not this method of violence and unreason at any moment thrust us back from the path of progress, destroy our dearly bought gains of justice and mercy, and, overthrowing the shaken pillars of civilization, bring back upon the world the dark and shelterless night of barbarism?

Undoubtedly it may, and probably it will, unless men of good-will unite their efforts everywhere, and work together to prevent war and to establish peace on strong foundations.

Two things will certainly help the wounded world to recover from its great relapse and move forward again on the path of progress. First, we must make a clear and definite endeavor to bring a regulative, disciplinary influence into the progress of education. We must try to bring up a new generation to understand and respect, not only the sanctity of justice and the beauty of human-kindness, but also the necessity of self-control. This work can only be done through individuals, in the home, the school, the church. It must be plain and patient, watchful and sympathetic, loving and uncompromising, satisfied with nothing less than the creation of a finer, stronger, more self-restrained man,—

"King of himself and servant of mankind."

Such men will do their best to avoid and avert war.

Second, we must carry the principle of self-control, (which is so essential in the social relations of the community that we protect and uphold it by law,) into the international relations of the world. We must learn to think of national sovereignty in terms of self-restraint as well as in terms of action. We must interpose every possible barrier between the cold ambition of rulers, or the hot passions of the multitude, and those aggressive policies and deeds which thrust war upon an unwilling world. We must devise practical means by which the cause of countries aggrieved or injured may have a prompt appeal to an impartial council of arbitration, or a fair and speedy trial before a high court of international law.

But, you say, we already have those things, at least in outline. Well then, all that we need is to make them work, and to put behind them the combined force, the concerted powers of those free nations that believe in justice, mercy, and self-control, as the vital elements of human progress.

In this good hope we labor. We believe that the world has grown better. We confess that it has suffered, apparently, after the weariness of a great trial the discouragement of a great relapse. *But we set our will and our work towards a great recovery, in which the world shall grow better yet.*

READING LIST OF ESSAYS

READING LIST OF ESSAYS

Abbott, C. C.:
    Days Out of Doors.
    Freedom of the Fields.
Abbott, Lyman:
    Problems of Life.
    Spirit of Democracy.
Addison, Joseph:
    The Spectator.
Arnold, Matthew:
    Essays in Criticism.
Atlantic Classics:
    Essays by various authors.

Bacon, Francis:
    Essays.
Baker, Ray S. (David Grayson):
    Adventures in Contentment.
    The Friendly Road.
Barrie, J. M.:
    Margaret Ogilvy.
    My Lady Nicotine.
Beebe, William:
    Jungle Peace.
    Edge of the Jungle.
Bennett, Arnold:
    How to Live on Twenty-four Hours a Day.
    Literary Taste and How to Form It.
    Self and Self Management.
    The Human Machine.
Benson, A. C.:
    At Large.
    Beside Still Waters.
    From a College Window.
    The Altar Fire.
    The Silent Isle.

Bergengren, Ralph:
    The Comforts of Home.
    The Perfect Gentleman.
Birrell, Augustine:
    Men, Women and Books.
    Obiter Dicta.
Black, Hugh:
    Friendship.
    Work.
Bolles, Frank:
    At the North of Bearcamp Water.
    Land of Lingering Snow.
Brewer, D. J.:
    American Citizenship.
Briggs, L. B. R.:
    School, College and Character.
Browne, Thomas:
    Religio Medici.
Bryce, James:
    Hindrances to Good Citizenship.
Burroughs, John:
    Accepting the Universe.
    Indoor Studies.
    Locusts and Wild Honey.
    Signs and Seasons.
    Wake-Robin.
    Winter Sunshine.

Carlyle, Thomas:
    Heroes and Hero-Worship.
    Sartor Resartus.
Chesterton, G. K.:
    A Miscellany of Men.
    Defense of Nonsense.
Cowley, Abraham:
    Discourses.
Croly, H. D.:
    Promise of American Life.
Crothers, S. McC.:
    Among Friends.
    By the Christmas Fire.

The Gentle Reader.
The Pardoner's Wallet.
Curtis, G. W.:
From the Easy Chair.
Prue and I.

De Quincey, Thomas:
English Mail Coach.
Flight of a Tartar Tribe.
Dobson, Austin:
Eighteenth Century Vignettes.

Eaton, W. P.:
Barn Doors and By Ways.
Green Trails and Upland Pastures.
Eliot, C. W.:
American Contributions to Civilization.
The Durable Satisfactions of Life.
Emerson, R. W.:
Conduct of Life.
Essays, First and Second Series.
Society and Solitude.

Galsworthy, John:
A Sheaf.
Another Sheaf.
Inn of Tranquillity.
Goldsmith, Oliver:
Citizen of the World.
Gosse, Edmund:
Gossip in a Library.
Portraits and Sketches.
Griggs, E. H.:
Self Culture.

Hazlitt, William:
Lectures on English Comic Writers.
Lectures on English Poets.
Table Talk.
Hearn, Lafcadio:
A Japanese Miscellany.
Out of the East.

Holliday, R. C.:
  Walking-Stick Papers.
Holmes, O. W.:
  Autocrat of the Breakfast-Table.
  Poet at the Breakfast-Table.
  Professor at the Breakfast-Table.
Howells, W. D.:
  Criticism and Fiction.
  London Films.
  My Literary Passions.
  Suburban Sketches.
Hudson, W. H.:
  Naturalist in La Plata.
Hunt, Leigh:
  Men, Women and Books.
  Table Talk.
  Wit and Humor.

Irving, Washington:
  Sketch Book.

James, William:
  Talks to Teachers.
  The Will to Believe.
Jeffries, Richard:
  Story of My Heart.
Jerome, J. K.:
  Idle Thoughts of an Idle Fellow.

Lamb, Charles:
  Essays of Elia, First and Second Series.
Lang, Andrew:
  Letters to Dead Authors.
Leacock, Stephen:
  Literary Lapses.
Lowell, J. R.:
  Among My Books.
  Fireside Travels.
  My Study Windows.

Lucas, E. V.:
    A Little of Everything.
    Character and Comedy.
    Cloud and Silver.
    Fireside and Sunshine.

Mabie, H. W.:
    Books and Culture.
    My Study Fire.
Macaulay, T. B.:
    Literary and Historical Essays.
Martin, E. S.:
    Windfalls of Observation.
Matthews, Brander:
    Americans of the Future.
    Inquiries and Opinions.
Milne, A. A.:
    Not That It Matters.
Mitchell, D. G.:
    Dream Life.
    Reveries of a Bachelor.
Montaigne, Michel:
    Essays.
More, P. E.:
    Shelburne Essays.
Morley, Christopher:
    Mince Pie.
    Pipefuls.

Newman, John H.:
    Historical Sketches.
    Idea of a University.
Newton, A. E.:
    Amenities of Book Collecting.
Nicholson, Meredith:
    The Provincial American.
    The Valley of Democracy.
    The Man in the Street.

Pater, Walter H.:
    Imaginary Portraits.
    The Renaissance.

Repplier, Agnes:
    Americans and Others.
    Books and Men.
    Compromises.
    Essays in Idleness.
    Points of View.
Roosevelt, Theodore:
    American Ideals.
    History as Literature, and Other Essays.
Ruskin, John:
    Crown of Wild Olive.
    Frondes Agrestes.
    Sesame and Lilies.

Steele, Richard:
    The Tatler.
Stephen, Leslie:
    Hours in a Library.
Stevenson, R. L.:
    Across the Plains.
    Familiar Studies of Men and Books.
    Memories and Portraits.
    The Amateur Emigrant.
    Virginibus Puerisque.
Strunsky, Simeon:
    Belshazzar Court.
    Post-Impressions.
    The Patient Observer.
    Thru the Looking-Glass.

Thackeray, W. M.:
    English Humorists of the Eighteenth Century.
    Roundabout Papers.
Thoreau, H. D.:
    Cape Cod.
    Excursions.
    Walden.

Van Dyke, Henry:
    Camp Fires and Guide Posts.
    Days Off.
    Essays in Application.

Fisherman's Luck.
Little Rivers.

Warner, C. D.:
    As We Go.
    As We Were Saying.
Wilson, Woodrow:
    Mere Literature.
    When a Man Comes to Himself.
Woodberry, G. E.:
    The Appreciation of Literature.